The Krays
The Geordie Connection

Steve Wraith & Stuart Wheatman

PAN BOOKS

This book is dedicated to George Davison Green,
my inspiration.

First published 2002 by Zymurgy Publishing

This edition published 2003 by Pan Books
an imprint of Pan Macmillan Ltd
Pan Macmillan, 20 New Wharf Road, London N1 9RR
Basingstoke and Oxford
Associated companies throughout the world
www.panmacmillan.com

ISBN 0 330 43750 X

1 3 5 7 9 8 6 4 2

A CIP catalogue record for this book is available from
the British Library.

Printed and bound in Great Britain by
Mackays of Chatham Ltd, Chatham, Kent

Foreword

My name is Dave Courtney and despite what you've heard about me... I'm a lot worse! I'm known as the 'Yellow Pages of Crime' but prefer to be known as an author after the success of my books Stop the Ride I want to Get Off and Raving Lunacy, and as an actor after my Cannes Film Festival debut with my own little production, Hell To Pay. Anyway this book's not about me, it's about my old mate Stevie, or as I like to call him 'Agent Number 4, The Geordie Connection'. Stevie is one of my knights of the round table. My house is called Castle Camelot and Stevie is one of my most trusted friends. I've painted the outside of my house and Stevie is there at the front of my little army in a suit of armour. Now if that isn't showing your respect for a friend I don't know what is! We first met in 1994 through the twins' elder brother Charlie, who was a mutual acquaintance, and from day one I loved the bloke. A big lad with a heart of gold like most Geordies, and a sense of humour second to none. We met up on several social functions where I beat him at pool on more than one occasion one handed. He'll hate me for telling you that!

In 1995 I arranged the security for Ron Kray's funeral, and was asked to pick two hundred flat nose geezers from up and down the country to make sure the biggest funeral in British gangland history went off without anyone trying to take a pop at the key players and faces. Stevie from New-Car-Sel (he hates that as well) was in my top ten geezers. I asked him to look after Charlie Kray on the day, and he didn't let Charlie or me down. I've been up to the 'Toon' on more than one memorable night out... what a place that Bigg Market is. Stevie and his boys have always made sure that me, my missus Jen and friends are always welcome up North. He has always been on the right side of the law Stevie, but he has a loyalty to me and the older chaps and that alone makes him our 'Geordie Connection'... We luv ya Stevie, man!

Dave Courtney OBE

Contents

1

East End Development

Many know the story of the Krays. Most people will know that the twins were locked up in prison in the sixties for murdering two people. Before covering my involvement with them, it is worth considering their background and upbringing. They have been studied in the past and no doubt will be the subject of studies in the future. The twins were born in a time when this country was beginning to go through a huge transition, socially and economically. Changes were taking place while they were growing up, and many of the changes that took place were due to the Krays.

The East End of London conjures up many different images. It has changed a great deal since the Krays' era but to go back just over a hundred years it was a very different place altogether. London in the early nineteenth century was a dark and dingy place. East London became industrialised at around this time and a working class population soon became established, as more and more people came to live and start families. The area saw a huge growth in size and population. Conditions were poor and soon became overcrowded. The narrow streets were filthy, neglected and barely even lit at night. Prostitutes, brothels, drunkenness, robbery and assault... it's hard to imagine what the place could have been like unless you were there. There were slaughterhouses, rendering plants, glue factories engineering works, loads of breweries... the lot. With all this being in the East of London the westerly winds would carry the smell away from the affluent West End. And I mean smell. Leather was another growth industry so there were many tanning yards in the area. To darken the leather hides, 'pure' was used. The charvers (wasters, scallies, losers etc) of their day would procure the 'pure' on a night, which basically means they would supply the leather workers with dog shit found on the street. Now you are starting to get the picture. Dog shit on the streets and pollution in the air.

East London was also the stomping (or stabbing) ground of the first world-famous serial killer: Jack the Ripper. In 1888, between Friday thirty-first of August and Friday the ninth of November, he murdered and mutilated five women so savagely that it caused fear throughout the city. All the victims were prostitutes and all were in or near Whitechapel. They were known as the Whitechapel murders. Once the newspapers picked up on the second and third victims, Jack the Ripper was born. He was no average serial killer – he was called that because of the way he would rip their organs out or literally rip them to pieces. He was never caught and has been the subject of much speculation and countless film adaptations, most recently From Hell, by the Hughes Brothers.

North of Whitechapel is Hoxton, or Shoreditch as it is now known. This is where another famous East End name would emerge. That name is Kray. Charles James Kray, the twins' older brother, born in 1927 at the first family home in Gorusch Street in Hackney. Ronald and Reginald Kray were born on the twenty-fourth of October 1933 in Stene Street. They were identical twins, born within an hour of each other – Reginald first then Ronald, at around eight p.m. that night. Already with one special son, proud parents Violet and Charles Kray had unknowingly given birth to three sons that would soon etch the name 'Kray' into the British crime hall of fame. They went on to become Britain's most notorious gangsters, securing the East End's infamy for crime and violence.

It's hard to pinpoint when the 'gangster' as we know it came into being. The whole gangster 'image' as in the look was borrowed from old American films and from infamous gangsters such as Al Capone. In London gangsters ran protection rackets down at horseracing tracks as far back as the 1930s, covered brilliantly in Graham Greene's novel Brighton Rock. In the racing game is where a lot of the names you hear about now stuck out – this is where the now 'retired' gangsters cut their teeth. These people were not fictional, they were real life characters. They started their careers by working for the racketeers in one way or another. Bookmakers were offered services they had no need for and would be persuaded that they did need the service after all. It was usually something like having someone come around and clean the chalkboards, but those who would not comply with demands would be made an example of... and the youngsters saw from an early age that crime could pay. Most would enter into this long before their teens and grow up into a world of crime. Other than protection rackets, there were safe crackers and smash 'n' grabbers, pickpockets, jump uppers – robbers who would target delivery wagons, conmen, burglars – most of which amounted to not much more that petty thievery. A good thief could make a good living. A bad thief could go to prison for further education and training.

In those days there was not really any security. Why should there have been? Society was not prepared for dishonesty but for those who knew all about dishonesty, it was open season. When you hear of people saying that 'the good old days' were safe, they were not really that safe at all. It was regularly said that, 'you could go out and leave your door open'– yes, that is true but it's only because there was never anything worth stealing in those days. Go out and leave your front door open these days and anyone will make off with three televisions, video recorders, DVD players, computer, music centre and jewellery... in 'the good old days' you could clear an entire house out for a few pence. The criminal is not a new phenomenon.

Pre-war underworld activities were not a patch on what was going on in America, but just like the Americanisation of many other cultures, the British criminal was soon to catch on. Instead of 'cracking' a safe with tools, thieves were now learning to (assume Michael Caine accent here) blow the bloody doors off. That's when the big money started to come in. Other changes taking place were in the police approach to solving these crimes, and also now the media was playing a big part with TV and newspaper coverage. Still at this time guns were unheard of. They were available, but there were still certain rules to adhere to... the police didn't carry guns, so criminals didn't; something that would all change in the not too distant future. Though there weren't that many professional criminals, they stuck together in the same drinking dens and were close knit just like all the other communities of the East End.

Mentally, Ron and Reg were inseparable; they had a bond where if one was happy the other one would feel it, suffering corresponded too. They even shared the same name. If one was around, it was assumed that the other would not be too far away, so they took on the name 'twins', becoming a single entity. They would share everything – even illness. They both caught diphtheria and measles at an early stage in their lives, which in these pre-vaccine times, children were in the highest risk group. This meant that they had to be separated for the first time and in different hospitals. Reg recovered quickly, but Ron almost died of the infection. Ron was kept in hospital long after Reg was discharged, but Violet brought him home against the wishes of the doctors saying he needed only her and Reg to put him back on track.

The Kray family moved to Vallance Road in Bethnal Green just before the outbreak of World War Two. They lived at number 178, which had the Liverpool Street Line running over the top of the backyard – perfect for a sleepless night. Violet wanted to be closer to her own parents. When she'd

8

married at seventeen, she was basically outcast by her family. The birth of Charlie eased the tension a bit and put them back on speaking terms, but the birth of the twins was the clincher. Vallance Road was quite typical of its time – overcrowded and slum. Houses had no bathrooms and toilets were always outside in the back yard. There were gambling dens, seedy pubs, billiard halls and brothels dotted all over. An area that was known for drinking and the love for boxing, it was also renowned for poor housing conditions and unemployment. After the twins had fully recovered from illness, Ron seemed slower and more socially reserved than Reg, finding it harder to get on with other people. He would spend time on his own or with the family's pet Alsatian, roaming around the bomb sites of Bethnal Green. Their illness was to play an important part in their early years because from Violet's point of view, she began to notice differences between them for the first time. In the family home, Ron would compete for his mother's attention. He felt disadvantaged in comparison to Reg... physically seeming bigger and clumsier. They would often fight each other, but would never allow a third party to come between them... squabbling but always sticking together. In Bethnal Green being identical twins gave them the edge over the other little tough kids. It unnerved them and it was something that Ron and Reg used to the their advantage. They became known as the Terrible Twins and were always fighting with their cousin Billy against others, against gangs, but nearly always against older boys... and they were fast learning how to handle themselves. When the war broke out, school was closed until they were eight years old, so this war torn and derelict world provided the backdrop to their countless fights and vendettas with other kids. It was the perfect setting. Always after a fight they would appear at home cleaned up as if nothing had happened, so as far as their mother knew, nothing had. They were experts at keeping this side of their lives from her. This is the side of them that their father was all too familiar with though. He was streetwise and knew exactly

9

what they were getting up to. The war and no school meant they could fight in their own wars. That was their education.

Without trying to sound too much like Uncle Albert from Only Fools and Horses, during the war was when crime really took off. The Blitz created many opportunities for crime, making way for the Black Market. There were shortages and plenty of deserters from the war to do any dirty work for organised criminals. Rationing was introduced and this saw a big turnaround in people's attitudes. There was temptation – mothers wanting to provide that bit extra, people wanting cigarettes, clothes, coupons for this and that... and the criminal was the one who could cash in on it all. They would supply anything and everything and were seen as heroes for being able to do so. This is where we can see similarities with America again. American gangsters were propelled into the big time through prohibition – they saw a huge opportunity at a time when many people were tempted to break the law. Never before the war would the housewives of Britain have even dreamt of breaking the law, but now they had to provide for their family by any means necessary. It was all about supply and demand. Because of the call-up to war, there was not a great deal of policemen around so it created a freedom for criminals to operate. There were people like Eric Mason who essentially invented ram raiding, Eddie Chapman the safe breaker from the North East (another Geordie Connection), once named as the most wanted man in Britain... but now criminals were starting to work as teams instead of individuals. Two men robbing a safe could get away with twice as much money; three or four men dressed as guards casually stealing the contents from a shop window and loading up a smart (stolen) car looked more credible than one man in a mad panic. In some cases the public even helped them load the cars up because they were that convincing. It was basically the birth of crime, but importantly, there was more and more organisation behind it. The South East of Britain was the centre of the war, leading to a population increase with in-coming service personnel, leading to an increased desire for drinking and prostitution.

Bethnal Green was bombed quite badly during the war. For a while, the brothers were evacuated to the country to avoid the bombing, but missed Vallance Road too much and were soon reunited with the rest of the family to become even closer. They were an old-fashioned East End family. Soaked in tradition, they were very close, devoted and self-sufficient as families were. They had to stick together and they had to be tough to survive. Their dad would either be on the run from the law, having refused to join up for military service, or would be out earning a living. After going on the run from his service or lack of, he changed his name to continue his work. It wasn't that he was a coward. He was a product of the East End – a fighter. It just happened that he wanted to do what he was doing instead of going to war, he had no interest in it at all. He was known as a pesterer – a travelling trader – who would roam the country buying and selling silver, gold and clothing. He earned quite good money so the family was able to live slightly above the standard of most others in Bethnal Green, though he himself was never cut out to be a 'family man'. He was well known and knew a lot of the East End villains. Also he was well known for a few other activities, drinking and gambling number one and two on his list. With this lifestyle he was seldom at home and the brothers went a great deal of their lives without a proper father, so the twins' early lives were hidden behind their mother or 'under her feet'. They were brought up in an environment without any real male role model and were strongly influenced by their mother Violet, her two sisters, and their grandmother.

This early nurturing in their lives moulded their way of thinking. Their dad, the times he was actually at home would often comment at their lack of respect towards him. He didn't agree with the way Violet had let them do as they wanted. His solution to this would be to discipline them. This was the way for families everywhere, but not for Violet's family. She knew from her own strict upbringing what the result would be. They would have arguments about it with the twins close by, not missing a word. Charles later blamed himself for the twins' behaviour. He said that he should have been more authoritative and taken them out of the area. Who knows what would have happened? You could look back now at the situation and see exactly what effect it would have on the twins. Their experiences with their part-time father increased their resentment towards authority. You can see the love for their mother, then their dad arriving on a weekend to make his mark. It was through him that they got their first taste of the underworld. Once he'd gone on the run, he would hide out with criminals and the twins would sometimes be sent with messages from their mother. It was Violet who held the family together in the war years. She was a warm and generous woman and looked after the three things that mattered to her the most: her sons. She taught them values and respect from an early age and instilled her strong sense of family values upon them. Violet's love for her twins was to practically smother them. When she'd returned to Vallance Road with them as the prodigal daughter, she had an enormous sense of pride. She dressed them the same – just like little dolls in a pram. Everyone was interested in them. People were not used to identical twins. With this in mind and with their mother's love the twins had a sense that they were invincible. She would accept everything they did, in doing so destroying their ability to judge right from wrong.

Every area of London had a reputation with the police for the different crimes it was associated with. Villains were known to acquire money by any means and have a total disregard for it once they had it. It was a means to an end... a night out and a chance to gamble and drink. They were known to live fast, die young and leave a not so good-looking corpse. They had a complete disregard for the family way of life and were categorically selfish. Crime-wise, it was the bank messengers (people who carried money from bank to bank) who were the target and violence was fast becoming a way of life for the robber. To blow a safe took skill and patience. Messengers were seen as easy pickings as there was little protection and little resistance. They would always surrender without a struggle, but would be given a few punches for authenticity. In time, protection increased and so robbing them was more of a risk. Bank robbery was the next step. Jump-uppers were also seeing a logic progression. They used to follow the cigarette wagons and make off with a few hundred cartons, the next step for them was to hijack the entire wagon and make off with hundreds of thousands of cartons. In those days, sentences for violence and robbery was by corporal punishment and a short prison term, usually twelve months maximum, and was considered to be worse than the usual four-year stretch. Prison was a lot different to what it is nowadays; it was a tough regime. The twins met robbers, hijackers, fighters and racketeers through their dad and also through him they had their first encounters with the law. On more than one occasion, they were woken up at night by police searching for Charles senior. Scared at first, they soon learned how to deal with them but also picked up a fear and loathing of them. Vallance Road was known as Deserter's Corner, so with all these people coming and going, the twins were constantly on the lookout for the law. It became a second nature and also acted in conditioning them further with hatred toward authority.

Crime in its infancy was mainly a family concern. With close communities, there would always be the local families who had a reputation and stuck out from all the others. You could have people on your side, but if you came from a family with a few brothers, you immediately had a tight trust. That's how the Sabini brothers became the first real organised crime family in Britain, they made a name for themselves on the racetracks in the forties. Then there was the Nashes from North London who paved the way for two other gangs – the Richardsons from South London who both ran powerful and feared gangs, and of course the Krays – they had firms made up of family and would stand by each other through anything. Family firms would build up reputations through fear to gain power... the power would lead to influence and so on. Brothers would start gangs or enter into one as a member of the next generation. The Krays were already beginning to drift towards this way of life, though they probably didn't realise it. As children they loved fighting and had a reputation amongst their peers... it was a reputation that would undoubtedly grow. It seems natural for it to have happened now. The Krays had rather unconventional influences in their early years, which was a major contribution to the business they entered into. Other than their dad, older Kray family members were also well known local characters in Bethnal Green. One of which was Mad Jimmy Kray, their paternal grandfather. He was a stallholder in Petticoat Lane and was famed for his drinking abilities nearly as much as his bar brawling. Their maternal grandfather, Jimmy The Southpaw Cannonball Lee was another character In his younger days he'd been a bare-knuckle boxer and then a music hall entertainer. He was a one-off in more ways than one – a non-drinker – and loved to tell the twins stories of his fighting days.

It was family influence that led the Kray brothers towards the boxing world as well. The twins' first real taste came when they were at the Victoria Park fair in the boxing booth. Men could win money by going the distance with the 'in-house' boxers, but not that many of them were successful, most would be half cut to begin with and would run out of steam or be sick within a few seconds. In the interval, the organisers allowed pairs of fighters to slug it out to keep the crowds hungry for more. Ron was quick to volunteer himself as a contender, but there was no one else of his weight division in the crowd for him to fight. The MC was about to refuse him a fight when Reg

14

stepped forward. They climbed into the ring and gave a no holds barred boxing exhibition in front of the bloodthirsty crowd. Neither would back down... they fought each other toe to toe as though they were sworn enemies. In the end it was declared a draw but the most important result for the twins was that the men – the fighters of the East End – were now made aware of who they were.

From then on, boxing took over their lives. It was all there was for them. Young Charlie had been the first to put the gloves on and the twins had watched as he sparred round after round in the back yard under the guidance of their grandfather. Although he was known as the more gentle of the brothers, the training paid off for Charlie and he went on to win a few boxing titles as a welterweight during his stint in the Royal Navy where he'd carried out his National Service. He was discharged from service because of severe migraine attacks, and the twins begged him to teach them the noble art. Charlie was becoming more involved in boxing and didn't need much persuading. Once they had talked Violet into giving them some space in the house, Granddad Lee set up a punch bag (an old Navy kit bag filled with rags). As word spread, Violet found herself with a house full of young boxing hopefuls and more gym equipment than she'd imagined... but she loved it. The twins must have been around ten years old when they fought that first time, and then they met again in the Hackney Schoolboy's Boxing Championship 1948, where Reg won on points. This was only a year or so later and they had came such a long way in so little time. Their dad had encouraged them to take up boxing, thinking it would discipline them and steer them away from the only other career option in the area. Hopefully. They went on to destroy everyone in their way. Ron was good but was only considered to be a brawler. He would just steam in using brute force. He fought with heart and would never give up. Reg was the better of the two and was an accomplished boxer with skill and a game plan. He studied it and saw it more as an art than an all out punching competition.

Local papers reported on the twins and they received rave reviews after each fight. A boxing career beckoned though it looked like Reg would be the only one to make it.

They soon turned professional... but it proved to have the opposite effect on them as to the kind one would imagine. Reg was Schoolboy Champion of London. He told me in later years that it was one of the proudest moments of his life, but it was the violence outside the ring that led to their downfall as boxers. They just could not help themselves. Managers would not touch a boxer with a reputation for street violence, but I don't suppose the twins saw it the same way. They were destroying everything they had worked so hard to build up. They got into trouble with the police on several occasions for Grievous Bodily Harm and other violent attacks. The stories about their fighting on the streets had became just as frequent as seeing them in the sports pages of the East End Advertiser. One attack even involved a police officer. Up until now, they had earned respect from people following their up and coming boxing careers, but now they were earning themselves a reputation as a couple of tearaways. The older generation considered the act of hitting a policeman as crossing the line. The post-war years were still very uncertain times and other than in the criminal community, this was a law-abiding area. Police were there to keep the peace and to protect – such behaviour was unknown. They were no longer known as the clean-living boxing hopefuls from the area, they had drifted into a world of violence. They narrowly escaped prison sentences each time they were on a charge, but they were lucky. For this to happen in their mid teens, they must have thought they could get away with anything. Why should they believe anything different? Even with witnesses involved evidence didn't stick, and their mother was always there to believe anything they told her.

Violet also looked to her family for support. Her sisters May and Rose, lived on each side of her in Vallance Road;

her brother Jimmy shared her home and slept on the settee, while Granddad Lee, his wife and son John, lived across the road above the café. Violet and her parents doted on the twins. As too did her sisters – they all wanted to be seen with the twins because of their uniqueness in the community. Everyone has a favourite auntie and Auntie Rose was the twins'. Famously, Aunt Rose told Ron his eyebrows were too close together, she told him that it was an omen. She said it was because he was 'born to be hanged'. She loved them but apparently had a bit of a temper and would often fight with other women (or anyone, really) in the street. Years later when she died, it is said to be the catalyst that finally tipped Ron over the edge; sending him into the world of madness that had been following him. Maybe this is true; it would certainly appear to be a contributing factor... a sudden loss of a loved one can affect people in different ways and there may well have been other elements adding to his state of mind.

Charlie married his childhood sweetheart, Dorothy Moore in 1948. They moved to number 178, which meant converting the gym back into a bedroom. The twins didn't get on very well with their sister in law and as Charlie spent more time with her, a space between the brothers began to grow, but boxing would always be their bond. In December 1951, all three brothers appeared on the same fight card at a middleweight boxing championship held at the Royal Albert Hall. This was massive and attracted more attention to the brothers, though the results were not as they would have hoped. Charlie lost his fight. Ron got disqualified and Reg won.

On March the second 1952, the twins were called up for National Service. Everyone had to do it. All fit men over eighteen were called up for two years. 'Fit' being a loose term – how do you think Mr Fraser became 'mad' Frank? Because he was 'unfit', of course. The twins were now Royal Fusiliers, for a day. They went AWOL to see their

17

mam, only to be brought back the following day. Their service to their country meant (a) doing a runner whenever they could or (b) they were locked up for doing a runner. Military service was just another authority figure that they had no respect for. Part of their service included a nine-month stretch in Shepton Mallet Military Prison, where they were able to meet up with like-minded people. For all they hated the army though, it did teach them something. Without their 'service', they would not have been able to organise people and plan strategically for their own battles on Civvy Street. It also led to them meeting and working with various criminals while plotting their escapes and hanging around with once they had escaped. This was the best networking they could have done. It was their dad who made their first introduction and it took off from there. On the run they would go to a club called The Royal, where the local gangs would turn up in strength to show who was number one. Fights were almost compulsory. Again, this was the twins' way of paving the way for themselves once their time was up; they were proving themselves as a force to be reckoned with as well as having the balls to do so while on the run.

They were finally (dis) honourably discharged from the Army, and could now go about their business. Fighting was now a way of life. They enjoyed inflicting pain on their victims and would always take the fight to the extreme. They would use weapons without a second thought and now owned their first gun. They leased a billiard hall called The Regal in Eric Street, off the Mile End Road in Bethnal Green. It was open all hours and became the meeting place for criminals whom the twins had built friendships with. The lease was taken out for three years at five quid a week and came about as a result of ridding the place of some unsavoury characters that had been hassling the previous owners. This may have been good been good fortune or good planning... it was their first step into their new world, and it meant that they could now start to write their own set of rules. It seemed quite fitting that they had a place called The Regal. They now had their feet firmly on the first rungs of the criminal ladder. Ron had now developed the image he'd been dreaming of and reading about for years. He started to dress gangster-style: The big chunky jewellery and wide shouldered suits, crisp white shirts and tightly knotted ties. He was adapting to a lifestyle that went with the job too. He'd sit in his own chair soaking up the atmosphere at the club. To anyone now, it was obvious that the twins had big plans for themselves. They would fight anyone at anytime and never lost... always on the move... and never seemed to rest or sleep. Ron was now at the forefront as the dominant twin. He had a network of young boys who were his information service – keeping their ears to the ground on his behalf. This was where he got the name The Colonel... because of his ability to organise and lead people, building up his own arsenal of weaponry, which was kept hidden at Vallance Road. Ron would show no apparent weakness... the only weakness he had was for young boys. He never showed an interest in women, but with boys he was gentle – a different person altogether. One thing he could not be in this environment was a homosexual... not openly. In such a world as the one they were entering it was unheard of. Ron didn't really want for much and had what was basically a simple life; living at home meant cooking and ironing was done for him by Violet. He had manicures, massages... you name it. It was his very perception of the gangster. He even started getting his hair cut at home, tailors brought in, started doing yoga... why? Because that's how gangsters lived their lives, isn't it? He didn't really have any want for material possessions, after all Reg was the one who could drive and owned an American car. Ron could live out some of his childhood dreams. It was like a reinvention... he had a new identity, a new persona... he was The Colonel and now he could act like it.

Reg began to follow suit (no pun intended) and took on the gangster chic dress code. This has significance to the twins as a partnership. Where once it seemed Reg was the dominant force, it was Ron who now emerged as the dominant twin. He was no longer reserved and awkward. Getting such a nickname as The Colonel was because of his drive, and now it seemed that Reg was in the back seat and was doing as Ron said. Reg strived for what he'd call the 'good life', meaning that he didn't see this lifestyle as a true retirement package. He wanted the respect, a showpiece wife, a nice car, comfort – the same goals the workingman strives for. He did not consider his 'job' as a long-term profession at all. In this instance they were very different. Maybe Reg was just in denial... all this may have been because of his want to be different to his twin, to have his own identity and to prove that he was not dominated.

Different desires would be something else that set them apart from each other... then in contradiction, Reg started dressing the same, so on the outside they appeared to be as identical as they were in the pram all those years ago. Those close to them knew they had many personal differences but visually, it was important for them to look the same and to an extent to act in a similar manner. It was all about image and presentation. To see twins dressing differently could hint towards conflict, and any suspicion of conflict between the Krays would be seen as a weakness. They now had a small team working for them, knock-off gear was stored in the club for money, little blags going on here and there – it was a small operation and was very literally a constant fight for recognition amongst the established underworld. By the time they were twenty-two, they were making good money through all kinds of activities, but it was always small time. They wanted bigger goals, and it was to happen possibly sooner than they anticipated.

The two major gangsters of the time were Billy Hill and Jack Spot Comer. They had formed an alliance to control the whole of the city and even called themselves the kings of the underworld. They had been ruling London for ten years as friends but sure enough they fell out and Spot had his faced carved up in a vicious attack in what became known as 'the Battle of Frith Street'. The odds were stacked up against Jack and he needed someone to turn to... he turned to the Krays. He offered them a pitch at what would be an historical gangland event – the 1955 Epsom race meeting. The twins could barely tolerate Spot anyway but took him up on his offer. The idea was that it would be a show of strength by Spot and would warn Hill off from trying anything. They may have been there as his 'ally' but showed contempt toward the gangs of both Hill and Spot. They were bored by the horseracing and showed no interest in the day, but at the same time showed no fear of anyone from either rival gang. These were the top gangsters in the country and the twins' behaviour was insulting to them and implying that they were has-beens. It was the proverbial two-fingered salute to all of them. The Italian gang was also there to observe what was going on – if there was to be a war they would certainly be interested in the outcome. Ron and Reg took their cut for the days outing and returned home. It was obvious to everyone that they had treated the day as a chance to show everyone who they were and that they feared no one.

Frankie Fraser was part of Hill's gang and was eager to fight it out with the Krays. If the twins wanted a war, then Hill's gang would be ready for them... a date was set and The Colonel prepared his army and gathered weapons in anticipation. This was the confrontation he had been looking forward to for some time, and now it looked as though he was going to get his chance. Both Hill and Spot heard about the battle and called it off. They had always exercised control without the use of violence and had an understanding with the police that if violence was kept off the streets, then they were okay to go about their business. It had been a good working relationship. Spot kept the twins at arms length after that incident. He was put off by their ruthlessness and wanted nothing more to do with them, but remained 'friends' with them rather reluctantly. They wanted to learn from him and to take over the West End, wiping out Hill and his gang along the way. Spot, however, was not about to give his secrets away to anyone.

The feud between Spot and Hill carried on and around a year or so later Spot was ambushed again, care of Frankie Fraser and Alf Warren. He called it a day soon after that, refusing the twins' help to rid the world of Hill's gang once and for all. Billy Hill also went into retirement... and the coast was now clear for someone else to step in. The Italians stepped up and the rumours were that they were not happy with the twins after they had favoured Spot in the power struggle. If they weren't happy with that, they would have been even less happy when Ron strolled in to a club one night with the firm in tow, took out a Mauser pistol and fired at them. No one was shot, but a few Italian suits would be at the dry cleaners the next day. They challenged the Italians on their own patch and they backed down immediately. It was a wise move. This had been the break that the twins needed and everything seemed to be falling into place nicely. Along with their firm, the twins were convinced they could fill the gap that Jack Spot and Billy Hill had left empty... it was now their chance to reign as kings.

Ron, on the inside now as well as the outside, was now a fully-fledged gangster. If the Italians were the main competition, he and Regwould be unstoppable. It was their graduation ceremony. 'Real villains' were now part of the gang... and that gang became known as 'The Firm'. Reason and calculated strategies would now need to come into play. They could not just fight for the hell of it anymore. In 1956, Ron shot someone for the first time. Knowing that he collected guns and had shot at people, it was pretty certain that one day he would shoot someone for real. He was identified by his victim and charged with Grievous Bodily Harm. The eleventh commandment 'thou shalt not grass' was broken, but friends in high places and the powers of persuasion meant that Ron walked. He could have been wearing Teflon suits at that time because no matter what was thrown at him, it would not stick. Ron loved it... it was another victory in the battle against authority. If you keep getting away with 'wrong doing', do you ever think about stopping? Not a chance. Neither did Ron, but he also never gave a second thought to the consequences. They soon earned themselves the tag of 'The most dangerous mob in London' and were getting money from all over the place in protection rackets, thieves and villains in the area offered them a cut of their action. Ron felt he was above the law... and in some ways he probably was... though not for long. In the same year he led a revenge attack on a man and ended up doing time for it. He got three years for GBH and found out first hand that you can't get away with everything, certainly not all the time anyway. The commandment had been broken again, and wouldn't be the last time as far as Ron's liberty was concerned.

Inside, Ron lived a comfortable prison life and Reg took care of business on the outside. This was the longest time to date they had been apart which meant Reg could now be his own man and run the firm in his own way. He had seen the dangers in Ron's battles but up till now had gone along with them. Fighting and shooting were certain to lead only to one thing and Reg wanted something different out of life. He took on a shop in Bow Road, Bethnal Green, which was turned into a club and became their new base... a new drinking club... The Double R, standing for Ron and Reg. So, he hadn't forgotten about Ron altogether, but while he was in prison, Reg could live his life as he wanted and go to work as a businessman. Helped out by brother Charlie, the club was becoming a huge success. Charlie had a good head for business but would prefer to remain in the background as opposed to running with the gang. This way he could get on with running the family business interests and not worry about the criminal side, which worried Reg.

Ron's prison life soon took a turn for the worse, he was heading for a breakdown. His constant mood swings and disruptive behaviour was doing him no favours... but this all pointed to a medical condition that was much deeper than originally thought. This is the point that it is believed that the death of Auntie Rose led to a breakdown. He was sent to the psychiatric wing of Winchester prison where doctors declared him insane. Diagnosed as a paranoid schizophrenic and his health deteriorating, Ron was moved to Long Grove Mental Institution in Surrey. At this point he began to panic; he had seen his friend Frank Mitchell in a similar position where he was to be held indefinitely because of his mental condition. Ron had begun to react well to his medication, but was still considered to be unstable for release and so a plan was successfully hatched to get him out. The law back then stated that if someone escaped and was at large for more than six weeks, they would have to be re-examined upon capture and dealt with accordingly... this is what they had in mind for Ron. They needed him out long enough to be re-examined, declared mentally stable and to serve the rest of his time in prison, knowing he would actually be released. The twins concocted a ploy to beat the system, which was simple but effective. Reg visited Ron one day where they simply exchanged coats. Both were wearing the same suits which meant Ron could just walk out whilst Reg sat at the table patiently. Minutes later Ron was on his way to freedom... as the minutes ticked by Reg sat in the visiting room waiting to reveal his identity. When he was asked where Reg had gone, the people at the institution were baffled when they heard the reply. One of their patients had just walked out to freedom so easily – it was their own stupid fault and had nothing to do with Reg he told them as he too walked out. The plan didn't run as smoothly as expected though. Ron's mental illness worsened after being holed up in a caravan in the country after the escape. Reg moved him back to Vallance Road to be with Violet but his mood swings and eventual suicide attempt gave the family no other choice but to surrender him back to the authorities. They didn't like to do it, but it was their only solution and was for his own good. Fate decreed that he should be returned to Long Grove and after a thorough examination, he was no longer certified insane. Bizarrely, the twins' plan had worked and Ron was returned to Wandsworth Prison to serve out the rest of his sentence.

He was finally released in 1959. The mood swings were still there... the paranoia... he'd pace the floor like a caged lion, ready to snap at any second. He was put on medication to calm him down but there were side effects. His speech and walking slowed and he put on weight. This 'calm' was really just the calm before the storm. Following that, just to top it all off, Reg got an eighteen-month stretch in prison for his involvement in a protection racket. This left Ron with the reigns to the Kray Empire. Up till now he was unpredictable but Reg had been there to smooth problems over and look after him when it was needed. Now Ron was dangerous, unpredictable, powerful... and in charge of the firm.

26

2

Cockney Rebels

Nineteen-thirties Britain was in depression, in the forties we had the war and rationing went on well into the fifties. The East End had proved to be easy prey for the twins and with London still very vulnerable, they could move on to other enterprises. Reg and Charlie had made some shrewd deals while Ron had been away, and things were picking up... they had clubs, illicit gambling joints, were making a name for themselves and the rich and famous flocked to have their photo taken with them. There was a need for glitz and glamour at the end of the decade and the Krays filled the void with their clubs. Whilst Charlie and Reg had built up and strived to operate on a more legitimate level, Ron had different ideas. Ron's philosophy was that of 'live by the sword'... he was a loose cannon and at times was uncontrollable. Everything he saw, he wanted and his way of getting what he wanted was by force. Ron knocked down relationships that had been built up with firms like the Italians with ease. He'd claim that people, i.e. Reg, had been getting soft in his absence, and his way of declaring he was back was to declare war. He'd be more aggressive and spiteful than usual – there was a definite change.

By the end of the fifties a new lease of life had engulfed London – there was a party atmosphere that brought about new ideas. *The Chelsea Set* met and socialised regularly to form the basis of a trendy new 'in crowd' made up of clothes designers, writers, fashion icons and photographers. *Lord John* opened in Carnaby Street; a boutique that catered for men, and set the scene for the growth of fashion central. David Bailey and Terence Donovan brought the models Twiggy and Jean *The Shrimp* Shrimpton... their faces defining an era.

Sixties London was the centre of the world for music, fashion, art... a whole new freedom that wasn't around in the war years. All eyes were on the capital as it was now one of the trendiest places in the world. *Swinging London*. There were only really a few happening places; the whole 'swinging' mania was, as usual, a media creation and it took off from there. Despite the media hype there was still energy creativity in the air. Go back just a few years and the mood was totally different. The youth of the country was realising they could have an identity and lifestyle different from their parents... traditions and rules of generations past were thrown out the window. This was the first time the working classes had any money in their pockets and were spending it as quickly as they were making it. There was spending power and a complete liberation from Victorian and post-war taboos. Even *Lady Chatterly's Lover* by DH Lawrence was allowed on general release... it was a great time to be young. As Paul Weller wrote, *life is a drink and you get drunk when you're young.*

The devastation of the war had made way for development. If recent decades had been bomb times, then the sixties was boom time... in the form of a property and gambling boom.

The Krays' quest to conquer the West End led to the acquisition of clubs such as *The Kentucky* and *Esmerelda's Barn* and an empire began to flourish. *Esmeralda's Barn* in Wilton Place was taken as part of a payoff. Reg was on bail after nine months awaiting a review of his case at the time the deal was struck. He was proving himself as a businessman... handling things with the help of Charlie meant money was being made whereas Ron on his own would act on impulse and never quite made the right decisions. He was good at winning arguments though, even if it meant arguing his way into a bad deal and loss of money. At this point in time, there were not that many people who knew the gaming business or knew about clubs and how to keep them 'safe' – The Krays were learning all the time and could see there was a market for this knowledge. There was a whole new nightlife culture centred on clubs and casinos – gambling was all the rage. London was the centre for gambling with a huge illicit economy, the Krays controlling clubs meant placed them in line for rich pickings. It was not all about gangland violence – they were savvy enough to know that it was a business.

Prior to The Betting and Gaming Act of 1960 there were no casinos or bingo clubs in the country and the law prohibited all commercial gaming of any significance. The idea behind the 1960 Act was to allow games of equal chance between friends and in clubs but to prohibit the commercial exploitation of gaming. There were so many loopholes to The Act... all of which were exploited in one way or another by such people as the Krays. Gaming as it was known then has always been associated with criminal activities but prosecution was difficult because the legislation was unclear. It was perfect for the criminal minded of the time. By the late sixties there were over a thousand casinos in Britain, offering instant membership and live entertainment by highly paid stars as a means of attracting people and inducing them to game. In 1968, the Government chose a system where commercial gaming could be properly regulated and controlled. The 1968 Gaming Act introduced a new test whereby prospective and existing casino operators needed obtain the Gaming Board's approval and a gaming licence. Many candidates failed on one or both criteria and so were no longer able to hold casino gaming on their premises. There were plenty of ways around this though; there would *always* be a front man.

Reg had been enjoying his freedom in recent months, but

it soon came to an end as the appeal against his conviction failed. He was sent to Wandsworth Prison for six months, but this was only a minor setback. Six months in that time of life didn't mean a great deal. Prison is always going to be a consequence for a career criminal, but the crimes that they were being locked up for were crimes that they should never have been doing in the first place. It was generally a result of Ron's hot headed behaviour or some petty crime they just hadn't thought through. Reg away for six months meant that Ron would be in charge again, and that would certainly give Reg cause for concern.

Running operations by himself, Ron was *Gangster No. 1*, organising his troops into battle from *Fort Vallance*... he was *The Colonel* after all and he had a name to live up to. He'd be forever planning his strategies, determined to prove he was back with a vengeance and no Reg meant he was hassle free... Charlie, while Reg was away, kept a low profile. Ron had a man called Leslie Payne working as an adviser for him in Reggie's absence and he helped as he muscled in on a various properties – gaming clubs were acquired with such ease it was frightening. He was also going through a phase where he would put his name to any venture, he would throw money into ludicrous schemes and wonder why there was no pay-off.

At the beginning of the sixties the twins were reunited once again. Ron had enjoyed his time at the helm with Reg away, but with him back, it was business as (un) usual. Deals were going on all over London and they were beginning to branch out... one deal was putting money into a seaside development in Nigeria. Leslie Payne and Ernest Shinwell (son of Manny Shinwell, Labour MP) helped set this up. An introduction took place between Ron, Leslie Holt and Lord Boothby, a Peer of the Realm. The whole venture fell through and the money disappeared... then by sheer coincidence, Holt died under strange circumstances. Ron had met Boothby at a gay party they'd both attended. Their friendship was even exposed by the *Sunday Mirror* under the headline 'The Gangster and the Peer'. It also alleged that the two were homosexuals. It wasn't that Ron went out of his way to hide the fact, it was more to do with the freedom of expression brought on by the sixties that word got around. This of course was common knowledge to the underworld already, but now the rest of the world was beginning to find out.

Considering the twins status... the lifestyle, the clubs, the fame... they may as well had huge neon signs above their heads taunting the police to investigate their empire. They were now mixing with some very influential people. Some thought that they were getting too powerful. The authorities were watching them constantly and one of the main reasons for this was their love of publicity. They weren't just courting publicity; they were engaged to it with big plans of marriage. Ron was the worst culprit – he loved being photographed with celebrities and sports stars who came to the clubs. He longed to be famous and longed to have the lifestyle that went with it. He would present himself as the stereotypical American Gangster just like he'd saw in George Raft films. Whilst American real life gangsters would delegate their dirty work... making sure that they couldn't be connected to crime, the Krays just couldn't seem to grasp the concept of keeping a low profile and letting others do their dirty work. Maybe it was all down to trust and the only ones they could truly trust were themselves. They were not unique in this – The Nash brothers were another firm who could not resist doing their own dirty work. Leader Jimmy Nash made news early in 1960 for receiving a Grievous Bodily Harm charge when he was blatantly guilty of murder... jury and prosecution witnesses were terrified for their lives and Nash escaped the death penalty. Soon after that, they retired from gangland activities leaving the other main name other than the Krays - the Richardsons – brothers Charlie and Eddie, scrap metal businessmen from South London.

The Richardsons ruled the South and were known as sadistic practitioners of torture to those who got on their wrong side. Frankie Fraser joined the Richardsons in 1963 as their number one enforcer after he was released from his prison sentence for the attack on Jack Spot and along with George Cornell, were a formidable force in the underworld. With Fraser on board, the violence escalated at a dramatic pace and their business interests like the Krays', were now beginning to prosper. Suppliers to most of the West End clubs with one-armed bandits, they also had friends in high places and found that certain crimes could be swept under the carpet. Another lucrative business venture at this time was known as 'long firm fraud', a market that the Richardsons also cornered. This is where legitimate 'fake' companies were set up, and goods such as electrical appliances, household items, leather goods – anything in fashion at the time – would be bought in from other companies. There would be businessmen brought in to front the operation so to anyone on the outside, it appeared a respectable wholesaler. They would pay for the goods up front and sell them on just as any other business would do and earn themselves the trust of the places they were dealing with. After paying these companies immediately, they would be given credit on their next purchase. That's when the long firm would get as much as they could on credit – and then disappear. It was such an easy scam to get away with. The goods would be sold on to market traders and huge profits made.

The Kray firm was also into long firm fraud though did not enjoy the same level of success as the Richardsons. They were still heavily into protection rackets and were subsequently arrested for demanding money with menaces in 1965, by Detective Inspector Leonard *'Nipper'* Read. They were demanding money from a club called *The Hideaway* and were remanded in custody to Brixton prison. At this point in time their level of influence could be observed... questions were asked in the House of Lords as to how long they were going to be kept locked up.

The questions, asked by Lord Boothby, caused outrage. Boothby was not their only high placed contact. When the case went to court, they walked out as free men and were cleared of all charges. They had used the threat of violence to scare witnesses into retracting their statements, and Nipper Read had to watch them slip through his fingers. A few weeks after leaving the courtroom they owned *The Hideaway* club and changed it's name to *El Morocco*. The more they got away with encouraged them further – just as it had in their childhood.

In the same year, Reg married the love of his life, twenty-one year old Frances Shea the sister of one of his friends. The marriage ended in complete disaster, lasting less than a year and Reg was hit hard by it. Frances could not handle such a lifestyle – it seemed to her she was in direct competition with Ron all the time, and to Ron it *was* a competition. Reg would still visit her, but Ron could now get his claws back into him and get his own way. He'd do his best to help Reg forget all about her, make him immerse himself into their business and keep him out at night as long as possible. Maybe Ron was doing all this for the good of Ron... he'd claim to be doing it for Reg, but all the time he would try to put a wedge between him and Frances.

The twins were now forming links with the American Mafia in New York. They knew the Americans were setting up gaming clubs in London and wanted to offer protection, which would be lucrative. Contact was made, though after an unsuccessful trip to forge further relations, Ron returned to the East End. Mafia talks were still ongoing, and they were optimistic that something could be salvaged. Ron had been introduced to all the wrong people courtesy of a friend he'd travelled over with. It was said that one reason he had not been introduced to the right people on his trip was that the Mafia thought the Krays' power was slipping... they needed to prove otherwise. They went on to provide protection for American celebrities visiting or performing in England on behalf of the Mafia. Frank Sinartra's son had been kidnapped while performing in London recently – another firm was supposed to have been protecting him and this was the perfect opportunity to jump in. Favours would let them know who was running things in England, it suited them down to the ground as they could combine business with pleasure. Performances were always in clubs... clubs had gaming facilities... gaming facilities had the Krays. Perfect. They came up with more elaborate plans to prove themselves further, one of which involved murdering someone who had crossed the Mafia to put them in the Krays' debt. This never happened though; it was another idea that fell at the first hurdle.

Complications between the Krays and the Richardsons were about to set in. Members of the Richardsons got into a fight with Eric Mason, a good friend of the Krays, who was out with two friends in *The Astor Club*. Insults were exchanged and one of Eric's friends knocked out one of the Richardsons. The police were called and the gangs legged it round the back of the club where Eric was overpowered by the Richardson gang and taken to a lock-up to be tortured. Eric was savagely beaten with bats, knives and an axe... they could not have touched him if it was a fistfight. Eric raised his hand as Fraser went for his head with an axe, leaving the hand stuck between the axe and his head, which it was imbedded into. He was lucky to survive. They also tried to cut his hands off in the torture session, saying he would never fight again. It was a sickening and cowardly attack, which to this day, Fraser dismisses as lies. In Fraser's story he beat Mason in a one on one fight before kidnapping him. Other people had different versions of events.

There was no real reason for conflict as both firms could quite easily co-exist and run profitable businesses. Both firms were already preparing to go into battle against each other before this incident. What happened to Eric was a result of the pent up anger that had built up between the firms. It was through greed that they had fallen out in the first place. Ron and Reg wanted a cut of the Richardson's long firm fraud success, but were told in no uncertain terms that they did not fit into their plans. Charlie and Eddie Richardson were also powerful and had no interest in sharing their fortunes. It was winner takes all, and no room for losers. Ron was livid... it was a tremendous insult to him personally and in true Ron Kray style, he wanted revenge. It looked like there would be another war... but it was settled in a very different way altogether. There was a successful drinking and gambling club ran by a local thief called Billy Heywood in Lewisham, which was attracting a lot of attention. It was on the Richardson's patch and they wanted a piece of the action – simple as that. It was making a lot of money and they believed they were entitled to some. It was taken for granted that the gamblers, who were mainly all thieves (a club ran by thieves *for* thieves), would not be as tough as a firm of gangsters, but the Richardsons greatly underestimated the resistance they faced. Eddie Richardson and Frankie Fraser paid the club a visit and were not given the answer they were looking for – Billy Gardner and Heywood stood their ground that night. As a result, they got a call informing them that the Richardson gang wanted to see them in a club called *Mr Smiths*.

On the eighth of March 1966, a gang from the speiler were rounded up and went to *Mr Smiths* to settle the score once and for all. They were heavily outnumbered as the two gangs squared up to each other... then the guns were drawn and all hell broke loose. Dickie Hart was part of Gardner and Heywood's gang and was shot dead. Eddie Richardson and Frankie Fraser ended up in hospital with gunshot wounds. This was the end of the line for the Richardson firm – the police instantly had enough evidence to put their top henchmen, including Eddie and Fraser, away for five years apiece for affray. Fraser was originally charged with the murder of Dickie

Hart but was found not guilty. It has been said that it was George Cornell who actually killed Dickie Hart, managing to escape before the police arrived, though no one can confirm this. Hart had been the only member of the Kray gang involved at *Mr Smiths* and murdering him was a liberty that would be avenged at any cost.

He may have evaded the police, but there was one person Cornell couldn't hide from. Ron Kray walked into *The Blind Beggar* public house the following night with Ian Barrie, armed with his Mauser pistol. Cornell was sitting on a stool at the far end of the room with his mate Alby Woods, and as Ron walked calmly over to him, he had only one thing on his mind. Cornell sneered for the last time as Ron levelled the gun to his head and pulled the trigger. *The Sun Ain't Gonna Shine Anymore* by The Walker Brothers was playing on the jukebox... and to Ron Kray this was poetic justice. But did he kill for revenge, or was it for the fact that he'd (famously) called Ron 'that fat poof'? Ron told me himself that he'd killed Cornell because he had killed someone close to him, but never would say who it was revenge for. It always sounded plausible that it was for Dickie Hart. Cornell was on Kray territory at the time, but it's not as though he was out to cause trouble. He was from the East End originally so he wasn't invading Ron's turf. Another statement Ron later gave me was that if Cornell had been anywhere other than *The Blind Beggar*, he would have lived. Ron couldn't stand the *Beggar*, so he had no qualms about soiling it with Cornell's blood. Ron would say so many different things about the killing when I knew him. He loved to discuss it – just as he'd done in the sixties. Everyone knew he'd did it. He made no attempt to hide the fact; he went as far to brag about it. It was his first kill and he revelled in the notoriety. This one-upmanship was something that he'd use in arguments with Reg all the time. He'd use it to dominate further; to taunt him, sneering and saying he didn't have the guts to go as far as Ron.

Within a year from being sentenced for affray, the Richardsons found themselves in the dock again. The evidence had been mounting up for some time – the first hand accounts of hideous tortures and revenge beatings had caught up with them at last. At first, they were being investigated for their long firm frauds but it was the extent of violence they had used in trying to silence people that led to their ultimate downfall. Charlie Richardson continued to go about family business in Eddie's absence, he had new people and the firm were as strong as ever. The torture they administered on their victims made the fraud look like a high street shoplifting outing and the police were hell-bent on making them pay. They would beat people who worked for them and who fronted fraudulent companies and torture people for information. More and more people were traced... a contract killing investigated... more tortures... the evidence read like a horror novel. People were scared to come forward because the Richardsons knew so many in the police force it was likely to get back to them. One bloke in particular was Jimmy Taggart. He'd been subject to one of the worst torture sessions anyone is ever likely to go through and live. He was prepared to make a statement only when Charlie was in custody. Charlie was remanded and the prosecution evidence gathered before he was given a twenty-five year prison sentence, but it wasn't over there. Evidence was pouring in all the time still; he was linked to a contract killing in South Africa where a man had mugged him off for a few grand and ended up paying with his life. Two hired killers were used. One of them disappeared but the other, Johnny Bradbury, was given ten years for his trouble. He also ended up telling everything he knew about the Richardson organisation and subsequently Eddie Richardson and Frankie Fraser were given a further fifteen years each. The Krays now found themselves in pole position. The Richardsons had effectively self-destructed. They were no more and now London was rich pickings for the Kray firm... all they had to do was stay out of real trouble. Just as in the era of Spot and Hill, the police were quite willing to let incidents go unseen provided they were not serious and did not upset the equilibrium of the community. By putting the Richardsons away the police force sent signals that gangsters were no longer above the law. They could not get away with murder.

The twins were still trying to portray themselves as the local boys who made good, but by now they were known for what they were – violent criminals. They used the East End ideals and values to their advantage; giving to charity and being seen with stars was a route to papering over their bad boy image, but the underworld were not so easily swayed as they knew Ron had murdered Cornell. They had immense power now, but the attacks kept happening and the use of sheer terror was used to extort money. Big Albert Donoghue had even become a member of the firm as the result of a Kray attack. He'd been shot in the leg and because he did not tell the police who had shot him, they put him on a 'pension' until he was fit enough to work for them. It was utter madness – they trusted him for not grassing them up, and he decided he could trust them after they had just shot him. The perfect working relationship. It was their reputation that they were becoming a victim of. They could never let it slip so the violence would escalate all the time; even members of the firm were beginning to worry if they would be next. I've heard from different sources that there were plans to kill the twins by the firm, as they were so unpredictable. No one felt safe and with Ron being trigger-happy, anything was possible.

At the end of 1966, the twins hatched a plot to free Frank Mitchell, the Mad Axeman, from Dartmoor Prison. Mitchell would be very useful to the firm if they could get him out, but the main idea behind it was to enhance their reputations by helping him campaign for a release date. Teddy Smith, an 'author' and Kray friend had put the idea to them and they went for it. It sounded like some of the bizarre schemes that were put to them twenty-five years later when they themselves were locked up. Teddy was also known as a madman, a trait not uncommon in their circle of friends and the plan sounded mad too. All they had to do was get him out of prison, keep him out long enough for the newspapers to run the story of his plight and have the authorities forced to investigate his case – then he'd give himself up and return to prison.

Mitchell was a huge, strong, fit and good-looking man, who had been certified insane. He was such a difficult customer even to the high security environment that he was basically left alone in, provided that he did not cause disruption. He had never been given a release date – he was there indefinitely. Albert Donoghue and Teddy Smith drove to the only phone box at Dartmoor to wait for Mitchell... all he had needed to do was walk over the moors to his freedom and into a car. It was that easy. They were in London before news of 'Britain's most violent criminal' escaping prison had broke.

The media interest was massive. They had greatly underestimated the impact the escape would have, and as a consequence were left with a very big problem. They had a huge uncontrollable madman holed up in a flat in London with an extreme dose of cabin fever. He wanted out. He wrote a letter to *The Times* hilighting his prison conditions. To keep him sweet, the twins supplied a woman for his entertainment and he promptly fell in love with her. He paced the room like a caged lion – threatening to leave and take his woman with him, and threatening anyone present at the same time. Everyone in the underworld knew the twins had sprung Mitchell and if he walked out of the flat, the world would find out who sprung him too. They could not let that happen.

Frank Mitchell was subsequently killed just before Christmas in 1966. He was taken out to a van where he was told they were going to move him abroad to start a new life. Inside the van, three hit men opened fire on him finally ending his life by a shot to the head. That was it – another problem sorted out the gangland way. His body was never found and no one was convicted of his murder.

The downward spiral had begun with the first killing. Ron would have said it was the complete opposite, but once the killings started, the overall outcome was not too difficult to predict. Then in 1967, Reg was hit hard by the suicide of Frances. At one point, things were promising and reconciliation between them looked certain. Frances was unwell and her mental stability crumbled. She had a breakdown, was hospitalised and soon after her release she committed suicide by taking a lethal dose of pills. Reg went into depression. He tore himself apart over her death and was drinking heavily to try to ease the pain. The drinking only made matters worse. It was too much for Reg to take. He was a sad case – a pitiful drunk and was easy prey for Ron. At the same time they were faced with another problem. This one was called Jack *'The Hat'* McVitie, there are very limited solutions in gangland.

McVitie had been making a mug out of the twins for some time. He was a loose cannon. He had no fear of the twins, was a drug user and a woman beater. He had taken certain liberties – was disrespectful to them in public, was said to have taken a shotgun to a club once drunk out of his mind, looking to kill them. McVittie had been given money to murder their one time associate Lesley Payne, but after a failed attempt, he just kept the money. He'd had plenty of warnings but had refused to listen. It was decided that he was becoming a liability and had to be disposed of.

Ron was the worst person in the world to be anywhere near Reg at this point in time. Reg was drunk, vulnerable and in need of 'belonging'. This was the perfect chance Ron could have hoped for – he could literally play the part of the devil. Reg was putty in Ron's hands and Ron was quick to take advantage – goading his brother further, "You can't kill anyone, you, you're useless." He would not let it pass. It was the twins against the world now and Reg

Kray had to prove himself against some petty thief who was making a mockery of everything that they had built.

McVitie was lured to a party in Evering Road, Stoke Newington, where Reg Kray stabbed him to death in a frenzied attack. The Lambrianou brothers, Tony and Chris, had taken him from a club where they had already plied him with drink. They had wanted to become a part of the firm for so long, and now was their chance to prove their worth. It was all calculated murder, though I doubt those present at the time thought it would evolve to be so. As they entered the room Reg had tried to shoot him but the gun failed, his motive now clear to a panicking McVitie, Reg could not just let him off with a warning. McVitie begged for his life. He was desperate and pleading for mercy. Most watching the scene just thought they were observing a bit of a joke. Ron was close at hand to wind Reg up further. One way or another, McVitie was going to die that night... it had gone too far. More taunting from Ron and soon Reg went too far. He grabbed a kitchen knife and stabbed McVitie through the face before finishing him off. That night Reg Kray finally achieved the same status as his twin. The entertainment over, they were both murderers. It was not necessary for them to kill McVitie. In the scheme of things, he was a no one. It was bad timing –McVitie was in the wrong place at the wrong time. He did more damage to them dead than he ever could do alive. The body was disposed of and the flat cleaned up immediately... more mystery, more cover-ups and more people to be silenced. The police were not aware of the murder until several months later, and it took a year to arrest them. Nearly thirty people in total were arrested as the police moved in on the firm. Nipper Read arrested the twins and the firm on the eighth of May 1968. Both were defiant and confident, believing that their name alone was enough to stop anyone coming forward and talking. The Richardson case had been a good learning exercise for the police though, and they too were confident this time. With the firm locked up, the fear was no longer instilled upon the community and the East End code of silence was ready to be broken. They didn't want the Krays anymore.

Amongst other charges they were tried for the murders of George Cornell and Jack McVitie. They had lost their grip. Members of the firm were willing to turn Queen's Evidence in order to save their own skin. They had been ordered to take the rap for the twins but refused, making them instant enemies. All of those arrested pleaded not guilty with the exception of Albert Donoghue. He was tried separately and was imprisoned for two years. Ron had ordered him to take the blame for the murder of Frank Mitchell but he refused. His only way out was to become a grass.

The downward spiral had continued... January 1969 saw the Kray trial begin which turned out to be one of the most expensive in British history. Of the ten men who stood in front of the jury, only Tony Barry was acquitted as an accessory to the of murder of McVitie. The remaining nine members of the Kray firm were charged with, convicted of and sentenced by Mr. Justice Melford Stevenson at the Old Bailey on the eighth of March that year, "I am not going to waste words on you. In my view society has earned a rest from your activities. I sentence you to life imprisonment, which I recommend should not be less than thirty years."

The firm was sentenced as follows.

Ron Kray, aged thirty-five, was found guilty of both the murders of George Cornell and Jack McVitie. He was sentenced to life imprisonment with a recommendation to serve at least thirty years.

Reg Kray, aged thirty-five, was found guilty of the murdering Jack McVitie and for being an accessory to the murder of George Cornell. Like, Ron he was also sentenced to life imprisonment with a recommendation to serve at least thirty years.

Charlie Kray, aged forty-one, was sentenced for being an accessory to the murder of Jack McVitie. He was sentenced to ten years in prison.

John 'Ian' Barrie, aged thirty-one, was found guilty for the murder of George Cornell. He was sentenced to life imprisonment with a recommendation to serve at least twenty years.

Tony Lambrianou, aged twenty-six, and Christopher Lambrianou, aged twenty-nine, were found guilty for the murder of Jack McVitie, were sentenced to life imprisonment with a recommendation that they serve at least fifteen years.

Ron Bender, aged thirty, was sentenced to life imprisonment with a recommendation to serve at least twenty years for the murder of Jack McVitie.

Freddie Foreman, aged thirty-six, received ten years for being an accessory to the murder of Jack McVitie.

Cornelious 'Connie' Whitehead, aged thirty, was charged with carrying a gun and complicity in the murder of McVitie. He received two years for the gun and seven years for the Complicity charge.

There was more to come, Ron Kray was charged with the murder of Frank Mitchell and was found not guilty. Freddie Foreman was also charged and found not guilty. The charge of murder against Charlie Kray was dropped. Reg Kray however, received five years for freeing Frank Mitchell from Dartmoor and another nine months for harbouring him. This was to run concurrently with his other sentences.

There was never any remorse shown by the twins. They were selfish and defiant to the end. It was partly due to the fact that they thought they were untouchable that led to their downfall. Instead of playing it cool and making a good living, they began to believe the hype – they thought they could get away with murder. Simple as that.

3

Likely Lads

The sixties in Tyneside were a big time for change too. We always talk of a North / South divide, but youth all over the world are never that different. Newcastle had a massive music and fashion scene in these explosive times, along with other Northern cities. Clubland and gambling was vast becoming big business. The Newcastle scene echoed that of the capital... a lot of the pubs were still very traditional, but it was the clubs and the music that made it different. We had one of the biggest bands of the time, The Animals who joined the likes of The Hollies, Herman's Hermits, Gerry and the Pacemakers and of course The Beatles and The Rolling Stones in the Brit invasion of America. Whether it was due to the fact that there was youth employment, football or the quality of beer – at long last there was an optimism that the city had not seen in a long while. We had clubs like *The Bird Cage*, *The Piccadilly*, *The 69 Club* and the *A Go-go* where you could go and see the likes of Shirley Bassey, Tony Bennett or Tom Jones. It was amazing... a modern world with a new breed of stylish young modernists pioneering what is now a world famous Geordie nightlife. With the increased spending power that the youth of the region were enjoying, clubs like those mentioned became the in places to be seen. There was a huge gaming industry too – casinos and slot machines were pulling the punters in and there was a lot of cash to be made. Along with clubs and gaming, there were other respects that made Tyneside and London similar... organised crime. It was going on in all cities, but most of the time people were only alerted to it when it made the headlines. There was no reason why the public should be aware of any organisation, it was something new and only those involved knew the full extent to the crime behind it. Clubs, casinos, gambling – the entertainment industry – went hand in hand with extortion, violence, protection and other criminal activities.

The Krays made to two trips to Newcastle in all, both of which have always been shrouded in mystery. The tales about the twins arriving in Tyneside have became folklore with so many variations as to what happened, the basics being that they came up mob handed to take over and were kicked out by *someone*. It's hard to actually find out which tales are true and which are false, *everyone* has their own version of events. One of the Newcastle myths is that Superintendent Jack Vinton was dining in the same restaurant as them and sent the waiter over with a train timetable with the trains to London highlighted, but again where this happens varies from practically every hotel to every nightclub and venue in the city. It needs to be noted that every big city in England has the same story or versions of, "The Krays came to [insert city name] and were met from the train by [insert the local crime family name]. They were told to get on the next train back to London and left immediately." Another one is that the police were there to meet them from the train and put them on the next one bound for London. The Krays were so notorious that their names could be used to enhance the reputation of the local villains. They or the police would be the ones who sent the Krays packing. On a larger scale though, it is not about the locals or the police, it's saying *our city* sent the Krays packing. I think that all these stories just prove that the Krays had a reputation that it would precede them anywhere they went. It shows the level of over estimation attributed to them and their physical capabilities. The Krays visiting a city would send it into panic – the city would think that they were coming to take over! They could not even visit a place for a few days on a social basis now. They were too well known. Every culture needs a bogeyman or a Keyser Soze... the Krays fitted in nicely as modern-day Britain's most notorious monsters.

From this point on, there are conflicting stories as to what actually happened when the Krays were in town, other than they *were* in town at *some point* in the sixties. I have heard so many of these stories, from Kray associates and people who were there or claim to have been there. It all builds up an interesting picture. To me, the intrigue lies in the fact you can never categorically say that they came to Newcastle and this is *exactly* what happened. Maybe all of the stories are true or maybe none of them are. There are always going to be people who disagree with what went on during those visits, but hopefully they are represented fairly within these pages.

One story is as follows... they arrived some time between late 1963 and March 1964; singer Billy Daniels was performing in the city and the twins were asked to look after him. His agent had phoned and asked if the twins could do it – they were told it was in a suburb of London, which would be handy... which then turned out to be Newcastle... a few hundred miles away. This was the protection they were offering for the American stars, which I mentioned earlier, though usually it was in the capital. It was the Mafia that they were ultimately working for by providing security. Many stars in those days had mob connections and with relations between the Mafia and the firm being forged, it was in the twins' interests to look after them. Reg phoned Eric Mason and asked if they knew anyone up there. Eric was probably closer to Reg than he was to Ron. It was Eric who set about organising the Newcastle trip; he made a few calls to Henry and Jimmy Young who he'd met in prison and pretty soon it was arranged for eight members of the firm to make their way to Newcastle. Ron, Reg, Charlie, Johnny Squibb, Mickey Forsythe with his mate Peter, Johnny Davies and Eric.

On their train journey, the gang had been discussing various business deals, Ron and Reg never seeming to take time off from it. The long firm frauds were a going concern at the time and discussions were conducted with enough slang words and phrases so no eves dropping passengers would know what they were talking about. It was business after all, and no one else's business. Names became 'the other fella' places became 'that club' and events were 'that thing in that geezer's place'. Even though the restaurant car had closed down, a generous tip ensured that they could still enjoy a meal – they were typical East End lads enjoying the fruits of what money can buy but were never arrogant with it. Eric Mason was great at organising such perks. He still lives by the same code: do things nice and with a smile and people will like you and do what they can to help you. Do it wrong and try to bully people and you'll get nowhere. The respect he commands everywhere he goes even today is testimony to that code.

The Levy brothers – Marcus, Norman and David owned the *Dolce Vita* nightclub where Billy Daniels was to be performing. They met the Krays et al from their train at Newcastle Central with a chauffeur driven Rolls Royce. Not a bad welcome... it was a gesture they appreciated. They were taken to the *Royal Turks Head Hotel* on Grey Street, which is where *Legends* nightclub now stands. At the hotel they checked in and Eric began making calls to people they knew in Newcastle to meet up for drinks.

That night they enjoyed an evening at the *Dolce Vita* where, amongst others were introduced to Angus Sibbet and Vince Lander. Angus Sibbet worked for Vince Lander and both were very well known faces in Newcastle. One theory behind this visit is that Lander had taken a thousand quid from gaming machines in London and fled to Newcastle using the money as capital to start his own business, which had flourished into the empire he now controlled. The gaming machines were said to have belonged to the Krays and they were not very happy about it; they wanted their cut. If this had happened, then yes, they would have been looking for their cut. They were the Krays after all. Maybe it did or did not happen... in the eyes of the public, anyone at that time who was in power and with a reputation was immediately linked to the Krays. Lander pulling such a stroke sounds more interesting than a man coming up from London, spotting a gap in the market and making good money from it. That theory aside, the twins, Lander and Sibbet were all in the same business, they enjoyed a spot of networking that night and kept in contact with each other. The Levey brothers were the perfect hosts that evening and the club was exactly what the firm were used to so they felt at home from the start.

On their second night they took the party back to the hotel. They were all socialising and enjoying drinks from the bar... the entire room was full of cigar and cigarette smoke as they exchanged stories and shared a few jokes. It must have felt even more like home for them with Ron sat amongst all the smoke lapping up the atmosphere and holding court just like in the London clubs. Billy Daniels, always the entertainer, began to recite poetry. He'd stood up and took to the floor as the room full of gangsters and hangers on fell silent. They listened intently, which must have been a surreal sight in itself. Before long, the party was bored and restless by it... they were East End blokes out to have fun and had no interest whatsoever in poetry. Ron did though. He made them sit through each rendition, hanging onto Billy's every word. Johnny Davies had enough. He got up to leave, "What are we sat here listening to this pratt for?" and was told by Ron to sit back down and listen, adding that the poems were good and to show some respect. Billy asked Davies if he liked the poems, "Can't stand them. Sing a song and I'll stay here all night, but your poems, you can keep them mate". Perhaps he was a little too honest. Ron had a go at him but Johnny stood his ground. Johnny was also a fighter and could be as stubborn as Ron if he wanted to. Now if the sight of the gang watching a poetry recital was surreal enough, then Ron Kray enjoying it and forcing others to enjoy it too would have been the icing on the cake.

As things cooled down, it was soon time for a different form of entertainment. Eric Mason had been seeing one of the girls from the *Dolce Vita* called Theresa (who later became friendly with Eddie Richardson on a visit), and had a contact in there who could supply girls for them, if they wanted. This seemed an interesting prospect, but of course Ron was a homosexual. Squibby gestured to Ron, "What about him? He's into poofs". (Johnny Squibb would always joke on with Ron in this way and it drove him absolutely mad! In the times of pre-political correctness, the word 'poof' was always used and caused no offence). It turned out that the kitchen porter was homosexual and was paraded in front of Ron who looked on approvingly. He eagerly took him upstairs to his room – I don't know whether the boy had much of a say – but they were soon interrupted when the manager barged in on them. Disgusted by the sight that greeted him, he threw the eight members of the firm out immediately. On their way out, Eric ripped the page out of the reservation book which had his name on it, destroying the evidence and any association with the incident.

From then on, they stayed at *The Imperial Hotel* in Jesmond, and enjoyed the hospitality of a bloke called Joe Lyle, a club owner and another well-known face in the city. On their third night, they were taken round Newcastle, courtesy of Joe who took them to his clubs *The Piccadilly* and *The 69 Club* and introduced them to everyone worth knowing. They were introduced to the manager of every bar they went to and enjoyed another good night out. Contacts were being made all the time, but not with sinister intentions. They were all in a profession where they needed contacts all over the country and that's exactly what they were doing – making contacts. I don't know if the police had been alerted to the presence of gangland's most famous brothers arriving in the city but it was certainly a secret that couldn't be kept for long, so maybe the police did have someone watching them as a precaution. The twins had respect for the

Levy brothers and Joe Lyle; collectively they had shown great hospitality and put themselves in good favour. They were well-known faces in Newcastle and the North East, but as businessmen. Sure, they were in clubland but saw no reason why it should include gangland. They certainly talked business with the Krays because it was their common ground, but that was where the similarities stopped. Reg and I discussed them on a visit one time, "They were straight people who saw nothing wrong with hanging around with people such as ourselves when we were there. They wouldn't have wanted to get involved with anything criminal we were doing. Vince Lander would have though" he said. Of the people they met in Newcastle, Reg described Lander as one of the only blokes who seemed to be a crook with good organisation. He said it was probable that the police were following him and were most likely alarmed by them meeting each other.

There were no take-over plots going on as far as the Krays were concerned. As hard as it may be to accept, this is what I'd heard from people present on that visit and from the Krays themselves. I do know that they were interested in starting up a clip-joint in Jesmond, but that's as far as it ever got. They were there for Billy Daniels' protection and to socialise. Of course they wanted to meet up with the influential people while they were here – they would have wanted to in any city. Memories will always be selective and can become hazy over the years though. I doubt there was any major conspiracy going on. It certainly puts the record straight about any gangs waiting for them and any police officers sending them back home. If they had forged any real links for business, I think they would have started making regular trips to the North East. As it was, their next visit was some three years later.

The next visit was a different story altogether. Angus Sibbet was a very well known man in Newcastle... known as the one-armed bandit king of the region; he worked for a man called Vince Lander (formerly Vince Luvaglio).

51

They were getting very rich from one-armed bandits, supplying to around four hundred clubs. The deal was that the clubs got forty per cent of the takings and the rest went to Lander, who paid Sibbet his cut from it. (On January the fifth, 1967, Angus Stuart Sibbet was found shot dead in the back seat of his mark-ten Jaguar under a railway bridge in a place called South Hetton in County Durham. He had been shot three times. Dennis Stafford then thirty-three, and Michael Luvaglio (Vince's brother) then twenty-nine, were both arrested and charged with the murder on the fifteenth of March the same year at Newcastle Assizes. Luvaglio was Sibbet's best friend and has always protested his innocence; Stafford was a career criminal who barely knew Sibbet and has always protested his innocence. The jury disagreed. They both received life sentences. *The one-armed bandit murder* even inspired the Mike Hodges' classic, *Get Carter*, starring Michael Caine. It was something that went on to define an era in Tyneside's criminal history. Gangland Newcastle was about to be exposed through the murder of Angus Sibbet. It was an eye opener to the people of the North East. Up until then, it was assumed that gangsters were just confined to London and any killing in London attributed to the Krays. Killings only took place in the capital and were ten a penny. Even today, killings are unusual but the circumstances become more and more familiar each time. The Sibbet murder was shocking because he was very well known and any criminal connections, though possible, were originally rumours and idle gossip from green-eyed sceptics. Gangland was alien to Newcastle in the sixties and even more alien to a pit village in County Durham where the body was found. It was alien to us because we'd never been exposed to it in such a dramatic way. Now those businessmen who dressed in immaculate and expensive suits like their cockney counterparts would be looked at differently. There is always speculation about people until they hit the headlines for all the wrong reasons. Lander was running Social Club Services Ltd and had Sibbet, Stafford and Luvaglio working for him. They supplied fruit machines, live entertainment and furnishings to clubs throughout the region and pretty much had it sewn up.) The Krays, though indirectly, played a part in the goings on surrounding it, but not in the actual murder itself.

Sibbet's body was found at five-fifteen in the morning of January the fifth in South Hetton by Tom Leak, a miner returning home from a night shift, and so began the investigation into Sibbet's flamboyant lifestyle. He was known as a womaniser (having two mistresses who were sisters) and was also married. He had enjoyed the fruits of his money, mixing with stars and entertaining friends in the clubs and restaurants of Newcastle. Years earlier, ex-soldier Sibbet had owned a Chinese restaurant with his brother James where he had fallen in with bad company. At that time, he was given a one year prison sentence for receiving stolen goods. The door to 'the other world' was opened and it appeared he had his foot in it.

The case itself is a curious one. Stafford and Luvaglio were together on the night of the murder and have never denied it. They left Stafford's house in Westmoorland Rise, Peterlee, at around eleven o'clock in a red E-type Jaguar, which belonged to Vince Lander. Twenty minutes after that, Sibbet was seen leaving the *Dolce Vita* in Newcastle. He'd been there for two hours with a group of friends sitting at his favourite table in front of the cabaret stage. He had settled the bill and left the others who stayed on till two in the morning. He was seen getting into his Mark-Ten Jaguar. The next hour in all their lives and what happened in it was the basis for the trial. It was argued that Luvaglio and Stafford murdered Sibbet in this hour, as prior to and afterwards they had watertight alibis. The police put it to the jury as this: at around eleven forty-five, the E-Type smashed into the Mark-Ten and both cars stopped on the A181, just outside South Hetton. Sibbet was shot three times with two other shots taking out the driver's side window, bundled into the back of his car and driven back into South Hetton where it was dumped. Stafford and Luvaglio then drove to Newcastle and were spotted together in *The Birdcage Club* now the *Stage Door*, on Stowell Street, at twelve-twenty. The police had to link the damage to both cars, which was caused in the collision, and prove that the murder happened before midnight. They were both arrested the next day as a formality to help the police with their enquiries.

This is where the 'stitch up' is said to have come into play. Luvaglio had never been in trouble with the law before, Stafford on the other hand had a string of convictions to his credit stretching back to 1956 where he was sentenced to seven years for housebreaking, receiving and possessing a hand gun. He escaped prison twice before being locked up again, this time for conspiracy to defraud and obtaining goods by false pretences, then onto car theft and possessing a pistol (he has indeed been in and out of prison most of his life, serving a six-year jail term in 1994 for forgery, released in 1998). He certainly had a criminal past and had a history of carrying guns, though it does not prove he did this crime. By coincidence, Eric Mason had got to know Stafford when they were both locked up in Dartmoor.

Stafford was linked from his past alone and because Luvaglio had been with him, he was in the frame too, but there seemed to be a way out for him. During questioning, Luvaglio was asked to sign a statement where he would be saying he was away from Stafford long enough for a murder to have taken place. In other words, they were saying they only wanted Stafford for the murder. He refused to do so, saying he was with Stafford from around eleven forty-five until half past two in the morning and was subsequently charged along with Stafford. This was reinforced when Luvaglio's solicitor went on record to say the police had told him to put the idea to his client – they knew he was innocent, but if he didn't say Stafford had left him for an hour and a half that night, then he would be charged with murder. Ronald Kell, leading the investigation, denies this ever happened. It was the first of many conflicting stories to emerge from a sensational trial.

Both men served twelve years of their life sentences, having three appeals rejected in that time. Stafford maintains to this day that at the time of Sibbet's murder, he and Luvaglio were at his house in Chelsea Grove in the West End of Newcastle, along with the red Jag which was parked outside. This puts the time at around midnight; a neighbour has since come forward to say she saw Luvaglio in his house talking on the phone and they even waved to one another through the window. This was apparently a call from Luvaglio's brother, Vince Lander, from Majorca where he was on holiday. From there, they drove to *The Birdcage* to meet up with Sibbet for a drink. They both have said that it was here that the red Jag was damaged, not in South Hetton, and the club doorman actually came out with Stafford to assess the extent of it. Stafford went out to the car to get some cigarettes, which is where this damage was spotted – maybe this was just part of the plan to make it look like the damage happened in Newcastle and not in County Durham. Stafford and Luvaglio then had a meal at the club before going home. Sibbet never showed up for their meeting. That, they say, is what happened that night. They had no knowledge of the murder.

During the trial, there was no motive for the killing established, no confession and no murder weapon to link them to it. It seems odd to me how they can still end up on a murder charge in that respect. Photographs of debris from both cars at the scene of the crime were shown to the jury, as too were photographs of bullet cartridges as well as Sibbet's glasses. There was nothing to suggest that Luvaglio and Stafford had *definitely* been at the crime scene – there were no eye witness reports nor was there any forensic evidence, which one would expect. It proved that the Jag had not been damaged outside *The Birdcage* though, experts pieced together broken plastics from reflectors, fragments of number plate – all of which suggested a collision on that road between both cars. This, it was said at the time, was the foundation the prosecution had produced but they failed to lay a single brick on it. The rest of the case was made up of circumstantial evidence. It has since been discovered that witness statements in direct conflict with the police version of what happened that night, were suppressed.

The police said that the car, with the body in it, had been abandoned at around midnight and lay unnoticed until five-fifteen the next morning. However, at twelve fifty-five another driver passed the Jag and noticed it was undamaged. One witness said that he passed the car at approximately one-fifteen in the morning. The lights of the car were on at the rear to indicate it had stopped, and as he approached in his car to pass, an arm extended from the driver's side to wave him on. One miner has said he saw the car (undamaged) and investigated it. He said there was no dead body on the back seat. Then at two twenty-five, three more witnesses passed and noticed no damage to the car. People were noticing the car because it was very striking and unusual to the area. Ronald Kell denies that any of these statements were 'buried', but the fact remains that none of them were heard at the trial, and forty people said they had seen the undamaged car. But, the Jaguar with Sibbet's body slumped inside was found damaged.

The police were pinning their case on the fact that the killing took place leading up to midnight but the pathologist confirmed that the time of death was between midnight and four a.m. They went as far as doing the same journey in the same make of car to prove it could be done. It started at eleven forty-five at night where they gave generous pauses for murder and moving a body and they arrived in Newcastle at twelve thirty-one. A 7.65 mm Walther PPK automatic had been determined as the weapon. Shots were fired from around three feet away, from one inch away and once with the muzzle of the gun actually touching the victim. Also, traces of blood were found in Sibbet's car which belonged to neither of the three men. This indicated that there must have been someone else there. Further down the road, blood was found in a phone box with blood that matched that of Sibbet's – this evidence suggested that someone had killed Sibbet, got his blood on their clothes and went to use the telephone. Neither of the accused had Sibbet's blood on them. Though upon Stafford's arrest, the suit he'd been wearing that night had been dry cleaned at nine a.m, the following morning, and still contained tiny fragments of evidence from the car damage. At ten a.m, he took the E-type Jag to a garage to be repaired.

There have been further explanations linked to the killing. A one-time thief in Newcastle

confirmed the theory that another man was involved in the killing. John Tumblety says he received a call, picked up and drove the killer from South Hetton to *The Birdcage* on the night. He said the man had a broad cockney accent and his clothes were covered in blood. He claimed the man had an injured leg, which would explain the blood in the car, and was determined to get to the club. The next night, Tumblety was approached by someone and told to forget what had happened that night in South Hetton; otherwise he would face a beating. There have been other theories too; one being a crime of passion where it was said that one of his women was unhappy with him and another one being the Krays were coming to take over (as usual).

The pair continue in their quest to have the verdict overturned many years on. They are desperate to clear their names. Stafford even confessed to it in one newspaper but said he just did it for the money. They want the evidence that the jury did not hear to actually be heard, believing that if this is granted, they will finally be recognised as innocent. It has also been said that Vince Lander had been linked to the murder. Lander was making millions and if he were in the frame for the murder and put in prison, then there would be a spot to be filled at the top of the ladder. After the trial, Lander's firm ran into financial difficulties and he disappeared for several years. During the eighties, Lander sank a hundred and fifty thousand pounds into a pub called the *Castle Inn*, in Durham, and later on was ordered to pay six thousand in unpaid fees to his financial advisor. In the early nineties, the police investigated an arson attack at his home, *The Lodge*, attached to Stanhope Castle in Weardale. Declared bankrupt in 1992, he accused Dennis Stafford of burning down his house and threatening to kill his wife and children. Now in his early seventies, apparently he is now living in the Daytona Beach area of Florida and is facing a legal challenge for various debts.

The whole case is fascinating, it was the first real taste of gangland activity in the region. It held the public's interest as it was reported each day in the local papers and on the news. I think it shows that the role of the gangster was now becoming recognised and associated with the club and gaming industry. It showed that Newcastle was catching up with the capital in criminal stakes. Violent crime is controversial enough and more so when it is on your own doorstep – it raises the stakes immediately. A gangland killing creates speculation and with such inconclusive evidence sealing the convictions of two men it becomes even more thought provoking. Many in the

North East have their own opinions as to who murdered Angus Sibbet that night. Many have said that the evidence for murder was far from conclusive and many have said it proved the two were guilty. The fact remains that they were convicted of murder and until it is proved otherwise, it will always remain.

There is a sub-plot to the one-armed bandit murder. In this sub-plot, three more characters enter the story; Irishman Thomas Patrick Hallett, known as Paddy Hallet... and Ronald and Reginald Kray. Paddy moved to London in the late forties and after doing his national service returned to London looking for a way to make money. He was a hard man, a good boxer and soon began working as a minder for the illegal street gamblers of the East End. If you are good at something you will always get recognised for it and Paddy was no different. The Kray twins approached him and soon enough he was making a living by collecting protection money for them. He got involved in a few 'heavier' jobs, and as a result he spent some time inside. In true Kray style, Paddy's family was well looked after while he was away and on his return he was generously rewarded for keeping quiet. Not long after his release, he met a girl from Newcastle, married her and decided to move up to become an adopted Geordie. He parted company with the twins but it was not on bad terms. They still owed him for not grassing on them and they reassuringly offered their help to him any time he needed it.

In Newcastle it was easy for a man like Paddy to find work. He had 'worked for the Krays' on his resume, which helped him secure a job working for Angus Sibbet. He was earning three hundred quid a week as Sibbet's bodyguard, which was a very tidy sum in those days. So, Hallett was now working for Sibbet, who in turn was working for Vince Lander. Lander had nightclubs, gaming clubs, was supplying the fruit machines to workingmen's clubs and was making a fortune from it with his brother, Michael Luvaglio.

It is clear that Sibbet was killed in a gangland-style shooting. This part of the story suggests it was a contract killing, and most fingers have been pointed at Vince Lander being behind it. There are certainly people around on Tyneside who know who ordered the hit on Sibbet and why it was ordered. It has been suggested that it was a 'Mr. Big' from the city. It is not possible to say who ordered it. It is clear that *someone* ordered it.

Ron and Reg were reportedly asked to carry out the killing on behalf of this 'someone'. They knew Hallet was connected to Sibbet so they met up with him to discuss what was going on. Again they made promises of loyalty to Hallett and decided not to get involved because they didn't want to rock the boat for their friend; end of story as far as they were concerned. Another means of killing Sibbet was employed successfully. Hallett appeared as a witness at the resulting murder trial, which did not go down well with whoever had ordered the hit. His boss had been killed and Paddy had been sworn in to tell his version of events on the night of the murder. There was no way he could get out of it. We must remember here that Hallett was Sibbet's bodyguard and was killed whilst under his protection. Naturally, a jury would want to know how that could happen. Hallett told the court that he thought Sibbet had gone to see one of his mistresses that night. This was plausible and would explain why he went alone. Subsequent threats were made after Hallett's testimony before he was attacked and had his face slashed. After hospital treatment he phoned the twins who came up immediately to show their support. They had relied on other people's loyalty in the past and now it was their chance to prove it was a two way street. Within a few hours they were in Newcastle and looking for revenge. They wanted the bloke who had ordered the attack on their mate, Paddy. The killing of Sibbet was by the by, the Krays had no interest in it but the killer had messed with the twins by messing with Hallett and they took it very personally.

A firm was quickly assembled and they went from club to club, scanning the dance floors and gaming rooms until they found who they were looking for. It was about to kick off in a big way until the police arrived. Jack Vinton bounded up with officers in tow and introduced himself to Ron and Reg. He nodded an acknowledgement to the man the Krays had came to settle their differences with and suggested to all concerned that it would be an idea to settle those differences elsewhere and in private. It was a polite warning which did the trick – the last thing the city needed was a gang war in the middle of a murder trial. They took it to a hotel.

The Krays outnumbered the other gang by far and it was easy for them to take control. With them they had Patsy Gallagher, a Glaswegian who was known to have a fondness for shotguns. As they filed into a room, Pastsy lined the rival gang up against a wall and told them in no uncertain terms that if anything happened to Paddy Hallet again, those responsible for it would be killed. He added that compensation to Paddy was overdue and that the twins would be expecting expenses for their trip as well. The money was paid on the spot, the score settléd.

I know the Krays came to Newcastle on two occasions – the first being to protect Billy Daniels, the second time was in 1967 where Ron was in the city with boxer Joe Louis. He was the only firm member to travel up and was looked after by the same people he had made friends with on his earlier visit. So, is the Paddy Hallett story true or another myth? Personally, I don't see any reason why it would be untrue. We know the other two trips happened because they are documented and there were photographs taken both times. In the Paddy Hallett story, they came up with haste for one night and for one reason only. It was not publicised. It would also tie in with other theories that Jack Vinton 'sent them packing' because technically he did. They were in a bar and he told them to get out. Anyone witnessing that would immediately infer that

Vinton had ran them out of town.

Krays' visits to Newcastle are a perfect example of their notoriety. The fact that there are so many different stories – all of them true, of course – has managed to keep their legend alive. I bet if each story were pieced together and believed, the twins would have been in Newcastle for six years in total. I know that after reading this, people will approach me to tell them what *really* happened. Ron, Reg and Charlie have discussed Newcastle with me in the past. Reg was interested in moving here if he ever got out of prison – I know this because he asked me to look for properties. Ron came here by himself that time with Joe Louis, so he obviously felt comfortable to be here without back up. Charlie enjoyed many nights out in the city and loved the place. Getting them to discuss Sibbet or Hallett was another matter. They could be vague and ambiguous when they wanted and they could suddenly forget how to name drop. The last thing they would wish to do would be to dispel the stories and myths, revealing their trips up North to be just a few social weekends. Such stories have kept the legend going... and stories are something that will keep the Krays going for a long time yet.

Reg Kray

Reg was the first brother I had contact with. I had sent a letter to both twins after the end credits of *The Krays* revealed where they were being held. I still remember that day the return letter arrived... it was a self-addressed envelope, so I knew where it was from immediately. I opened it carefully so I wouldn't rip anything inside... unfolding the piece of paper carefully; then there it was: a letter from Reg Kray. In the top left corner was a photocopied newspaper cutting about Reg's forthcoming book, *Born Fighter*, and beneath that was a childlike scrawl which at first appeared to read, 'From B Cell Reg Kray'. After re-reading it, it took the form of 'Steve, God Bless. Reg Kray', and beneath that it said I could publicise *Born Fighter* in my magazine if I so wished.

The magazine in question was *The Mighty Quinn* (named after Newcastle United's centre forward at the time, Mickey Quinn), which I started up with my mate Steve Cross from Scunthorpe. We were both passionate about the Mags (Newcastle play in black and white strips and have a mascot of a Magpie, hence the Mags), and the magazine evolved from our love for the team. After three months in production, our very own soapbox was ready to hit the streets at forty pence a pop, undercutting our rivals by ten pence. Five hundred issues were sold in an hour and a half and we made a profit of a hundred and sixty quid! After that we enlisted some helpers – my dad, brother Rob and mate Rob Blaylock. The next issue did a lot better and *The Mighty Quinn* began to grow in popularity. As far as I was concerned, I was just like Robert Maxwell... well, after a decade on Slim Fast, that is.

I received Reg's first letter on fourteenth of November 1990. I was ecstatic. I read the letter again and again, hoping for it all to sink in. Then my friends and family read it again and again. Then I did again, for good measure. I doubt Reg was thinking along the same lines when he was writing, I mean, God knows how many letters he must have received day in day out, but to me it meant something. I had not anticipated how I would feel if he wrote back, but a big part of my feelings that day was nervousness. I think. I hadn't really prepared for a reply. My head was spinning; I had a huge adrenaline rush as I poured over the signature again. Reg had bothered to write back... he'd written to *me*.

It was like the impossible had happened. It was surreal. Now that I had a reply I wanted more. I wanted a visit. Straightaway I began another: "Dear Reg, Thanks for the letter..." Within two days I received another letter from Reg in an envelope he had addressed himself. How it arrived I will never know; it's surprising how mail gets to your door at the best of times, but miracles like this tend to restore your faith in the postal service. Again, the adrenaline took hold of me... shaking but opened with care. Then the initial joy turned to disappointment. The second letter was almost identical to the first. It was just a run-of-the-mill mail shot he sent out to everyone. My hopes of a friendship with Reg Kray were beginning to fade before my eyes. A day later my reply from Ron arrived with a clear message, "I will not be able to keep up a correspondence, God Bless. Your friend, Ron Kray". Again, this was a standard reply; it was typed with Ron's barely legible signature at the bottom. Two days later another letter from Reg saying the same thing, in what appeared to be a new form of hieroglyphics. They were both pleased I was thinking of them, supporting them even, but that would be the extent of our contact.

I was gutted. After such a promising start, it was a let down to get such news. I could see that my parents were relieved so I decided not to dwell on it and to get on with my own life. I'd had some form of contact, brief though it was. There wasn't much I could say about either of them at this point. I was a bit surprised at Reg's handwriting but that's about it. Maybe there are handwriting specialists who could use it to decipher his personality. At least they had the decency to say they could not continue writing instead of just leaving it. So there were no hard feelings from me as I was sure they had to send dozens of these letters out every week.

Three months passed until the name Kray found it's way into the Wraith household again. My mother handed me a copy of a magazine, *Take a Break*, with an article about a schoolboy who was hoping to become Reg Kray's adopted son. This lad, Brad Lane, had visited Reg after a pen-pal relationship... and lived not too far from Scunthorpe where my friend Steve Cross lived. Time to put plan B into effect (you *always* need a plan B) I wrote to Brad and asked about his 'dad' and sent some copies of *The Mighty Quinn* down. Then it was the waiting game again. A long waiting game. A *four-month* waiting game! A letter arrived along with apologies, and my quest continued. I know I have just said that I decided to get on with my life, but the curiosity was still there. If there was still a *slight* chance, then I wanted to take it. I had got so far and wanted to have another crack at meeting the twins. I have no idea what was spurring me on at this point. What is it that makes a teenager want to meet two convicted murderers? In a way, I did see them as heroes. I was fascinated by their notoriety, the way they dressed, the cars, the celebrity status... I suppose this was something I wanted for myself. Some may say I was obsessed. If I wanted something badly, I made sure I gave it my best shot.

My next step was to visit Steve and time it with a trip to see Brad and his mother, Kim. This was the first week of April 1991. I called them from Steve's and was told by Kim that they were going to visit Reg. "Come tomorrow and we might be able to get you on a visit to see him." I nearly dropped the phone; unable to contain myself... those were the words I'd wanted to hear. The next day I left Steve's and headed for Doncaster. Brad and Kim met me off the train, though I could see Brad had reservations about me turning up. I was probably seen as a predator who was there to 'take' Reg away from him. I think Kim was a bit embarrassed at his behaviour, but he became a bit more at ease as the day progressed. We went back to their place where Brad took me up to his room – or shrine – to look through some of his Kray memorabilia. He had a large oil painting by Paul Lake signed, 'to Brad from dad and Uncle Ron.' I was green with envy. It was excellent to see all this, but at the back of my mind I was thinking this is all well and good, but I want to meet him. Kim said he'd be phoning soon and that he'd been asking about me. It felt eerie... not in a scary way though, just the fact that Reg had been asking about me... what did he want to know? I was sitting on edge till he phoned, then it happened: The phone rang and I could feel my heart thumping against my chest. "That'll be dad", said Brad and as Kim answered I was straining to hear the conversation above the Edgar Allen Poe-esque heartbeat inside me. Everything was a blur till she turned to me, saying he wanted a quick word. I have to admit that I was shaking when I took the receiver from Kim, I said, 'Hello Reg' into the mouthpiece.

"Hello, who's that? Is that you, Steve?" he asked.

"Yes Reg. It's Steve from Newcastle."

"Newcastle, eh? How far is that? About three hundred miles, is it... that's a long way, was it a long journey?"

"Yes Reg, but it was worth it." I seemed to be gaining my confidence now.

"Good, good. Well, you look after Brad, he's a smashing kid, be like a brother to him, okay, and I'll see you soon, okay. God bless."

I handed the receiver back to Kim. That was it – my first conversation with Reg Kray. My first impression? His voice was a lot easier to understand than his handwriting.

He was softly spoken with his unmistakable cockney accent. I was trembling with excitement. Kim hung up the phone and told me I had clearance to visit him the following day.

There was speculation of a move, but my first visit to Reg was when he was still at HMP Gartree in Leicester. I had an overwhelming sense of fear entering the prison. The sheer enormity of the place... you are in a different world immediately, reassured only by the fact that if you can get to look out of a window you still share the same sky, and you know you are a visitor. It is too easy to forget yourself in such a short space of time. I can't imagine what it must be like to be locked up in a prison – people say there are tough prisons and easy prisons, but I think any situation where your liberty is taken away is tough.

Kim was asked for the visiting order, then I had to record my personal details. Why a nineteen year old would be married and have a long string of convictions was beyond me, but those were the type of questions I needed to answer before we could sit in the waiting room; soon after we were led out by an officer to see Reg. We were taken through a series of what can only be described as contenders for the biggest, widest iron doors in history, each one of them thumping shut to send a rattling awareness of doom through you. I'm sure they probably *do* shut quietly, but the officers are not there to make visitors feel at ease. Quite the opposite, as I was now beginning to realise. Through another iron gate and we were there. I wasn't quite sure what to expect, but was surprised by what I saw in the visiting room. Four straight lines of six tables each with four chairs around them. I suppose it was the openness of it all... after seeing too many films with thick glass partitions and telephone headsets to communicate. Brad and Kim made for a table which was slap bang in the middle of the room. Brad said that 'dad liked to sit there', I was bemused that he'd prefer to be in the middle but this was all new to me. I was expecting to be sitting in a far corner, backs to the wall, a clear view of the door, and the entire room. The other visits were in full swing now and there was no sign of Reg. Now I was beginning to shuffle in my seat – anticipation... nerves... the lot. I was up a height. It seemed to have happened that quickly that I'd had no time to think about the situation. The contact I'd made already, meeting Brad and Kim had been a long process – but now I'd spoke to Reg one day and was meeting him the following. I trained my eyes on a small door at the far end of the room, and as I stared a well-built, grey haired man appeared. At first it didn't register that it was him. Kim and Brad stood up to greet him but I was fixed to my seat. I'd made the effort in a suit and tie, but etiquette wise, the situation was so surreal I just couldn't react. Reg wasn't bothered... he extended his bony white hand from his prison shirt, shaking my hand in what was a vice-like grip.

"Pleased to meet you Steve, glad you could make it. How are you? Did you have a good journey?" He asked, as he looked me in the eyes. I regained my composure and greeted him. The first thing I was aware of looking into Reg's eyes was power. He had a self-assured look with piercing eyes. As he sat, it struck me how small he was. I was just over six feet tall at the time, a few inches taller than Reg. I suppose that is what *everyone* thinks when they meet someone like this for the first time, 'you can't be Reg Kray, Reg Kray is seven feet tall'... it is expected from mythological characters.

Still in my mind was that black and white picture of the twins by David Bailey, both of them looking like towering giants, staring down at everyone, which I suppose, was the effect they wanted. For a man on the wrong side of fifty, he was an awesome sight... physically fit having never missed a training session since being locked up. He asked how I was getting on with Brad and what I did in Newcastle, or Newcarsel as his accent pronounced it. I hate it being pronounced like that, but this time I kept it to myself. I was explaining to him that I ran a post office and a magazine for Newcastle United fans when he stopped me mid-sentence. "That's it! I knew I had something to ask you. I'll write to you about it." With that, he turned his attentions to Brad who was sat on his knee. He turned away and left me thinking, Eh? Reg Kray is interested in my post office job? Wait a minute... *post office job?* No way.

Throughout the next two hours, Kim made her way back and forward to the canteen collecting cartons of orange squash for Reg... he'd take a drink before Brad would produce a small bottle from his pocket and top it up. I later found out that it was being topped up with Scotch, although the way he began slurring and repeating himself was a dead give-away that it was some sort of alcohol. He also acquired a nice colour to his face in this state of merriment, which was compounded by the fact that Kim was quite subdued throughout the visit. Even though drunk, he still asked what was wrong with her... Kim just shrugged each time, silent. As I got to know her better, these sorts of mood swings were commonplace, so I didn't pay them much attention. I knew a lot of women used to write to Reg with wild ideas of forming romantic relations with him – whether it was because they liked him or the notoriety I don't know. As time went on, I often wondered if Kim had similar feelings. Maybe Brad was a way of getting to know Reg... I'll never know... I used to think about it sometimes when she was in a mood, thinking that she was like that because I was there and was jealous because I was becoming friends with him. True or not, I wasn't bothered.

During that visit (and others), Reg spent a lot of his time elsewhere – literally. He was like a sideshow... shaking hands with everyone... having a quick word with someone... leaving the three of us in an uncomfortable silence till his return. With around fifteen minutes of the visit remaining, a familiar face approached our table. Paddy 'Joe' Hill, one of the Birmingham Six came over and greeted us. He shook Reg's hand firmly saying he'd be praying for him to get out. Paddy himself recently being released after a severe miscarriage of justice meant he'd spent the best part of his life in jail. Reg was visibly lifted by Paddy's words and this meant that my first visit was left on a high. Paddy had been locked away for sixteen years after confessing under torture... he was finally awarded a million pound in 2002 for what he went through, but a million pounds does not come close as compensation for such a loss of time to an innocent man.

As we got up to leave, I shook hands with Reg again; "You must visit my brother, Ron. I'll try to sort something out. Thanks for the smashing visit, look after Brad and have a safe journey home. I'll be in touch." Then he hugged me just like Brando in *The Godfather*. This demonstration of affection made me feel important, not just that he had done it, but everyone in that room saw it too. The last of his 'squash' was then swigged back and he made his way back to the far end of the room, pausing for a second to wave at us then was gone.

As we waited to be escorted out, I had time to think about what had just happened. He was a middle-aged man, physically and mentally fit as I was. He was not bitter about being held there, though neither was he remorseful for why he was there either. I was quite sad to leave him but at the same time it was not like he was begging us to take him with us. He was established there, he was a survivour, and that meant he had adapted to his environment. Though in this case, it looked like the environment was adapting to him. I knew he was no stranger to prison; but I felt the length of such a sentence would have been enough to crush any man's soul. Not this man. I can look back on it now and know that it's not sympathy he wanted, sure you can feel for his plight, but to him it was just about serving time. It wasn't the situation where you could say, 'poor Reg, locked up like that.' He did his crime and he was doing his time... fair cop and all that. He knew he had a lot of time to serve, so he made the best of it. At first when he'd been locked up with Ron and the firm, he was an angry young man. He'd get into fights with cons as well as officers and was letting everyone know who controlled the inside – the two who had controlled the outside. There were newer kids on the block now though and fighting is a young man's game. Reg had done enough to ensure he was respected wherever he was, he didn't have to prove himself anymore.

Once I got home I put pen to paper again; wanting to strike while the iron was hot. The next day I received two more letters from him telling me to keep an eye on Brad, and insisting I visit Ron as soon as I could. After the first visit, local newspapers ran stories on my Kray friendship and it became a bit of a novelty in the area. Media interest was something I could use to my advantage, I made sure to mention the magazine in interviews, which helped to shift a few copies. I could sense from that visit that we'd hit it off, then a few days later, Reg asked me to look out for a large house or a mansion for him in Newcastle with plenty of land. He had told me he'd been interested in an affluent area of the city on their infamous visit in the sixties, but hadn't done anything about it. He'd had thoughts then of a speiler but now he was thinking long term about the future. It wasn't the first time he did this. Years on I'd even put down a large deposit on a house for him which he lost interest in. The deposit was the sort of sum that would buy a comfortable house at the time.

Early on during my visits was when the requests and favours started. They were subtle at first... on the twenty-fifth of April 1991 Reg told me to tell Ron that he disliked Kate (Ron's wife) and not to trust her. In September 1991, he asked if I had heard any news on Charlie Kray, as they aren't speaking... every visit I can remember since I started 'working' for them began with 'any news?'

I kept up regular correspondence with the twins. I could see that I'd made an impression and I also started to visit frequently. Reg was a Category B prisoner that meant he was only allowed two visitors a week, so I felt honoured to be invited round about once a month to see him. Ron in Broadmoor could have two visitors a day. The only problem I had was the travelling. As I don't drive, I had to catch the train to visit him, but it was worth it. As time moved on, I fell out with Brad and Kim – I'm not sure if it was resentment or jealousy over my friendship, but that's the way things go I suppose. You can't be friends with everyone.

Then the visits began to change slightly... I was visiting Reg on my own, my friendship was independent of Kim and Brad. It also meant that there was not someone else there to fill the uncomfortable silences... not that there were any. We got along fine as friends and he was intrigued by the fact that I was running a post office and editing the magazine at such an early age. He could see that I was entrepreneurial and took a chance... he told me he had a warehouse full of merchandise and wanted me to help advertise and sell it – for a share of the profits, of course. He gave me the number of a bloke called Pete Gillette, who would 'supply me'. It was one buzz after another in Kray World. It seemed like no time had passed since my first visit, and here I was talking openly with Reg and now being asked to do favours. I didn't really have to think about it... it wasn't that I was bullied into anything or felt pressured, it just progressed that way.

I phoned Pete Gillette as Reg had suggested. I didn't feel out of my depth, but this was all new to me and I suppose I wanted to make a good impression. It was the rush of being part of something that made me feel a bit edgier than usual. Reg had trusted me enough to do this and I didn't want to let him down. It would look bad for him to befriend someone who would mess up first time, and wouldn't do my confidence much good to know I had ruined a friendship in such a way. Pete had shared a cell with Reg and was a close friend of his. I told him what Reg had said. He seemed a nice enough bloke and said he'd sort something out. Now, there's sorting out, and there's *sorting out*... his impression of sorting out meant sending six huge boxes of merchandise to my door. I couldn't believe it. I took the boxes in and had a good rummage through them. I was like a kid on Christmas morning. There were hundreds of copies of the twins' autobiography, *Our Story*, tee-shirts with Reg's face on and the words 'Enough is Enough' printed beneath, and some copies of an artists impression of the twins which were selling at two hundred and fifty quid each. There was a note with the pictures in Pete's handwriting: 'Steve. Keep up the good work. One of the prints is for you from the twins. Be lucky, Pete Gillette.

I made the post office my base and began advertising my new stock from there. At first, the response was slow, but once word spread I was snowed under with orders and phone calls. It just needed to be rejuvenated slightly to get the ball rolling. I bought some sticky labels, sending half each to Reg and Ron to sign, then stuck them on the books. Now, the demand for limited edition signed copies of Kray books is a lot higher than your common or garden Kray book, isn't it? And that's what everyone else thought, as they were quite prepared to pay extra for them as well. They went for twenty quid each – it was amazing. The twins were over the moon and so was I. I knew I was pretty clued up on making fast money like this but I also learned something else that day: The twins may have been behind bars, but it was business as usual for them. It took time to realise exactly what I was doing – I mean, it was a favour I was doing. Reg asked me to do him a favour, right? So I did him a favour. It was little favours like this that kept Reg's mind busy behind bars. A lot of people doing such favours would amount to quite a tidy little sum. 'Favours', as he would put it, were business and people prepared to do favours for the twins meant they never went out of business. That first venture netted them a four-figure sum, and true to their word I was given my cut. Reg suggested that it might be useful to advertise in my magazine, which was still called *The Mighty Quinn* at this point – a suggestion that I took on board, but I wanted something in return. I wanted him to write an article on football for it. He was a bit hesitant at first, but two days later, I received *My Football Recollections*, reproduced here in entirety.

Though I have never been a fanatical football fan, I have had the pleasure of seeing some of the great players. My earliest introduction to a football match was when I was about ten years old and an uncle of mine took Ron and I to Tottenham Hotspur's football ground to watch them play. There were thousands of people present on this day, packed together, and my first impression was that such a gathering of people could be dangerous for the sake of their safety, if they were not controlled properly. Those days there were not the same seating facilities as there are today. The other thing I noticed was that the footballers wore very long and baggy shorts and I wondered to myself why they did not wear neat shorts the same as boxers. At the same time I was fanatical about the sport of boxing and so would read all the boxing magazines, and so saw all the boxing photographs and how the fighters dressed in their shorts and boots for their bouts. One of the greatest footballers I ever saw was the great Stanley Matthews. I remember how he would dribble past each player on the right wing until he was in a position to pass across the goalmouth. His dribbling was uncanny, and the way he would swerve was a pleasure to watch. Another great player that I saw was the late Frank Swift. He was obviously one of the world's greatest goalkeepers. I remember how he would pick up the ball with one hand and throw it toward one of his side. Around about that time, I witnessed the great playing of Tommy Lawton, who could head a ball better than any other player I have seen. He was the best centre forward that I ever did see. I was also fortunate in that I saw the Compton brothers Denis and Leslie. I recall either one or both of them were associated with the hair cream Brylcreem, in that it was said that they used Brylcreem daily. Many years later I met Malcolm Allison the player manager at the Astor drinking club just off Berkeley Square in the West End of London. In one of the books I have written there is a photograph of Malcolm and I, along with others, taken on this occasion. Sometime in the sixties I met Dave Mckay and used to go to his shirt and tie shop to buy ties. When I was first convicted I spent some time in Leicester Prison and there I met Frank O'Farell. He came to Leicester Prison to give a lecture on football to the inmates, which he did on a regular basis, and I know that he gave his fee to charity. Frank is one of the nicest people it has been my pleasure to have met and we became firm friends to this day. Frank has been one of the best player managers in the game. Sad to say, some years later, after my first introduction to football and my perception of the crowd dangers, there was a disaster at one of the stadiums when the crowd got out of control. On reflection I feel that if a ten year-old could foresee a crowd control problem then the safety people at the time should have seen the same. On a happier note, I was pleased to say that my fashion consciousness did come into effect, by the wearing of shorter shorts and better all round attire. I seem to recall that it was mainly down to the Italian teams that footballers did become smarter in general, because they copied the Italian teams. About five years ago my friend Pete Gillett influenced me into becoming an Arsenal fan, so I will be rooting for the Gunners, and wish them a successful season. Last but not least, I would like to take this opportunity to wish all football fans, regardless of which team they support, an enjoyable end to the season. God Bless, Reg Kray.

Reginald Kray, May 1991

I couldn't thank him enough. It showed that he was not just on the take and that he could return a favour to me. That again was an important sign. I did receive a bit of criticism from the local press for my association with the twins, but sales of *The Mighty Quinn* increased following the article, and that's what counted. I don't believe in bad publicity; never have done.

Something was bugging me about the Reg tee-shirts that Pete had sent me along with the other stuff. I couldn't put my finger on the reason, other than I just wasn't that impressed by them. I knew they could be better and I knew that there was a demand for Kray merchandise. I suggested to him that I knocked up some designs for a new tee-shirt and see how they sold. The cut would be seventy-thirty in their favour and I got cracking as soon as I could. A month later we not only had a new tee-shirt design but also shopping bags, t-towels, calendars and mirrors – a whole range which once approved, was snapped up almost immediately. A fanatic will buy just about anything but I had to draw the line on a few items out of respect. For example, Kray condoms... a pack of three personalised by each brother – the ultimate protection racket. Reg supplied me with lists and lists of names and addresses he'd collected over the duration of his sentence and told me to mail shot them. I used freebie post office envelopes (thank you, your Highness) and received excellent feedback. It was amazing how much interest there actually was and that people would feel they needed these things because they carried the Kray name on them. The tee-shirts were really popular and I got a lot of praise from satisfied customers.

It wasn't long into our working relationship when I received a call from Reg. He would only tell me that it was urgent that I went to see him, so putting it like that, I didn't really have much choice. He'd just been moved from Gartree to Nottingham Prison so it was a bit easier to get to. The atmosphere in Nottingham was pretty relaxed as we shook hands and embraced. Something was on his mind. Still in contact with Brad and Kim Lane, Reg was concerned for Brad and it seemed that he was really beginning to go off the rails. Reg put it down to not having a distinct father figure, something that Brad needed in his life. I couldn't agree more, that is until he went on, "I can't be Brad's father cos I'm a lifer. I'd like you to move in with Brad and Kim and be a father to him". I couldn't have disagreed more. I was gobsmacked... you could have knocked me down with a feather and then invented a few more clichés in a vain attempt to express what was going through my head. Put yourself in that position for a second... I was looking right at him in disbelief, hoping he might crack up and tell me he was kidding. There was silence... still I stared as he looked at me for a reaction. What the hell could I do? He was actually being serious! I sat stunned as he talked. He took out a folder containing what looked like legal documents. It was as outrageous as anything that Ron could throw my way – in fact, more so.

I had no intention of going along with the idea, and luckily it was never mentioned again. It was certainly one of the most bizarre things I've ever heard in my life. I really don't know how to explain the logic behind it. It was a harebrained scheme where he had given absolutely no thought to anyone or consideration to anyone's lives. I could probably look at it from different angles and say it was an honour that he thought so highly, then the other angle is the complete opposite. He wanted me to move in and take care of these people who I'd already fallen out with, be a father to an out of control teenager (it wasn't that long ago that I'd been one) and be a husband to someone I barely even knew. On that visit we (thankfully) discussed other business. Real business. He wanted my help in republishing a book of his called *Thoughts, Philosophy and Poetry*. My ears pricked up immediately, as there was more potential in this one happening. Originally, the book had been a flop and he wanted me to help repair the damage. I jumped at the chance. Just being connected to the project would have been good, but financially I was offered a better cut than I expected. Reg was keen to split the profits straight down the middle and I was keen to let him. I was on a high as I travelled home; it certainly was a much more appealing prospect than becoming a father with a ready made dysfunctional son.

The next few months were spent sorting out copyright clearance and other contractual commitments that had been signed for on the book's first release. Once that was out the way there was just the task of reading an entire manuscript in Reg's handwriting. I lost count of the hours I spent on it, but after six months I was happy with the final draft copy. It was back breaking, eye straining work but I'd done it. Then came the next bombshell... "Steve, I've decided not to re-release *Thoughts*, but could you help me with my new book? Its called *Villains We Have Known*. I'll go seventy-thirty with you."

I was outraged to put it mildly. I mumbled something to the effect that I'd be unable to help him on that one and put the phone down. The thing that hurt the most was that he didn't even apologise for wasting my time. I had learnt a very hard lesson. I had wasted near enough nine months on the strength that we were going to re-release the book. It just showed how far removed from reality the man was... he was so out of touch with the real world that he thought time meant nothing to everyone else. I'm not sure how true that is, or whether he just didn't care that I had my own life on the outside. Whichever one it was it meant he was inconsiderate. I'd also began to publicise the book in the newspapers, and the *Sunday People* had ran an article on it. I learnt that Reg was like that – his moods changed like the weather. He could ask you to help with something on one visit, you'd set the wheels in motion and go into the next visit well prepared... then he would have changed his mind and it was over. Just like that. This was usual for Ron as well, it was all par for the course. To have one friend like that was annoying enough, but two of them was too much at times.

One consolation I got from the book deal, or the cease of, was that there were ten unused poems that he said I could have and use as I saw fit. I knew him well enough by now to let the book deal go. On a few occasions we got on each other's nerves or let each other down; it meant that we would stay clear of anything similar in the future. We always needed a cooling off period. So Reg asking me to help on a different book was out of the question for me, even if it was a ninety per cent cut in my favour. Once bitten, twice never gonna waste my time for Reg again, as they say. He could see I wasn't taken by the Brad and Kim idea, so it was forgotten about as well as the book. Life with the twins was like a rollercoaster... full of ups and downs so you knew that when you were on either that it wouldn't last forever, and the opposite was on it's way. Still, I knew there was always money to be made as far as they were concerned, so wasting time on the book was all it had been. At least I hadn't lost any money. He still wouldn't give up on the idea of *Villains* though. On the fifth of February 1992, Reg asked me to introduce him to Chris Donald, the bloke behind *Viz* magazine, or *Fizz*, as Reg called it. He wanted Donald to buy into *Villains We Have Known* and also to buy a share in *A Way Of Life*, another book Reg had in mind. The interest in '*Fizz*' came from the fact that they had ran a spoof story on the Krays and Reg assumed they must be supporters. In consecutive months, I was asked if my mate Paul Hollingshead would print *Villians* for a ten per cent cut and then to print and promote it with Paul Marcus Henry. He was like a man possessed, changing his mind all the time and phoning me to ask whether I'd ask people to get involved. I'd already given him my answer and I was sticking to it.

Celebrity visits when I knew Reg were a far cry from the fifties and sixties. Back then the Twins were celebrities through association, they met everyone who was worth knowing, but now 'celebrities' would only ever visit the twins for one reason – to raise their profile. An ageing comedian / now has-been soap star and a washed up actress are two that spring to mind. Their respective careers were at an all time low, so what better way to get your name in the papers than to visit dear old Reg? It really annoyed me, because when their help was needed they were otherwise engaged. Reg would not have it though, like me he believed that any publicity was good publicity so people used Reg and vice versa in the end. They would argue that there was friendship and say they knew the twins from the old days, but friends are there all the time, not just in the run up to Christmas when they are in pantomime and want publicity. You could almost start a poster campaign with that: 'Reg Kray is in for life... don't just visit at Christmas'.

Speaking of Christmas, the twenty-second of December 1992 became a date that I would remember for a very long time. Mrs. Dodd, the Governor of Blundestone prison's secretary, wrote saying that Reg wanted me to visit him on what was known as Family Day. This was a day where lifers could spend some quality time with their loved ones as a sort of Christmas present. Lifers tend to get such privileges and I considered it an honour to be invited. It would be a six-hour visit. I got the letter two weeks before the visit, so I'd had time to let it sink in and also to panic slightly at the same time. All kinds of thoughts were running through my mind... Would we be able to fill the visit with conversation? That was my biggest worry as often Reg struggled not to repeat what he'd already said, so how would he cope with a visit three times as long? I was half an hour late for the visit due to the bad weather causing rail delays. I called the Prison but should have known that my message wouldn't have reached him. The various security checks and leaving a few bits and bobs at reception for him just slowed me down even more, but eventually I was escorted to the large visiting room. The room was *alive*... Children's voices and all the decorations made it just like Christmas Day. Reg was at his usual table in the middle of the room, and sitting with him was the prison's vicar and a nun. I waited until they had finished and Reg stood up to greet me. He said his goodbyes to them and then he hugged me like a long lost brother.

"Thanks for coming Steve, you look fit and well, your filling out nicely,"... I braced myself for the inevitable... "You do know your half an hour late, and I've had to listen to their rubbish for all that time." I tried to explain that the weather had caused delays, but excuses didn't interest Reg. He had no concerns about the weather... I was late and that was that, no point in dwelling on it.

We were scheduled for two meals; at midday it would be a three-course meal of soup, followed by turkey with all the trimmings and ice cream or jam roly-poly for dessert. Then at three o'clock it would be a choice of sandwiches and crisps followed by fruit or cheese and biscuits... sounded good to me. The first two hours flew over as we discussed business deals and talked about people on the outside that Reg wanted me to get in touch with. The Christmas atmosphere had engulfed the prison. As we began our first course, I couldn't help feeling that this meal could be taking place absolutely anywhere. To take a photo and look back on it, you could have passed it off as a family Christmas dinner at home. It was quite poignant as I took a look around and saw all these families tucking into turkey. For that one day in the year, they *were* at home. I also thought about Reg as we ate. For him to invite me that day was like saying I was a member of the family. It wasn't something that we openly discussed, but we both knew what it meant for us to both be there.

After lunch, Reg began to reflect on the past and speculate about the future. He didn't often talk about his past, so I decided to seize the initiative and ask him if he would have changed his life in anyway. He took a deep breath and stared right at me, "No, I wouldn't Steve. If I hadn't done what I done, I would never have met people like you. You and others who visit me would never have written to me if I had not been in prison. My one and only regret is not to have made it as a boxer, but it was obviously not meant to be."

On a roll I asked if he regretted killing Jack McVitie. His

answer was short and sweet, "No, he got what he deserved and I have no regrets." Reg never showed any remorse for his crimes and I feel that this was the sole reason that the Home Office never showed any compassion in releasing him earlier. If he said he was sorry for doing it, then he'd be saying that he shouldn't have done it and that it was a mistake. In his world in past days, decisions were made on the spot and you stuck by that decision. It was gangland... there is no remorse in gangland and no going back. To someone outside of this world – people like you and me, or a grand jury – just cannot comprehend that someone can say the wrong thing or wind someone up and as a consequence, *deserve* to die. It's as alien to us as it would be for one of them to take a nine to five nice safe office job. The Krays have always portrayed Jack McVitie as a pill-popping-good-for-nothing bloke and tried their best to make him look bad to justify killing him. He took pills so he could stay awake for twenty-four hours at a time. He loved life and hated the night coming to an end; pills and booze were his vice. He had taken liberties with the twins – he was supposed to have fulfilled obligations which he had not, he was forever borrowing money and not paying it back. It was felt that they couldn't let him get away with it anymore. The justification was that he was making a nuisance of himself in gangland – he became a problem they needed to get rid of. The decision was made; they stuck to it, end of story.

Reg introduced me to a few of the others lifers on the same visit, and as usual he would walk from table to table playing the host to other visitors. As I watched this, I could see he was completely in his element... shaking hands, hugging, laughing and joking and talking business. It was quite sad in a way. I thought of Ron and how his day may be panning out. I always thought of Ron as the one who was stuck in his former life, now it was just like Reg was reliving the days of glory as well. As twins, I found them both quite different, but in this mode there was no difference at all. In this mode we weren't in prison, we were in the *Double R* or *The Regal*. At least we were for those few valuable minutes. It was such a sight to behold – everyone there couldn't wait to meet him. All looking up from their family time to introduce him or to let him pick their child up, shake his hand and say 'Merry Christmas'.

Just after we'd finished our sandwiches, Reg motioned to one of the officers who brought down a large brown box. "I got you a few things for Christmas Steve, have a look at that little lot." He sat back in his chair, smiling proudly as I opened the box. It was crammed full with socks, shirts, pens and pencils and books by all sorts of people including two boxing books featuring the twins by Harry Carpenter and Frank Bruno. I was gob smacked... looking up I thanked Reg before diving straight back into it. They say that Christmas is about giving and not receiving, and when I looked up from that box with my amazed expression, I could tell that Reg had got a lot of pleasure from it. So, here's me rummaging through all this incredible stuff and then it begins to dawn on me. A lot of people would send stuff into Reg – socks, shirts, pens and pencils and books by all sorts of people. My 'present' turned out to be the stuff he obviously didn't want. Still, it's the thought that counts and it's not like he could have nipped over to the local Megastore to buy me The Wonder Stuff's new CD, is it? At least he'd put some thought into putting it all into a box.

The six hours that I had worried about filling came to an end. Reg thanked me for a 'Smashin' visit', and we embraced and as I picked up my box and made my way to the exit. The floor was littered with bits of wrapping paper and streamers as I walked toward the door, the other visits had came to an end and the sound of the children playing became a memory until next year. Reg stood at the table and waved, a visible tear in his eye. It was actually a sad moment. This had been his Christmas. I always think of Christmas as a time for family – it's what Christmas should be all about.

I thought about this a lot more on my way to the station. It puzzled me why Ron and Reg could not spend this Family Day together as they had no other family to enjoy it with. I couldn't help but laugh inside as I went through my Christmas box again on the journey home. I opened the first few pages of the Frank Bruno book to see that it was signed... not by Bruno, but by another boxer, 'God bless. Reg Kray'. It had been a great day, though. One that we'd both never forget. Presents or no presents, it was an honour to spend such time with Reg Kray.

Sometimes arranging visits was difficult due to work commitments, but it meant when we did catch up we had a lot more to talk about. In the new year, I visited him again in Blundestone Prison and immediately I saw the glint in his eye... obviously there was news. As another con brought over some refreshments and left the table, out it came, "I've proposed to someone, Steve." Amazing. I couldn't believe it. Rumours of Reg spending 'quality time' with other inmates had been doing the rounds for years – Reg liked to spend his hours with the younger prisoners rather than the older lags... but to actually propose to one of them? I think Reg had read my mind and put me at ease when he announced that he had proposed to a *female* prisoner by the name of Linda Calvey. Linda was known as *'The Black Widow'* and was serving a long sentence for murder. A match made in heaven, I hear you say. Quite. He had kept up a long-term pen-pal relationship with Calvey and had decided to pop the question. He hadn't received an answer for a time but was quietly confident. I don't know about you, but if I was proposing to someone called *'The Black Widow'*, the last thing I would be was confident. He then talked of his first wedding to Francis Shea. There was no question that Reg doted on Francis and I don't think he ever let go of her or their special day. Having his bride buried in her wedding dress after her tragic suicide was testament to that. The wedding to the Black Widow never happened, but I later learnt from Reg that Charlie Bronson had also proposed to Calvey in the same week. She declined on both counts. Women, eh?

With both twins there were always urgent press duties to take care of. It may have been campaigning on behalf of one of them or setting the record straight for both of them, but always *something*. I was glad to help out if and when I was asked to write to a newspaper. There was one occasion that Ron had asked me to write to John Major, who was the Prime Minister at the time. Ron loved it, but Reg went mad saying I'd played into the hands of the press and had jeopardised their chances of parole. Ron was keen to keep the ball rolling though, saying to me all the time that Reg should not be kept in prison any longer and to help get him out. I mentioned it on my next visit to Reg, suggesting a march to Downing Street to deliver a petition to Major. At first he wasn't keen on the idea and he killed the conversation dead. Fine – I knew not to pursue it any further. We discussed all the other usual business, and then towards the end of the visit he asked, "How many signatures do you think you could get?" Bingo. That was the sign I needed to start an official campaign. Reg and Ron had hundreds of friends and thousands of addresses of pen-pals, so once the forms were printed by Steph King, one of Reg's closest friends, we set about sending them to people who would be willing to go out and collect names. The forms were returned in their hundreds over the next few weeks and by the time the last sheet was returned there was over ten thousand signatures. Steph organised the walk from Hyde Park to Downing Street, whilst I organised the press and media. The date was set for October the ninth 1993. As expected there was a low turn out of 'faces', but over two hundred supporters turned up to justify the heavy police presence. The petition was handed over to the Prime Minister and all the major television channels and newspapers were there to capture it. It was a job well done. The twins were happy, Steph and I were happy. It was a shame though because for all the effort we had put in, I knew it wouldn't make the slightest bit of difference to possible release. It did succeed in keeping Reg Kray in the media spotlight and showed that he could still pull the crowds in.

There were always con men, crooks and cranks popping up all the time, and I was always given the 'pleasure' of meeting them. Of course I also met a lot of genuine people who shared a belief that the Krays should be released, many of whom I am still in touch with to this day. Once I was introduced to a fellow con, "Steve, this is Paul... he's a good burglar." He just looked like a hanger on. I said to Reg that he couldn't be that good if he was in here. Reg had no answer. There was no answer. The 'burglar' then got up and left us. As we talked, another inmate caught Reg's eye. He beckoned the man over and introduced him to me. His name was Ron Stevens. Ron was a good friend of Reg and had first met Reg in a billiard hall on Mile End road. He later became a regular at the twins' *Double R* club, and they had kept in touch for years until their paths finally crossed again, this time behind bars. Reg was always full of business ideas and as I got to know him more I began to wonder if he was losing his marbles. He asked me to meet up with an assortment of nutters and oddballs the length and breadth of the country to 'square a deal' as he put it. These were the scams or 'business ventures' where I became the point of contact.

First up was a trip to Wales to meet the Frayne brothers. These two lads looked the business. Reg had asked me to pick up some merchandise from them and check them out. They took me around the pubs and clubs where they were running the doors and were good company. They handed over the stuff that Reg wanted and that was that. A pleasant time was had by all. A year on and they were arrested and sent down for robbery. The papers said that the brothers revelled in the Kray story and that they had convinced themselves that they were the new twins.

Next on the loony tour; Mike Peters from Birmingham. He had arranged a charity do in aid of a young lad with brittle bones disease and wanted to use Reg's name to publicise the lads plight. No problem there. Reg sent down some signed artwork. He then asked Reg if he would be interested in a fifty-fifty partnership in a used car business. Reg gave me an address and asked me to go and have a look at the place to see if it was kosher. To enter into the partnership Mike wanted twenty-five grand up front from Reg. I knew a few lads in Birmingham and asked them to take a trip around spaghetti junction a few times to find out what this lad was all about. When I got the call back I wasn't surprised to hear that our man was known in the area as a con man. Formerly known as Steve Fowler, it was said that his office was a brick wall with a door; the rest of the building lay as rubble behind it. Reg was fuming but grateful that he had asked me to check out the man's credentials in advance.

Scaffolding was next up on the Kray business plan. Jonathan Parlin had set up a company in Essex but felt that because he was such a fan of the twins that the least he could do was offer Reg half of his business and twenty-five per cent of any profits. All he wanted in return was Reg to say that yes he was in business with him. Reg duly obliged and was confident that this man was kind hearted and genuine. Another promising sign was that Jonathan even changed the name of his company to incorporate his new business partner's name. Instead of *Parlin Scaffolding* it was now *Par-Kray Scaffolding*. He even sent Reg a few sheets of headed paper and business cards to prove he was doing things above board. Reg was proud to be a partner again. I wasn't convinced. I decided to check out Mr. Parlin with the help of my mate Christian Simpson. Christian knew Essex like the back of his hand and it didn't take long to track down Mr. Parlin. Unlike Mike Peters in Birmingham, Jonathan Parlin did own a scaffolding company, unfortunately he also owed half the population of Essex a lot of money, and we were talking the bad part of Essex not the good part. So now it was coming together. He owes a lot of bad people a lot of money... so he calls in Reg Kray. What better way to frighten off those people he owes money to than introducing his not so silent partner? After a visit from Christian and me, *Par-Kray Scaffolding* folded. No amount of industrial strength support would be able to re-build Mr. Parlins reputation after that one.

I lost track of the number of different ventures that fell through for various reasons. A lot of the time they fell through because they were so off the wall there was no way they would ever get anywhere. Reg had his own ideas – producing Champagne, or 'Campaign Cocktail' as it was to be known, red roses in plastic tubes with his name on a card inside – and those are some of the tame ones. Quite often, these harebrained schemes would come from an associate of the twins as a money earner and it wasn't always just Ron who would jump in feet first without looking. I said I would act as an advisor for Reg, for both of them... kind of like a mediator to suss out the money makers from the time wasters. If I knew then what I know now, I wouldn't have bothered. I was getting calls from all over the place with offers, offers and more offers... practically every trade you can think of. Some of them turned out to be very profitable for him and others of course, turned out to be con men after Kray money.

There was the time I was called by a Scotsman going by the name of John Miller. He wanted Reg to put his name to a business venture called *School Dinners*. He wanted a five-figure sum that would see Reg earn his money back in no time and promised a lot more on top. Now, those kinds of promises sound good – some bank managers may argue that such a business plan and turnover sounds good enough to warrant a nice start-up loan in fact, which was the first cause for alarm. Reg was quite keen to get involved, but somehow the name John Miller sounded familiar to me. I'm quite good with faces, which comes from doing the door, but names don't mean that much to me unless you are important. For some reason this name had stuck in my mind, but why? I started flicking through all the indexes of my Kray books, then onto other books till I reached Ron Biggs' autobiography, *His Own Story*. And there he was... Miller, John. I flicked through the pages and began to read about how Mr. Miller had attempted to kidnap Ron Biggs in return for a reward. When I reported the story to Reg, the deal was dead. Our friend John had also claimed to have found Lord Lucan prior to the Biggs kidnap. Maybe the twins were his next targets, who knows? He was certainly a tryer. The *School Dinners* scheme did go ahead though, without Kray involvement. It was so successful that I read about it in the newspapers. It was alleged that he had prostitutes dressed up as schoolgirls to serve more than just food in his eating establishments. What a bloke. It was a close call and would have been an absolute disaster if I hadn't looked into John Millers background first.

Reg was always interested in what was going on in the outside world. He was fascinated by the fact that you could now get takeaway food delivered to your door and loved to hear about other cultural developments. I mean, last time he was free, a Big Mac was something he'd hide a shooter in. One development he was really into was the music scene. He was heavily into rave culture and had even experimented with drugs such as ecstasy. One story about his drug taking even leaked to the press via 'a trusted cellmate', which was titled 'Reg E Kray'. In September 1996, I took dance band QFX to meet him in Maidstone, along with my mate Ray Cann. Ray was panicking as Reg had asked for a pair of training shoes and Ray had been unable to deliver. This was Ray's first visit, so as soon as we arrived he made for the nearest sports shop while Jacquie, Kirk and me went for a drink. Just as we were finishing our drinks, Ray came in out of breath but smiling. He had a bag with a pair of training shoes in - panic over. The security inside the prison was a lot tighter than it had been in the past. We were searched but luckily had decided not to take in the bottles of scotch as requested. We took our seats in the visiting room and Reg appeared looking fit and well. He took an instant shine to Jacquie and said he'd ask a warden if she could stay the night with him. Reg looked a bit unsure of Ray at first though making him sit on his 'deaf side' as he did with most new people. After small talk it was down to business... Reg brought a portfolio of songs he and cell mate Bradley Allardyce had written, which were surprisingly good – a lot better than his poetry, which was more or less what I was expecting. QFX were interested in taking things further on the strength of his songs. Reg then asked us all to swap seats so he could talk other business with me. It was the usual mish mash of merchandise, Kray parties, phone cards and sending money to people. He was in a very good mood on this visit, and business-wise it had been productive too. He left the visit early saying he wanted to beat the rush back, which is exactly what Ron always said! They were too similar sometimes. It was eerie. Before he left, we swapped training shoes with him so he had a new pair – Ray got the left, I got the right.

Through my involvement with Reg, I'd been present at some memorable visits over the years. The Christmas Day visit is one I'll always remember, the first time I met him is another... the best one of all was a visit at Maidstone. Thinking back about it I was in such a privileged position, but at the time it was just the sort of thing I took in my stride. It was only after such an event that the relevance of it all hit me. Here I was in the middle of something huge... this visit in particular made gangland history. Present at this one were us younger associates Christian Simpson, Dave Courtney and myself along with Frankie Fraser, Charlie Richardson, Charlie Kray, and Alec Steene.

So, here I was in amongst one of the most important meetings in British criminal history. As we all checked in with our respective visiting orders I had a terrific sense of occasion. We all knew that this was a first and definitely a one off. As we waited, I wondered what was going through the minds of these ageing gangsters. They had not all met each other like this in over thirty years. The last time there had been any talk of the Krays and the Richardsons meeting was to go to war... to fight it out to the death... the winners having control of London. None of these men were strangers to prison, so while it was like a second home to them, I can imagine it was bringing back some bad memories. They had clocked up well over a hundred years of prison time between them, and that's not even including Dave! We made our way through the sequence of security gates and checkpoints and were led into the large canteen that was the visiting room. Reg wasn't there yet. We made our way to a couple of tables in the middle of the room. People on visits had stopped talking and could do nothing other than stare at us. Dave and me pulled the two tables together, we all took our seats and chatted amongst ourselves as we waited for Reg to appear. He didn't keep us waiting too long. He was wearing his regulation blue and white pinstripe shirt opened to his chest revealing a chunky gold cross, a pair of Levi's and a brand new pair of white Reebok trainers. He smiled widely as he approached... first he embraced Charlie Richardson and then the rest of us in no particular order. As we took our seats the conversation from the other cons and visitors started back up. It was an unbelievable sight.

I didn't really get a chance to speak much with Reg, but for once I couldn't care less. It was fascinating to see Reg with Charlie Richardson after all the stories I had heard and read about them. The rivalry and hatred was not just set aside, it was left firmly in the past. Dave made me feel at ease with his jokes and laughter even when sitting with some of the biggest villains in the country. I also chatted with Alec Steene. Alec always had a lot of time for me and I appreciated that. He wasn't a villain but a man who loved the whole gangster lifestyle and was proud to be associated with the chaps, particularly the twins. For once Reg didn't get up and start talking to other cons – he was full of questions... wanting to know who was alive, where they were and what they were doing. They discussed old times, looking back on those days with fond memories. I decided to get the refreshments in and asked what they all wanted. Charlie Kray wanted a biscuit as did a few others... "What do you fancy Charlie? Penguin or a McVities?" asked Fraser. We all burst out laughing. It was great to see they could laugh about the past like that. The visit lasted two hours and it was an emotional Reg who said his goodbyes to his friends. They had tears in their eyes knowing that this would probably be the last time they would see each other alive. In a way, that was the main reason for the visit. None of them were in their prime anymore and it was a way of making up before time ran out. It was good to see them make the peace after many years and while they still could. I also think that it was a good show for the media –there always talk about the rivalry between the two gangs but now they had put it to rest once and for all.

My last visit to Reg was in December 1999. The visits had been getting less frequent over time and we both knew that they were drawing to a close. We didn't fall out or stop doing business fully, it's just that there were other things to be getting on with and we had drifted apart like friends so often do. In not seeing him as often, I noticed the physical changes more. He'd lost a lot of weight over the years and didn't look like the healthy Reg Kray in the prison gym photograph, which he was still sending out to people. He clung onto the image of the powerful gangster for all he was worth.

Ron Kray

It was round about two weeks after I had visited Reg that Kim phoned me to say I'd been given a visit to see Ron in Broadmoor; an institution which was built to house the type of criminals that normal prisons and hospitals couldn't handle. It was originally called Broadmoor Criminal Lunatic Asylum, changing from prison to hospital in 1948. It still resembles a prison rather than a hospital though. My mam had already prepared me for what the place would be like, but deep down I was a bit uncertain. It was daunting to say the least; I was visiting a mental hospital... visiting him in a psychiatric visiting area. I was glad that my mam could tell me a bit about what to expect as she'd been in and out of them over the years, and glad too that I would not be alone on my first visit. Oh, by the way, my mam is a nurse... that's how she knows... I could tell you were wondering.

I went to Brad and Kim's the day before the visit to find there were a few problems. Brat – I mean, Brad – had been going slightly off the rails of late, and while down there, he dragged me into a situation which I didn't appreciate. He got drunk, acted stupid and let his mouth run wild with all kinds 'beer talk'. The worst part was that he started saying he would get his dad to sort me out. His 'dad', being Reg Kray of course. I didn't feel threatened by it... but the fact that some little kid started going on like that was a disappointment. Now I was on the eve of my first visit to Ron with this stroppy kid trying to threaten me because he couldn't get his own way. Over the years I've heard enough 'I know Reg Kray and he won't be happy' stories to last a few lifetimes, to hear it come from a stroppy kid was just the start of it.

Friday the nineteenth of April 1991 was the day of the visit. Armed with two hundred John Player Specials (Ron

93

's brand of cigarette) we drove through the Berkshire countryside and arrived at Broadmoor with half an hour to spare. The approach to it is something else... dense woodlands surrounding it with trees looming over the narrow winding roads till you reach the dark and imposing Victorian building. Immediately your mind starts playing tricks on you... you double check the petrol gauge... you see movements in the shadows... you lock your door... stop for no one... it's the sort of place Stephen King would award five stars to if he ever went into the hotel and leisure industry. Although I knew what to expect, I was still taken aback by the place. It could easily have been mistaken for a stately home, but the bars on the windows certainly gave me the feeling that there were some people in there that society was better off protected from. We headed towards a part of the building that had obviously just been modernised. We entered through an automatic door, where behind a reinforced glass 'reception' area, two officers sat reading newspapers without so much as looking up as we approached. Kim explained to them that we were there to visit Ron Kray and after filling out form I was in. Kim had to sign to leave the cigarettes for Ron so there was a bit of a hold up before an officer led us through the secure doors, gates, courtyard and corridors to an original Victorian part of the building. All the time I was noticing the colour scheme... light blues and pale yellows... calming colours... something that is essential in this institution. Pale yellow is associated with the feeling of harmony and stability and blue with feelings of tranquillity and the resolution of conflict. Green is also supposed to be a calming colour – apparently when the Blackfriar Bridge in London was painted green, suicide jumps dropped by thirty-four per cent. I was slightly cynical about the whole concept, as my post office interior was also of a 'calming' colour scheme, which never really had that effect on me.

From there it was down another calming corridor and through to a large sunlit room containing around twenty tables, each with four chairs around them. There was a large stage to the left of the room where theatrical productions must have taken place. We dropped anchor at a table in the middle of the room. I found it strange that both twins preferred the middle, maybe it was something to do with wanting to be the centre of attention. Brad and me were barely speaking at this point, so the long wait took even longer. There were ten or so nurses positioned at different vantage points around the room, which was unnerving at first but considering where we were, it was another essential.

As we sat in silence, I noticed that most of the other visits were going on around us and still there was no Ron Kray. It was also at this point that I noticed something else, something inside myself. Up until now, I had been told about what to expect the institution to be like and the general environment and atmosphere of the place. I had not thought much about the reason why I was in that environment... to meet Ron Kray. What did I expect from Ron ? Did I expect anything at all? What preparation had I done? What should I do and not do? What should I say? I didn't go in there with a game plan and I wasn't quite sure what to expect. I didn't think it right to preconceive anything about him. I had read plenty of books and articles, and now it seemed logical that I would meet Ron after meeting his twin brother. I was just going to go with the flow... I was dressed well, he knew of me, I'd known about him for years... let's see what happens. Eventually he appeared at the same door we had entered through and made his way over to us. He was immaculately dressed in a blue suit tailored from Saville Row, a crisp white shirt, silk tie and solid gold tie pin. He was wearing polished Gucci shoes and gold tinted spectacles to complete the look. Here we were sitting in the visiting room of a hospital for the criminally insane, and the man we are visiting is the best-dressed person you are ever likely to see for years. The sight of him amazed me as he approached us. He was very charismatic and obviously stood out from everyone else in the place. He could easily have been mistaken for a wealthy businessman there on a visit himself. This time I made no mistakes, I greeted him properly. I stood along with Brad and Kim. He was barely audible as he greeted them and I decided to introduce myself to him and shake his hand. His grip was firm and cold, "Good to see you Steve, Reg has told me a lot about you."

We all sat down with Ron taking the seat next to me. The second thing to strike me about this man were his eyes – small, dark and piercing. Similar to Reggie's but there was something more here. I got the impression that this stare could turn a man to stone in an instant... there was something menacing beneath the surface, but I couldn't quite put my finger on it. He took out a pack of John Players and clicked his fingers. Immediately his cigarette was lit by one of the nurses and while he was there, Ron ordered him to bring us some tea and 'the usual' for him. It turned out that his order was non-alcoholic lager – four cans worth, so at least he wasn't going to be as tired and emotional as I remembered Reg was. The nurse returned with the drinks and Ron stood up and did the honours by adding milk and sugar to the teas. Brad and Kim were sitting there like it was nothing and here's me with my eyes practically popping out! I had seen every photo and read every book on the twins; to have Ron Kray pouring tea for me just as he'd done for Reg in a picture taken at Vallance Road... well, it was heart stopping.

I was still savouring the moment during the small talk when Ron leaned forward and put his hand on my knee, "You don't mind that I'm bisexual, do you Steve?" I wish he had waited till I didn't have a mouthful of tea before he asked. Composing myself, I told him I wasn't bothered so long as he didn't fancy me. I just came out with it... and luckily he saw the funny side as he removed his hand and whispered, "Good, good." I could see that I'd have to be alert at all times.

It was always a strain to make out what Ron was saying,

but as time went by, I could see that this was how he spoke normally. Probably another misconception about the twins – I suppose you just assume that with such a stature comes a bellowing voice. Ron spoke just like any other polite middle aged bloke on the street. He was keen to know what was going on in the outside world and Kim passed on different messages from friends and associates. His reply was mainly the same each time, "Good, good." Every now and again he would turn to Brad and me and ask if we were all right, conscious of the fact that we were still there. Sitting there in an awkward silence, we would nod and say we were okay before he turned back to Kim to catch up on business, "Good, good." He started to talk about a book he was reading which was all about world cruises. One thing you need in a place like that I thought would be escapism and something to look forward to. I imagine that's why so many prisoners take to painting, as a way of visiting other places inside the mind. It's a well known fact that such activities are therapeutic, and with mental illness these forms of expression are encouraged. He talked of how he'd go on a world cruise when he was released and how he'd love to take Brad and myself along with him. I could see his face light up as he told me, it was like he could taste the fresh sea air right there and then he came back to earth, still with a slight sparkle in his eye. He promised to send me a brochure. I found this slightly unusual as I'd just met him, I mean, I just couldn't tell if he was serious or not but it was a gesture I appreciated.

Fresh air was something I would have killed for on a Ron Kray visit. On that first time I met him he must have chain-smoked an average of around thirty John Players. He would smoke half of it then stub it out, clicking his fingers for another one to be lit immediately. It seemed to say that he was in a hurry – quick movements, not enough time to finish, moving on from one thing to another, eager to get to the end – but time was one thing he did have. It seemed to me like it was mimicking his thinking, with a certain restlessness and always needing to be on the move, almost agitated. He talked to me quite a lot for a first time visit and I felt more at ease in his company than I did in Reggie's. Ron seemed to have a genuine interest in what I had to say and would listen to me, that was quite a big difference... you can always tell when someone is listening and when someone is talking *at* you as opposed to talking *to* you. On subsequent visits he would enquire about things in my personal life that we'd discussed weeks earlier – he listened and remembered details like my mother's name or where I'd been on a night out and who I was with. Ron seemed interested in the fact that I liked to keep fit by playing football, circuit training and boxing. The gym I went to was run by former cruiserweight champion and friend, Glen McCrory so we talked about boxing for a bit and he asked if I had any pictures of me weight training. I said I could sort some out and send them on. I was quite chuffed that he was keen to find out things about me.

After an hour and a half, Ron made his way back. He liked to get back to his ward early to avoid the rush. One thing that never happened in there was a rush, but each to their own. We shook hands and said we'd keep in touch. As we walked back through the tranquil corridors, I went over some of the things we'd discussed. The world cruise; the photographs of me all sweaty in my training gear... I dare say it was naivety on my behalf. I now know the true reason for him wanting such pictures and why he'd want to take younger men on a cruise with him, but that was Ron just being Ron . I wasn't angry with him at all. At least he was honest about who he was.

As we were leaving one of the officers called Kim over. He had something that Ron had left for her. She signed for it and Brad carried it to the car; it was a box. Inside, it was opened up and we found it contained a huge collection of A4 sized black and white photographs. They were all of the twins in their heyday; a lot of them from Reg and Frances Shea's wedding day and were unseen by anyone outside the family. As we looked through them on the journey back, another thing that struck me was the similarity between Ron Kray *then* and Ron Kray *now*. Obviously they were the same person, but the way he dressed then compared to now was exactly the same. The way he'd held court with his soft voice; a voice that was just quiet enough to make you pay close attention, always active and on the move... but definitely the way he was dressed – nothing had changed. He was exactly the same, only he was older. He was living as Ron Kray the well-dressed archetype of London gangland, because for him, he still was that same person. It was as though he'd been frozen in the late sixties and then thawed out later in life. His suits and mannerisms all in tact but he'd aged with time. What did I make of all this? To be honest I wasn't too sure myself. It could be unhealthy to live in the past, but he was certainly in control of his faculties. I didn't necessarily think it was sad to see him like that, the only Ron Kray I'd seen before then was the exact image of what I'd seen now. Psychologically, it could have gone a lot deeper due to his illness. In dressing the same and trying hard to appear the same may have been some form of denial. He was still *The Colonel*, no matter where he was... he was still very active, but he was still very much trying to relive his better days. A few days later, I received a letter from him dated the day after that first visit. In it he said he'd be sending me two hundred quid to cover my expenses and again he asked if I could send him any pictures of myself weight-training. I didn't send any because now I knew why he wanted them. I also received a brochure through the post days later from him. It was full of different cruises like he'd mentioned on the visit. This I learned was quite a normal thing for Ron to do when visited by a new boy or man. I didn't agree with it, but as I say, each to their own. Each time I hear people saying they visited Ron and they were that close that he offered to take them on a cruise, I have a chuckle to myself. It was standard procedure whether you looked like Johnny Depp or Johnny Merrick. Ron was up-front from the beginning; he didn't hide anything like this and was not backward in coming forward. He was always honest with me, or as honest as a convicted murderer in a mental institution could be.

I was soon making solo trips to see Ron, and likewise Reg. I visited Ron alone on July the twentieth 1991; this was the first time that I had seen him look distressed. He was like a different person. He had been shown a newspaper cutting about a tragic young boy named Colin Budd who had idolised the twins. Colin was nineteen years old and his ambition was to emulate his idols... Ron and Reg Kray. He had a collection of cuttings about them and a tattoo etched onto his body. One day he walked into a gunsmith's store in Colchester, Essex, in an attempted hold up. During the hold up, the owner managed to load a gun and shot him dead. The story upset Ron and on the visit he opened up to me, "If I have any regrets Steve, it's that we are looked upon as heroes by some kids today. There's nothing clever about ending up in here. Kids today have a lot more choices than me and Reg ever had. You make sure you keep on the right side of the law. Don't end up like me. You hear me?" This was proof for me that he was aware of the things they had done and was aware that they were wrong. I knew all about their younger days and how their mother had conditioned them – the way that they could not differentiate between right and wrong. I can never believe anyone does not know the difference; there are probably extreme cases, but most of the time it sounds like a cop out to me. Here Ron was telling me he knew they had done wrong in their lives. It's not like he was sorry though, it was just sounding like he was sorry they had been locked up for those crimes, and not the crimes themselves. For the Krays in their day, there were not many choices – there was petty crime with the ambition to go further, there was boxing and there was show business. Or all three. Ron could accept that their crimes hadn't paid but it was their 'destiny'. He hated reading things like this... that young people were wasting their lives and their freedom because of some romantic vision that crime was glamorous. Crime had been glamorous for the twins, but not for long. A thirty-year stretch was not glamorous, nor was being shot dead in a hold up at nineteen years old.

It was a tiring nine hour trip to spend an hour and a half with Ron but it was still worth it. After I took the initiative to produce merchandise that first time round, Ron was so taken by the idea of the Kray mirrors, he mentioned it in his book *My Story*. Working for them in this capacity was not really the money-spinner you'd imagine. Yes I got my cut but it was always the twins who benefited from such deals. Right then for me, the money didn't seem to matter. It was the buzz… the association of working for them on a business level that kept me going. I didn't treat this as a full time position – I had my own job and my own life, but I was definitely enjoying the notoriety that came with it. Who wouldn't? It was a good sideline, money on top of what I was earning and becoming known for different reasons other than my day job.

Both twins always made sure that my expenses were looked after. Our friendship took off at a tremendous pace with Ron writing or calling a few times a week. I seemed to get on better with Ron as our visits were all about conversation. Unlike Reg, he had no reason to get up and start socialising with other patients while I was there. He'd phone me to ask if I could look into different ventures he'd been approached about, could I send some money to this person or that charity or did I get that money he'd sent up. On the twenty-ninth of April, I received a letter from Kate Kray with a cheque for two hundred quid in it and on the same day, another letter from Ron saying a further two hundred would be coming my way shortly. It was good to see that it wasn't just a one-way friendship of me visiting all the time and using my own money. Receiving expenses meant he was thinking about me. As money was now a major part of our relationship, I contacted Ron to ask what I should do with the money being made (I was careful to make sure that every penny was accounted for and listed in detail any expenses I had). He told me to open a bank account up and keep any money they were owed there until further notice. No way. I had visions of putting a thousand quid in one week and being asked 'where's my ten grand?' the next. I didn't need that sort of hassle at any stage in our friendship. We could be good mates, but enemy status is only a mood swing away. He was still the same person who had been locked away in 1968, and I had to keep it in the back of my mind no matter how well the present situation was panning out. I hung back from the idea of a bank account for a while, then as more money started to come in Ron was always telling me to send it to this boy and that boy, the bank account forgotten about. It began to feel like a race to get rid of the money as soon as it was earned... it was going out all over the country to any Tom, Dick, Harry, Larry or Barry.

Ron would never cease to amaze me. Quite a few times he asked me to make statements to the press highlighting their plight or just commenting on a current affair on their behalf. A lot of the time the stories didn't make it to print, but when they did I was always rewarded for my effort. One day I received a call from Broadmoor and Ron was seething at a news report he'd just heard on the radio.

"That bloody rat Major (John Major] is trying to jeopardise our chances of parole! He said he doesn't want today's kids being the Krays of tomorrow! It's slander. The slag. I want you to make a statement on our behalf, use your discretion, Steve. I'll be in touch. God bless".

With that he was gone. I barely had a chance to speak. This was how many of our 'conversations' would take shape when he was in this mood. Once the 'God bless' was spoken, I always knew the conversation was over. I tried to get in touch with Reg to talk it through first but was unable to do so. So, it looked like I had to put my Kray Media Liaison hat on again, and take on the most powerful man in the country on their behalf. The press release I put together was as follows:

"In response to Mr. Major's speech we would like to say that in our day, no one would dream of mugging and battering old ladies, stealing from their next door neighbours or molesting and killing innocent women and children. The people of our day would not tolerate any such behaviour. To be compared to people like that by our own Prime Minister saddens and hurts us deeply".

Ron was so happy with it that he told me to 'tell all the papers'. It got good coverage the next day in the broadsheets, giving the twins their right to reply and hopefully making John Major take note for any future remarks. I got a letter back from Ron saying I'd done well with the write-up and that it worked out for the best. He was always urging me to campaign on Reg's behalf as well. He'd say that Reg didn't deserve to be locked up like an animal and to help get him out. Reg on the other hand, wanted them both to be released though I think he knew deep down that it was highly unlikely.

It felt good to be trusted to such a degree by them, I just had to remember to be cautious. Ron was obviously unstable at times and Reg could also be unpredictable. Anything I went into with them would have to be carefully considered. Whilst many of the visits were filled with talking about nothing in particular, I felt quite honoured that they had brought me in as an unofficial business adviser. They wanted me to cast my eyes over deals and give them an honest opinion as to the money making potential of them. I knew that I wouldn't be the only person who would have their say, but to be asked whether I thought they should part with their cash for various deals was quite a responsibility. In their position, they needed to rely on people. I saw straight away that they were surrounded by 'advisers' who couldn't care less about them. Many of these people were just out for themselves and could not be trusted. I'd need to be on my guard at all times, there was a lot of talking behind backs and playing people other off against others for personal gain. There were some decent blokes though and I made some good friends, but some of the others made me wonder what the twins were thinking of to even talk to them.

I took my old mate Matty to visit Ron in Broadmoor one time. On our way down we were involved in a serious car crash. A drink driver had skidded in front of an articulated lorry that had to break suddenly, forcing Matty to break hard and swerve to avoid it. We clipped the back of the lorry and spun three times before crashing through the central reservation and landing on the other side of the motorway. The car was a total write-off. I don't know how, but we were okay apart from a few cuts and bruises and a rip in my new suit. We counted our blessings that it was only seven in the morning and not midday, because rush-hour traffic would have been a lot different. I had my camera that day and took some shots of the car because I couldn't quite believe that we escaped with so few injuries between us. I called Broadmoor to let Ron know that we wouldn't be able to make it, and got my mother and grandmother to do the same. I sent some pictures of the car and an apologetic letter to Ron, asking him when the next available visit was. Over the next couple of'days I received four letters from Ron calling me a rat and a slag and telling me that he was 'right disappointed in me'.

I didn't think it was right that we were in a crash and here he was mouthing off to me like this. I hadn't known him for that long, so this was our first 'falling out'. It made me think about what I was into and how deep I was in. I know there are friends who can fall out and once things are off their chest and all is said, it's back to normal and the friendship is still there. I know others where they can argue and the friendship is over. It was a learning curve for me. I could have taken it to heart and ended it all then, or I could let it go, knowing it had come from an emotionally unstable criminal who had been away from society for some time. It seemed he couldn't take disappointment well at all. In his eyes I'd let him down and upset him.

That's when I found out that Ron had been sitting in the visiting room at a table by himself for the full two-hour visit. Whether it was a breakdown in communication or some form of mental torture I wasn't sure, but I hoped at least the photographs would reach Ron. Luckily they did and he was quick to apologise and arrange another visit. He also wanted to know if he could do anything to help us with any costs we had incurred. After refusing money a cheque still arrived for two hundred quid. It was a nice gesture, and said a lot about the real Ron Kray. Sure he was disappointed and I dare say humiliated at having to sit there for two hours... I'm glad to say that when he knew I was on the level, he showed a different side to his personality. If this was a guilty conscience or real concern, I was unsure at first but now realise it was a bit of both. There was never a conventional apology, but I knew he knew. Just like Reg though, once something like that had come and gone, that was it. It would never be mentioned again... it was in the past. It seemed slightly ironic to me that the 'immediate' was gone in an instant, yet they were both firmly stuck in their own past and they were still hanging on to it every day.

The rearranged visit took place two weeks later and this time we decided that the train was the safest option. The journey went without a hitch and we reached Broadmoor with an hour to spare. We left Ron some John Players at reception, and were escorted to the visiting hall. We made our way to the table in the middle of the room and pulled up three chairs and waited for Ron to join us. Within five minutes the familiar dapper figure of Don Ron appeared in the doorway and he looked over his gold rimmed glasses to see where we were sitting. waving him over we stood up to greet him. I shook hands first, "Hello Steve good to see you, good to see you." in his customary whisper and I introduced him to Matty as we sat down. Ron clicked his fingers to attract one of the nurse's attentions. He ordered six cans of non-alcoholic lager and Matty and I had tea. He had his first cigarette lit and we were off... then a silence seemed to fall over him and I was beginning to wonder whether we had picked a bad day to visit. He was hunched up and tense, I could see something within him starting to rise, his eyes fixed behind me.

It was then I felt someone nudge my chair from behind trying to squeeze past, which distracted me from Ron for a second. Turning sharply to see what was going on, I could see it was a patient. No problem, but no 'excuse me' either. He stared through me and pulled up a chair at his table where an elderly woman was sitting. I turned back to Ron who was livid, "Slag... the fuckin' slag". He was staring right at the patient who'd knocked my chair, seriously wound up – his anger was like volcano about to erupt. I tried to calm him down by telling him it didn't really matter, but I sensed it was nothing to do with that. Ron continued, "He's fuckin' a rat. He's a slag and a rat."

I'd heard this kind of talk from Ron before, and recently had been on the receiving end of it but had never seen such hatred in Ron's eyes since I'd known him. Matty was as intrigued as I was. I asked who this bloke was, "Sutcliffe, Peter Sutcliffe, The Yorkshire Ripper. He's a no good slag." I already knew that Ron had a dislike for Sutcliffe. In 1983, Ron organised an attack on him and Sutcliffe was left with one side of his face slashed open. The pair had never fallen out over anything, or had ever exchanged words for that matter. Ron despised him for his crimes against women; he needed no excuse to feel how he did.

Hearing Ron in what sounded like he was preparing for a fight was an unreal experience. Matty and I turned to each other in disbelief. There was total silence between us as it began to sink in. Suddenly, Ron jumped up... we flinched as the chair legs scraped back... looking up at him, I realised what a powerful force he would still be against any opponent. The anger just seemed to leave his whole being within a millisecond; he turned to Matty and said, "Well thanks for coming Matthew, I'd like to have the rest of the time with Steve now, we have business to discuss." We never did talk about it but we both thought he was going to do Sutcliffe right there in front of us, it was something where you just had to read the other's expression to know there were no words to describe it. You could feel the relief in the atmosphere as Matty shook Ron's hand and we arranged to meet back in reception. His visit had lasted a mere fifteen minutes.

Ron had something on his mind and he wanted to tell me. He was a talker anyway, but the past was his favourite topic. Get him on a good day about the old days and you could forget about getting a word in edgeways. Once we had discussed a few more merchandise ideas Ron revealed that he had just finished reading a book by a former member of the so-called Kray firm and he wasn't happy with the inaccuracies that had appeared in it. "I'm sick of people writing lies about us Steve," he said. I listened intently as he started to talk about his life at the top of the criminal ladder. "People think I killed George Cornell because he called me a queer. That's rubbish. I didn't like him Steve, he was arrogant, but Cornell got his because of what he told me. You see, he told me he killed Freddie Mills." I was taken aback by Ron's frankness, he continued, "Cornell and I were not always enemies, and we had confided in each other. He and Mills fell out and George killed him, simple as that. He told me this in good faith and I have kept it until now." Ron was being deadly serious as he told me, and that is word for word how I remember it. No one was ever found guilty or convicted Freddie Mills' murder. Ron was certainly sincere when he told me, though I still wouldn't like to guess one way or the other. It was something else I was unsure of – a mind game? I don't think so. It would also tie in with what I discussed in *The Swinging Sixties* chapter. It was said that Ron shot Cornell because he'd killed someone close to Ron – maybe that someone was Freddie Mills and not Dickie Hart. At the time of Cornell's murder, it would have been easy for Ron to just go along with the 'fat poof' theory as his motivation. All his spies would tell him Cornell had been heard saying something about him *just* to put themselves in favour, but at the same time, anyone heard badmouthing Ron Kray was reason enough for him to put a bullet in their head. I can only share what he told me and can't prove it one way or the other, but Cornell – if it was true – had confessed to an unsolved murder.

Ron went on to describe how he had walked into *The Blind Beggar* Public House and shot Cornell through the head at point blank range. "It was great Steve, I can play that moment over and over again in my mind, I can smell the fear. Good, good." With that Ron had another Player lit up and patted my hand with his. He was revealing different sides to his personality like this all the time. I knew he'd murdered in the past; everyone knew, but I'd never heard him describing it so graphically before. It's unusual to hear someone reminisce so fondly about murder, I'd read about this murder many times but hearing of the pleasure that committing it had brought really disturbed me. He went on to describe it other times after that. He said he went through it over and over in depraved sexual fantasies, using the scenario to reach orgasm. I found it sickening. I think in today's society, people can be desensitised to murder and crime through being constantly bombarded with it through film and TV. When faced with it in such cases like the Rodney King incident or September the eleventh, you can see the media effect on whole nations and society as opposed to just a community. Many people can feel distanced from it because it can be an everyday occurrence that does not affect their lives, and then an event like the twin towers unites everyone in shock, grief and repulsion. I'd say this was the effect Ron describing a murder had on me. I could read a murder... a murder... a murder all day and not be moved by it. I had no personal connection with the bloke and it happened before I was born. Now I'd got to know Ron Kray and he was telling me how good it felt to murder – to actually physically end someone's life in such a violent and ruthless way. To see his face light up as he told me was a real eye opener to some of the repressed thoughts that could resurface from the mind of a paranoid schizophrenic. It was one side to Ron I didn't like. It's almost impossible to hide a reaction to something like that, but obviously I would try to keep my true feelings to myself. The eyes and the hands of a person are always a giveaway. You can tell when people are lying or telling the truth, if they are guilty, embarrassed, angry... you name it, just by things they do subconsciously.

He loved to tell stories though, he could sit or hours losing himself in recalling memories about events or scrapes they'd been in – the good old days – or tell me of his dreams for the future, people they knew, had taken on in battle or were just good friends with. I remember these stories because it was Ron's sixtieth birthday when he told me. (His best present was to follow two days later with a visit from Reg. They were allowed only four visits a year under supervision, a grand total of eight hours... how the authorities spoilt them) As usual he was immaculately dressed sporting a jazzy pair of crocodile shoes and a grey pin striped suit, from Saville Row of course. He was on top form and was keen to introduce me to his fellow patients on this visit. I met everyone from Hannibal Lecter to Freddy Kreuger; they were all good to their mums and were just misunderstood according to Ron. Maybe some of them were. We sat down and Ron poured me a cuppa and started to recall other inmates he'd had the pleasure of doing his bird with. One of those people was none other than Michael Peterson a.k.a Mr. Charles Bronson.

The twins had first met Charlie in Parkhurst in 1978. They were on C-wing together. Ron said that he could see the potential in the young Bronson and that he took him under his wing. He would give the young Charlie twenty quid a time to exchange for baccie (tobacco) so that he could have a more comfortable life inside. They built up a good relationship and I think that the twins could see a hint of themselves somewhere within Bronson. Ron wrote him a letter when he was locked up in solitary confinement after one of many misunderstandings with a screw. In it he told him to 'Slow down, don't end up like me, life is too precious to throw away your young and full life. Think of your mum when you feel bad. I don't want to see you like this. God bless. Ron.'

He told me he remembered writing the letter in his cell at the time, but described his cell as *The Lagoon*. It threw me a bit at first, I didn't know if I'd heard right or whether he'd lapsed into the past, but I didn't recall *The Lagoon* as one of their clubs. He continued... remembering writing the letter so vividly as his cell had been decorated like a small nightclub. All the other cons called it *The Blue Lagoon*. He smiled as he told me how cons would pop in and share a drink and a smoke with him. I could picture it... the smoky atmosphere, the drink flowing, the conversation, the business... not unlike one of the clubs on the outside... always with *The Colonel* holding court. This was what he'd loved on the outside; sitting in his clubs in amongst all the smoke and soaking up the atmosphere. He loved being the host. To hear such a story made me smile too – to me it signalled more escapism for Ron. Being in *The Blue Lagoon* was like being a million miles away from Parkhurst. It was good to see that there were things he'd enjoyed as a free man that he always hung on to. He could lose himself whether it be five minutes or five hours.

Ron explained to me that prison life wasn't for him and that it was slowly driving him mad, eating away at him all the time. Violence could erupt at any time on C-wing and in Bronson the twins had a valuable ally. He recalled with such joy the days when he would bash a screw or a con and then Reg would follow up the attack. Again I found this interesting as it seemed that when they were in prison together, it was still Ron who was the dominant of the twins – still leading the way in battle. Once Reg even had to restrain Bronson from bashing up a con called Dave Simmonds who had slighted him. The twins were not bothered about the con, but the more damage Charlie inflicted the greater his punishment would be when he finally stopped. Ron inevitably bashed one screw too many and was sent to isolation, losing his sanity all over again in the concrete coffin. Bronson remembered Ron's letter of support and returned the gesture, 'Keep it together, be strong and don't let the authorities grind you down.'... something that Ron would never forget. In solitary the screws tormented Ron. For them it was like having some wild animal in captivity that they could have their fun with. The hardest thing for him was that he felt for Reg. He knew that the same screws torturing him would be dealing with Reg in the normal manner, he knew that Reg would be suffering mentally, not knowing how his twin was. No doubt they would have had their fun with Reg too, getting their revenge by taunting him about Ron. After the incident, Ron was admitted to the hospital wing for assessment and was finally categorised as a mentally ill patient who could not be treated by the prison authorities. There was no other option but to transfer him to Broadmoor.

Ron was actually happy in Broadmoor. A lot of people couldn't understand why as Broadmoor is not well known for releasing patients. He was allowed more visits than he could have dreamed of in Parkhust. He also had a locker full of tinned salmon, fruit, chocolate – you name it Ron had it. When you have everything you want, why would you want to change it? It was a regime that would suit him a lot better than prison ever could. It wasn't long before Bronson joined Ron in the nut house and their friendship started back up. Charlie became an unofficial minder to Ron fending off a lot of the lunatics that would harass him and in return Ron would arrange for a lot of good looking females to visit Charlie. Ron was always bemused by the attention and fan mail that he received from women all over the world and was never short of love interests in

Broadmoor. Not a bad arrangement if you ask me. With Ron in Broadmoor and Reg in Parkhurst, visits for Violet were very tiring and time consuming, but as Ron used to say, "She never let her boys down". It must have been one hell of a strain on her; first to have both twins locked up, then one in a mental hospital, and then have to visit them separately. It proved their love was strong and the family ethics that bonded them during the war years shined through. Violet would even send in items for other cons that the twins wanted 'looking after', so Charlie never went short of tracksuits and training shoes thanks to Mrs. Kray.

Ron when talking about Charlie said "I told him he still had a fighting chance in the outside world. If he had the chance on the outside, then it was a fighting career he should go for." He could see the potential in him and Charlie obviously listened to the advice. Bronson was eventually transferred back into the prison system to serve the rest of his sentence. When released, Reg put him in touch with a bloke by the name of Paul Edmunds who was a boxing promoter from Canning Town. Edmunds arranged a fight in East London but needed to give him an alias as the fight was not what you would call a legal show. That day Michael Peterson became Charlie Bronson, and Charlie Bronson became a legend. Ron and Reg called him before the fight to wish him luck and made sure Charlie Kray was at ringside to cheer their mate on. Ron laughed loudly during the story... he had ran a book on the fight with the other patients on Somerset Ward and Bronson won with convincing ease. Bronsons brief taste of success (and freedom) did not last long however, and shortly after another resounding win in the ring, he found himself back behind bars.

Ron, just like his brothers, loved to name drop into conversations and stories. The countless names of toyboys and lovers Ron had in prison would be reeled off, all just names to me, but I would listen all the same. I don't ever think that listing their names was ever meant to shock me because I know that he was comfortable with his sexuality and had been for many years. He'd already tried it on my first visit anyway, so he knew I wasn't bothered by it. There was one story he told me about an artist he used to know. I guessed the time of this to be around 1964 when the Lord Boothby scandal had broke. I know Ron paid weekend visits to Brighton and was quite taken by the place. The circles he'd began to mix with at that time, 'The Chelsea Set', would invite him down to parties as a lot of them had country retreats and what have you down that way. He'd get that glint in his eye as he'd start to tell it... "You know Steve, when I used to go down the South coast, I used to know this artist. Lots of talent. A bit of a drinker, but always full of ideas." He looked back on it with fondness as I tried to picture the scene. Here's how it went.

One day while the two of them were sat on the pier, his artist friend was almost in tears. "What's wrong?" asked Ron. "Oh nothing," came the reply "It's such a grand sight. The high tides, the rocks, the gulls, they bring back such sad memories." Ron told me how they couldn't pursue a meaningful conversation out in the open, so they found shelter in a nearby pub and he elaborated on his tale of woe. They sat down with a couple of Brown Ales and Ron listened to the story just as I was, as the artist went into more detail.

He'd met this beautiful girl at a dance, they courted, and he found out that it was soon to be her birthday. He wanted to give her a special present and as she had come to mean so much to him in such a short space of time, he wanted to show her in the best way possible. She was very fond of a particular part of the bay where they had first met, and being an artist, he decided to capture it in a watercolour. He waited until the next beautiful sunny day before he made his way down to the bay. The thing was, he realised he'd forgotten to take water along with him once he sat down in front of his easel to paint.

Instead of going all the way back home to get some water, he decided to just use some seawater.

He did so and the painting turned out well. Very well indeed... Ron went into detail of how he'd caught the sea crashing against a ridge of rocks with the water spraying up into the air, each drop catching the light of the sun on it's way down... the untouched and golden sandy beach, the deep blues of the sea on the horizon, vibrant yellows and the pale blue cloudless sky. In due course, the painting was presented to the fair maiden on her birthday. She loved it – absolutely adored it – and hung it up in her bedroom in pride of place.

I was intrigued. Ron lowered his voice to his barely audible mode. I leaned in so I could hear him. "The thing is Steve, that the part of the painting that depicted the sea, yeah? Well, because it was created with seawater, it was subject to the attraction of the moon, which meant it was tidal. This meant you could see the sea in the painting coming up over the rocks by the shore's edge, and then down again at low tide."

I'd had my head slightly cocked to one side to hear properly, but now I turned to face him. What on earth was he talking about? I looked at him in disbelief as he went on...

"One night it was the highest recorded tide in the country's history. The entire South coast was hit with thunderstorms, rain, hurricanes... everything. Next day my friend went to visit his girlfriend. The whole household was in a state of complete despair. It was the watercolour, see. The watercolour had overflowed during the night and it fucking drowned her in her sleep. And since that day, after what had happened, he could never paint anything again."

He timed that story perfectly. Just as he finished it, he stood up to leave and we said our good-byes. He was smiling to himself, knowing he'd had me believing the whole thing all along. I stood and watched his exit; the other visits now drawing to a close with Ron 'beating the rush' back to his room. I smiled as he turned back to wave. He really was a man of many dimensions. That story proved he had a wicked sense of humour, but to anyone else listening, it probably confirmed his insanity. There were so many times he'd have me in stitches with his sense of humour. He'd be so dry in his delivery, sometimes I'd have to think first before knowing I could laugh. There would always be a slight pause and he'd look at me as if to say, 'Have you not got it yet?' Every time I visited he would always ask what I wanted to eat and drink – usually tea and most often I'd join him in a snack. I remember once I declined the offer of food as I'd had something on the way down. Ron didn't eat either. I thought he was just being polite, but he said the reason why he wasn't eating was because working in the kitchen that day was none other than Graham Young, *The Bovingdon Posioner*. Young was convicted in 1972 of murdering two workmates by Thallium poisoning and administering poison to four others. He'd already poisoned his stepmother to death and attempted to poison his father, sister and a friend for good measure. And now he was working in the kitchen at Broadmoor! I couldn't believe it; I know people in there have mental problems, but if this was true, then the Governor must have been as mad as a box of frogs. It was insane. In 1995, the same year as Ron's death, a film called *The Young Poisoner's Handbook* was released, which was all about Graham Young. I watched it with interest to discover he'd died of a heart attack while serving a life sentence in Parkhurst on the first of August 1990… a year before my first ever visit to Ron. I couldn't help but laugh at the fact I'd believed him all that time. Broadmoor was surreal enough at times, so I was glad to wipe that particular vision from my mind.

Speaking of extremes… Ron's mood swings were exactly that. He could go from one to the other as quickly as he went through his cigarettes. In his environment, I don't suppose there was room for any beating around the bush, there was no time to waste in building up to something with Ron. I was summoned to a visit with him one time and he was absolutely seething. On this visit I got to see a chilling side to him I hadn't seen since he'd described the Cornell murder. This visit was similar, he had the same frankness, the same cold and serious expression... he moved closer and asked me to arrange the deaths of Kim Lane and Pete Gillette. This was not just an off the cuff remark. He wanted them murdered for upsetting Reg and he wanted me to do it. This was definitely the Ron I'd read about in the sixties... in this mood he was relentless. I could picture him now giving the same orders to the firm. He insisted I organised it. I had to keep a calm exterior but inside my conscience was screaming for me to get the hell out of there. We discussed other business, but I couldn't take any of it in; I don't think I even heard anything else he'd said. The visit came to an end and as far as Ron was concerned, their death warrants had been signed and he could go back to his room a happy man. I left the place a very unhappy man. At that time, the only hit man I knew was Pete Waterman and although his music was bad, I'd never heard of it killing anyone. I'm joking about it now but at the time this was serious. I knew what his moods were like and I was banking on him changing his mind. I left it a few days. Nothing. I spoke to him on the phone. Nothing. I knew he wouldn't discuss it over the phone, so I could be a bit more relaxed in talking to him... but he was phoning to arrange another visit to see if I had 'sorted that thing out'. In a week's time he'd be expecting to hear results. What could I do? It was a no win, no win situation. I'm not sure if he had realised exactly what he'd asked me to do, but there was no way on this earth that I could even contemplate doing it. It was constantly on my mind leading up to the visit, then on the journey... and eventually the visit itself.

We sat facing each other at the usual table. He got his cigarette lit, keeping his eyes firmly fixed on me all the time. After the usual small talk, he asked if I'd sorted the pair of them out. I told him I hadn't and I didn't elaborate any further by saying I needed more time. "Good, good" came the reply. It was as casual as that. He'd called it off as casually as asking me the time. Imagine now if I had been mad enough to get in touch with someone to carry out his order. I wanted to tell him he could not just go around ordering two murders and not even think to tell me he'd changed his mind... but I realised how ridiculous it would sound. It would sound as ridiculous as the murder request. I was just glad it was over. He had no right to even ask me in the first place. The more I thought about it, the more I wanted to tell him – but it was in the past now, forgotten about. Thinking about it now though, he couldn't have been serious about killing them at all. He knew I was not even a petty thief, never mind a killer; and he knew I was not the type who could live with myself if I had arranged for such a thing to happen. If he was that serious about it, he had his pick of anyone throughout the underworld to carry it out. In which case it would have been over within days. It was all about mood swings. He had already managed to get to Pete Gillette in another way though, through the film *The Krays*. As Charlie was an adviser on the film, Ron had made sure he got a favour out of him before renaming him Mr. X. In the film there were a lot of 'real' extras used – friends and associates connected to the family. As Gillette had shared a cell with Reg it was a perfect guise. Charlie, under instruction, secured a part for Gillette. The part was one of two blokes who get beaten up by Reg, played by Martin Kemp. On screen, Reg catches him and the other bloke as they admire Frances sitting in his Mercedes as he emerges from a shop. Reg gives them both a severe kicking and leaves them both semi-conscious on the road as he and Frances drive off. Charlie had suggested to Martin Kemp that during fight choreography, sometimes people *can* get hit for real, and if it happened that Gillette *did* take one or two enthusiastic shots then he would merely be suffering for his art as an 'actor'. Apparently Mr. Kemp was only too happy to help out, though I'm not sure how many takes were needed to get it right.

Ron acted in the same manner with Dominic Anciano, producer of the film. As you know, the twins were less than happy at the deal they received, so as well as blaming their elder brother, they blamed Anciano. The fact was that it was all down to Charlie that they got such a bad deal. They already held him responsible, but couldn't really do anything in way of revenge to their brother. They looked elsewhere and found the producer. Ron told me that they had been mugged off and that he should be 'done over properly'. The anger would build but he would never raise his voice or lose his cool. You could see a rage burning within him ready to explode, but somehow he kept it under control, if you call ordering a hit on someone a form of control that is. I learnt to spot the signs. He'd be agitated... fidgeting... anxious, looking at me like it was an inconvenience for him to be there after I'd spent nearly ten hours travelling to see him. Again, the chain-smoking would give the impression of anxiety, whether he was anxious or not. I don't think Ron ever actually *wanted* anyone killed. Not really. It was just his reaction and once he'd said he wanted them killed, it was his way of eliminating the person and the upset they had caused from his mind. Once he'd 'killed' them, the anger left and he could go relax.

Next on his hit list was his own wife. I, along with most others, knew Ron was gay. I never asked any questions about his reasons for marriage, as it was obviously a business arrangement no matter which way it was disguised. This visit was on the twenty-fifth of September 1993. It seemed that during most of my visits, he was at odds with somebody and I found myself playing the part of agony uncle. This was one of the few times I'd seen Ron not wearing a suit. He appeared in a black jumper, white shirt, dark slacks and polished shoes and looked distinctly dishevelled. Saying he was in a bad mood comes nowhere close. This was the worst I had ever seen him, he was like an animal. His first and only topic of conversation was Kate Kray and her book. She had upset Ron by including revelations of an agreement they had over sex in her book, *Murder, Madness and Marriage*. The book had been serialised in a tabloid newspaper and she had revealed very personal details about an alleged 'sex pact' between them. Again, he changed his mind eventually but this was the most wound up I'd ever seen him. I knew that he would drop it once he'd vented his anger, but this time he took a lot longer to vent it. His fists were clenched tight, the white knuckles bulging as he kept calling her a slag throughout. He said that a lot of things revealed in her books, like having in her possession the gun that killed Cornell, were all lies and that she had just used him for his name. I don't know if she said she had the gun, but I do know that it resides in the Black Museum at Scotland Yard.

On a visit on the third of June 1992, Ron again was not in the best of moods. The trial of Lindsay and Leighton Frayne was receiving a lot of media coverage at the time. The Fraynes were charged with robbery and conspiracy to rob the Halifax Building Society in Gwent. The thing was, they had also become involved with the twins and taken it upon themselves to become some sort of updated version of them. They dressed in sharp suits and visited all the old haunts in the East End but didn't really rate as bad imitations. All the ambition was there, but they just came across as an outdated pastiche. Their naivety in getting caught meant that not only were they looking at a long sentence each, but they were also attracting a lot of bad publicity for the twins. Bad publicity was the last thing they needed with the parole board looking for the slightest excuse to refuse them each time, now the Frayne brothers were handing the authorities an excuse on a plate. As more and more was revealed during their trial Ron was getting angrier, "I can't believe these boys, Steve. They've done Reg and me a lot of harm. Do you know they tried to kidnap your pal Gazza?" He was referring to the footballer Paul Gascoigne, this I had to hear... "Yeah, they tried to get his body guard, Paul Edwards who used to be in the SAS, to help them kidnap him and hold him ransom. How stupid can you get Steve?" I had to agree. Reg had told me about them too, although didn't know if there was any truth in the kidnap part. I'd heard that the Frayne brothers were connected to the Krays a lot further than the Krays would ever let on. The Krays are said to have made an arrangement with them to help maintain their stronghold on the underworld. They would give them all the contacts they needed with the intended plan that the Fraynes would take over London and hand control over to Ron and Reg when they were released. Knowing of the deals the Krays got involved with this does not surprise me. It was reinforced when I'd heard that the Krays funded the Fraynes too. They would travel to London each day in a bashed up car and eat pitiful meals in order to save every penny they could for themselves. The plan failed though and it was easy for the Krays to deny all knowledge.

In 1993, just over a year to the day of that visit, Ron's behaviour was still up and down. It was a sad sight to see, as he could be calm and in control on one visit, then agitated and irrational on the next. He was in a good mood but made it quite clear that he was becoming increasingly irritated with a fellow patient by the name of Lee Kiernender. As I drank my tea and he his non-alcoholic lager, he pointed Kiernender out to me and I thought nothing more of it. He told me that he had an annoying habit, which I must admit is one of the most annoying things in the world... he whistled whenever Ron was within earshot and always out of tune. Ron told me he was on a reduced drug treatment and as a result he felt unstable and irritable. The rest of the visit passed without incident and I left him feeling happy and upbeat. Two days later I picked up a newspaper to read that Ron had taken exception to out of tune whistler and tried to strangle him. Five nurses were needed to drag Ron from him. I could not believe it... I rang the hospital for an update; as I was quite friendly with one of the nurses she told left: 1991 - Broadmoor, first visit by Brad Lane and Steve Wraith

above: 1995 - Charity night on Tyneside,
L-R: Carl Carty, unknown, Charlie Kray, Steve Wraith.

below: 1994 - Charity night at Hackney,
L-R: Charlie Kray, Lennie McLean, Tony Lambrianou,
Gary Kray, unknown, unknown, Steve Wraith.

1995 - Ronnie Kray's funeral (pictures by Tony Furby)

top - left, Ray Cann, centre, Charlie Kray & Steve Wraith, right, Reg Kray talks to Jamie Foreman
bottom: left, Charlie Kray, centre, Steve Wraith, right Reg Kray, far right, Gary Kray

top: At the Queen's Theatre, Hornchurch (picture by Colin Fanning)

L-R; Steve Wraith, Tony Lambrianou, Freddie Foreman, Alec Steen.

centre: L-R; Stephen Sayers, Steve Wraith, John Henry Sayers.

left: 1997 - Steve Wraith and dog "Nipper" named after the cop who arrested the Krays.

top: Back row - wish to remain nameless,
Front row - L-R; Darren Newmass, Christian Simpson,
Tony Lambrianou, Steve Wraith.

bottom: 1999, L-R; John Lillico, Dave Courtney, Steve Wraith,
Brian Whitfield, Graham Borthwick.

top: Charlie Kray's funeral "I miss Charlie the most..."
(picture by Colin Fanning)

bottom: 2000, St James Park - L-R; Nick Reynolds, Alan Parker,
Steve Wraith, fomer great train robber Bruce Reynolds.

top: L-R; Nicky Lambrianou,
Frank Fraser, Fred Foreman,
Steve Wraith, Tony Lambrianou.

centre left: 2000,
L-R; Steve Wraith, Gary Tiplady,
Rob Wraith.

centre right:
Howard Marks, Steve Wraith.

left:
2000 - Wreath for Charlie Kray
L-R; Ian Freeman, Steve Wraith,
Graham Borthwick.

top: Steve Wraith and freinds
- Gateshead Car Park 2001.

left: Steve and Dawn
- Benidorm 2002.

below: L-R; Andy Walker,
Billy Jones, Steve Wraith
on the door at the Groat
House, Christmas 2001.

top: L-R; Dave Courtney, Steve Wraith, Ian Freeman.

bottom: Steve Wraith, Eric Mason, Stuart Wheatman, 2001

me that Ron had been moved to Abingdon Ward and was stripped of all privileges. He was allowed to call those on his phone list so I passed on a message to him. He phoned me a couple of hours later... still sounding as upbeat as when I'd left him. "I just flipped Steve. I told you they were messing with my drugs didn't I? Still that's that. I'm better off here anyway. I'm off gardening and kitchen duties. No privileges see. But it means I've got time to think here. I get forty quid here from the NHS so that's a result! Anyway I have to go. Will you do me a favour? Phone the papers and tell them that this attack is the last act of violence Ron Kray will ever carry out." It was as good as done. Bizarre.

In the same year Diana, Princess of Wales, visited Broadmoor. The visit was publicised in all the newspapers, with the tabloids making out that she was having tea with the Ripper and Ron. Not so. I visited Ron a week later and the first question I asked Ron was, "How was the Princess?" Ron glared at me over his spectacles and then said, "She didn't want to see me." Further questioning revealed that she had the option of visiting Ron but had declined. He wasn't impressed, "I'm just as mad as everyone else in here!" Maybe it was for the best. It was unlikely that any member of the royal family would have been permitted to visit one of the Krays, or Sutcliffe for that matter. The press would have a field day and the public would see it as an unforgivable act of condoning their crimes. They were too high profile. On the same visit he asked me to pick up an envelope on the way out that he'd left at reception. It contained an old newspaper that he wanted me to send to Reg. In it was a photo of the Queen Mother visiting the East End in the 1940's. There in the background was a young Ron Kray. His non-visit with the Princess had jogged his memory about this paper and he wanted to send it to Reg to remind him of his brush with royalty.

I definitely enjoyed my visits more with Ron than I'd had with Reg. Ron was a likeable man most of the time. Making my way home after the visits would always be my time to reflect – The Ripper incident, the murders he wanted arranged, when he spoke about killing Cornell were all added to the times when he would tell me all kinds of funny stories, listen to my life outside, learn all about my family and even ask me to help produce greetings cards with a polar bear on the front and one of his poems inside. He was a hard man to work out. I found him to be very different to Reg, but they would always be 'similar'. They had a tight bond that could never be broken by distance.

Ron was the youngest of the twins and had emerged as the dominant one. Within the firm, he was the more dominant of his other older brother too. His life was a very troubled one that seemed doomed by his illness. He changed physically too, the medication, giving up on exercise, chain-smoking... but he always appeared to know what he was doing. Even when agitated, he knew it was down to a change in medication. Many people have asked me whether I think he would ever have been released – I don't think he would have. Patients in Broadmoor are at a disadvantage to begin with. For example, if locked up in prison, a convict can abide by the rules and stay out of trouble to increase his chances of parole. In a mental institution, the criteria are not that well defined. They don't know what is the best way to behave to increase their chances and different behaviours may evoke different responses in the observers. Mental illness is not something that should be taken lightly – it should be treated and not just swept under the carpet. We hear all the time of mentally ill people committing murder and all the time the signals were there to the authorities. Ron Kray had been accurately diagnosed in prison in the fifties yet did not receive any treatment for his schizophrenia. Locked up for murder, it took the authorities around eight years to take him out of a conventional prison and transfer him to Broadmoor where he could receive help. He was a lot happier there even with his ups and downs. He had his own clothes and could dress like the London gangster he'd always be remembered for.

Charlie Kray

I became good friends with Charlie Kray. He was a good bloke who would do anything for a mate. I got to know him well through first getting to know his brothers, meeting him at parties and later when hosting our own parties. He would always be the life and soul and would make anyone welcome. He was very image conscious as well... always wore a suit, always had his hair dyed and groomed and always had a year-round suntan.

There are plenty of misconceptions about Charlie. He was always going to be in the background compared to his notorious brothers but he was still very much 'a Kray'. Like many East Enders, he'd been a boxer and was very streetwise. Taking more of a silent partner role in the firm meant that he could be the business brain behind operations and leave Ron and Reg to run the public relations angle. It was a perfect partnership, all three were happy with the arrangement. Ron and Reg could mingle with the rich and famous in their clubs, while behind all the glitz and glamour, Charlie would be doing all the real work – the work that nobody saw going on. He would make sure everything ran smoothly and he was good at doing so.

The happy partnership was unsteadied one night in *Esmerelda's* though when the silent partner was anything but silent. *Esmerelda's* was a good earner for the firm; it had a discotheque on the first floor and a gambling joint on the second. It was in Belgravia in London, a particularly affluent area. The usual arrangement was that the sons and daughters of the rich gamblers would go to the disco while their parents would enjoy themselves upstairs. Charlie was the right face to be running this place. Gamblers wanted a relaxed atmosphere; they didn't wish to know about the gangland side of things and didn't want to feel threatened. Charlie fronting the operation was enough to put anyone at ease. He would be the perfect host as usual, ensuring everyone was happy. Charlie mixed with everyone, suited up with his overcoat hanging on his shoulders, shaking hands and welcoming his guests.

One particular night all three brothers were there, and the customers began complaining about the behaviour of one of the patrons – it was obvious there was going to be trouble. The person they were complaining about was Ron Kray. He had been going to the disco, made unwanted advances to young men so the relaxed atmosphere became tense. Ron's behaviour was upsetting people. Charlie was not amused. Business was good but Ron was going to mess things up by acting so stupidly. Charlie took him to one side and told him the score but Ron was stubborn; he could not see the problem. Charlie picked a chair up and hurled it at the bar, "We may as well smash the place up now then!" He began smashing the bar up and hurling abuse at Ron. Reg stepped in to try and calm Charlie down, but this time neither of them could stop him. He clearly made his point. Charlie was always known as the easygoing Kray brother. He *was* easy going... until he was wound up to the point of eruption. After that night, everyone knew he could be as dangerous as the twins if pushed. He silenced a lot of people that night by standing up to both twins at once and proving that he certainly was not a man to be messed with.

When considering my memories of Charlie... I met him many times in London and Newcastle. In all the time I knew him, I never saw a side to Charlie that wasn't likeable. He was always a gentleman – an East End character with a lust for life and always seemed to have a smile on his face.

On the first of August 1996, I heard news concerning Charlie that was so unlike Charlie that anyone who knew him could not believe it. He was arrested for his involvement in a thirty-nine million pounds cocaine deal.

It was shocking enough to hear that he was caught up in the crime, but to hear that he was the mastermind was difficult to comprehend. To the general public, it was as sensational as ever but to people who knew him it was a different story all together. The 'quiet' Kray brother, an OAP no less, caught in a huge drugs bust was something that the news teams and tabloid reporters around the country could not wait to jump on. Video footage of Charlie at a party with undercover policemen was shown on the national news... it was as though there was a huge sigh of relief that the third Kray would be safely locked away. When I heard, it just didn't sink in. As far as I could see the situation, a man who couldn't cover his tracks on a poxy tee-shirt scam was hardly a criminal mastermind. It was as though what I was reading and hearing about involved a different person all together.

Charlie and two others, Robert Gould and Ron Fields had been arrested in an elaborate sting set up by two Geordie police officers. He was allegedly caught on tape offering to supply cocaine to two business/policemen who he had met and become friendly with.

On two occasions, Charlie had asked me to meet up with him to check his new friends out but I couldn't make it due to other commitments. On hearing that it was those friends who turned out to be undercover policemen made me feel sick and the fact that they were from up here didn't help. I could just picture him telling them how much he loved Newcastle and these two policemen just reeling him in. One part of me was saying that if I'd met up with them, then just maybe I could have sussed the pair of them out. *Maybe*. And then *maybe* Charlie would be a free man. The other part of me was saying that if I had been present at *any* of those meetings, then the chances were that I would be in a cell next to Charlie. In that sense it was a huge relief.

He was remanded at Belmarsh High Security Prison in Woolwich, I kept in touch with him by letter and spoke to him on the phone. He was being held as a triple A category prisoner on twenty-three hours lock-up, high risk and likely to abscond... at seventy years of age. I tried to keep his morale up and to let him know that we were all thinking of him. He wrote back saying how much he appreciated my effort. He remained as positive as he could in his situation, but he knew that if things went the wrong way for him the consequences were not worth thinking about. On the sixth of August, he wrote to me asking if I could sort security out for him if he got bail. *That's* how positive he was about his chances. Inside he had the likes of Charles Bronson and Dave Courtney as company. I was in touch with Dave as he was waiting for a court date too.

Charlie was coping well and in telephone conversations he always sounded upbeat. I could always read between the lines though – he would never say it outright but he was very worried beneath his 'typical Charlie' exterior. He talked a lot about his girlfriend Judy Stanley, he asked me to send her cash and make sure she was alright. He was never selfish in that respect. In one letter dated the second of December 1996, he said he wondered when it would all end... that he sat on his own, thinking, contemplating the future and said he didn't know what he'd do without Judy. It was obvious that his thoughts of her kept him going.

When Dave walked free from his appearance almost a year later, we both agreed to meet up in June to stand as character witnesses for our mate Charlie. Charlie had written to me just after Dave went free saying 'what a result' it was and that he was pleased for him. He said it must be the best feeling in the world. Now he had to prepare himself for his own trial.

I travelled down to London by train and arrived in Kings Cross on June the fifth 1997 to attend Charlie's trial the following day at Woolwich Crown Court, next door to Belmarsh Prison. It was nearing a year since his arrest now. Christian met me off the train just after midnight and we went for a drink. We made our way to a quiet shady looking snooker club just outside the station and as we reached the bar, I couldn't help but feel we were slightly out of place. We were the only white people in there, the rest of the punters were oriental... then it dawned on me that we were in Triad territory. The snooker club was one of their many after hours dens but after initial apprehension and a few drinks, I began to feel quite at ease. We played snooker for a while and had a quick bite to eat, leaving at three-thirty am. We talked a lot about what we'd each been up to recently, what other friends had been up to and just generally caught up with things. Chris is one of those people that no matter how long it has been since you last met, you can catch up immediately like you only saw each other last week. Always one for surprises he then told me that we are sleeping at *The Hammersmith Apollo*. He was working there for a security firm, so he was able to get us into one of the dressing rooms to doss down for a few hours before the trial. The dressing room had just been used by Sir Cliff Richard during his *Heathcliff* show but we tried not to let that bother us.

After a restless sleep we made our way to Woolwich. We arrived on time and were greeted outside the court by Frankie Fraser and Charlie's QC, Mr. Goldberg. Frankie said that another solicitor Michelle Haeems was looking for me to clarify a few points relating to the evidence I was due to give. Not knowing which way to go I followed Frank and Goldberg into the Court buildings. As we entered we went through the security checks and emptied our pockets for inspection.

I found Michelle Haeems waiting for me on the next floor up. She asked if in May 1996 had I ever met Charlie or arranged to meet him. I told her I had spoken to Charlie but couldn't meet him due to a prior engagement. Michelle was happy with that and told me to wait in the canteen and my name would be called on the speaker system when I was needed. The trial was to be held in Court number one. The canteen was full of familiar faces

– Frankie Fraser, Charlie's close friend John Corbett, Eileen Sheridan the former Miss UK, Bill Murray from ITV's *The Bill*, Ray Burdis, director of *The Krays* and Les Martin, one of Charlie's biggest supporters.

Whilst seated in court with a tense atmosphere, this was the first point that I let the enormity of the situation hit me. I could see the anxiety in peoples' faces and that made me stop to think. When I first heard about the charges, like many others, I just dismissed the whole episode as a mistake or another attempt to get the Krays that was so absurd that it would be laughed out of court. When encountering the scale of security, the police, the hype, the press turnout – it began to hit home. The conversation centred on Charlie's chances. We all made positive noises, but there was an underlying feeling of a long, long sentence. We seemed to be spending too much time in the canteen and as I downed my fourth cup of coffee at ten past eleven, an announcement informed us that council had been removed from court. The clock ticked slowly... at twenty past twelve an early lunch was called... at one-thirty another announcement... there would be no evidence heard that day due to legal arguments. We were told that a member of the jury had either recognised or had had an encounter with a defence witness the previous day, so as a result the juror was removed and the jury reduced to eleven. I felt deflated. There were bad vibes throughout the day and this was the icing on the cake. On leaving the canteen, I met up with Christian, sank a few pints and then caught the train back to Newcastle. There didn't seem like that much to talk about as we sat in the pub. We made small talk and arranged to meet up on the following Tuesday when we would be going through it all again.

Tuesday the eleventh of June arrived; I had travelled down on a late night train again. I went to the court the following morning. Already there was Fethi, a Turkish restaurant owner from Birmingham, and Jon Ivey the director of a recently released play based on Tony Lambrianou's life and book called *Inside The Firm*. Today there was a prompt start. As we reached court one we were all flanked by armed officers and were once again searched thoroughly as we passed through the security cordon leading to the court and the public gallery. I was led through to the defence witness waiting room, where I made polite conversation with Fethi and Jon and we discussed Charlie's chances. The atmosphere once again felt gloomy. No one actually sounded positive about the outcome; sometimes people put on a brave face and say that everything will be all right when they know it is unlikely,..... well no one even bothered going through the motions.

I was the last person called in the morning session. The usher called out my name and I got up and walked to the packed courtroom. The air was stifling, making me immediately uncomfortable as the court usher led me to the witness box. It was a tense situation to be in. I caught a glimpse of Charlie behind a glass partition standing between two burly prison officers. If I felt this uneasy after a few minutes, I could only imagine how he was feeling. I swore an oath and was questioned by Goldberg for the defence. Goldberg, like Charlie, was suntanned and expensively dressed. I thought he seemed a bit smug, almost arrogant as though the case would win itself. I just hoped his overconfident manner was justified.

After confirming my name, address and occupation, Goldberg went straight into asking about the magazine, *Number Nine*. I wasn't too sure where the line of questioning was leading. I was asked about how many copies I'd sold and was asked about Newcastle United – had I met them, did I know them... then was handed an autographed football and was asked to comment on it. I said that it looked like an autographed football, but after looking closely, realised they were all fakes and told the court that none of the signatures were genuine.

He then asked if I'd heard of autographed footballs being auctioned, and how much one would fetch if it were genuine. I replied, "Anything up to one hundred pounds, I have also seen footballs like this autographed by Sunderland's team, but they don't make very much, Sir." I don't think they understood my attempt to be court jester.

He then asked how I had got to know Charlie... "Basically through my magazine. Others involved sent copies to sporting heroes such as Kevin Keegan and Peter Beardsley, I sent mine to Ron and Reg Kray as I had heard a lot about them and was curious as to their response. They replied to my letters, and to cut a long story short, I visited the twins in prison and was then introduced to Charlie, it was a natural progression. I spoke to Charlie on the phone at first."

When did I first meet the defendant? The twenty-fourth of February 1994 at *Guvernors* pub in the East End of London.

What was Mr. Kray doing there? He was playing the host, meeting people and generally socialising. It was a charity event in aid of a young child suffering from cerebral palsy.

Was it true that I held a party at which Charles James Kray again played host? Yes it was. I organised a party for a young boy called Terry Moran at *The Elysium Lane social club* in Bensham, Gateshead. Terry had suffered eighty per cent burns in a bonfire night accident, both Charlie and Tony Lambrianou agreed to travel to Newcastle to help support this event.

I also told the court that Charlie did not receive any payment or travelling expenses and that a member of his family was quite ill at the time, while others may have cancelled, Charlie honoured his agreement and attended. I went on to say he socialised and was a great host. He posed for every photograph, signed every autograph, and said it was one of the best nights he has ever had.

Was footballer Paul Gascoigne at this event? Paul was invited, and indeed his mother two sisters and Aunties were there, but Paul could not make it as he was signing for his new club, Glasgow Rangers, at the time. In summing up, I was asked to describe him. I said he was affable, friendly and a good host. I am proud to call Charlie Kray my friend.

No further questions.

I looked over to Charlie. He winked and smiled; he was obviously pleased with my performance. I reluctantly call it a performance because it hints that you are putting on a show or lying. I'd told the truth throughout. I glanced around the courtroom, it was such a strange feeling standing in the box defending one of the Krays, I couldn't help but imagine what the people in the court room were thinking, especially the jury. I just hoped that I'd helped in a small way to réduce whatever sentence Charlie was going to receive. Judge Carroll interrupted my thoughts by asking QC for the Prosecution, Mr. Kelsey-Fry, if he had any questions for me. He did.

Kelsey-Fry was very straight to the point. He certainly knew what he was doing throughout. He had a Kray in court and knew he would be the one to put Charlie in prison. He asked me if I had ever let Charlie Kray down, arranged to meet him and not turned up or ever arranged to meet Charlie Kray for a drink in Croydon. I replied no to all three questions. He and the Judge thanked me, and I was free to go.

With that I looked towards the jury, then Charlie, who once again gave me a reassuring smile, and I was led down from the witness box and escorted up to the public gallery. All the chaps who were present congratulated me. On my 'performance' as that's how court is always perceived in gangland; compared to a stage. Act innocent... make him sound like a good person... do this, do that. I was just glad it was over for me. I had done my bit now it was up to the jury to see that justice was done. I was curious as to Kelsey-Fry's line of questioning. I now know that Charlie was recorded on tape arranging to meet a Steve (not me) in Croydon and the prosecution just wanted this point clarified. Goldberg with his questions wanted me to portray Charlie as a kind hearted man who would do anything for anybody and make out that the police were liars intent on setting Charlie up. He was trying to build a case for entrapment, and I personally didn't think that was the greatest of ideas, but I was only a post office manager not *Columbo*. As far as I was concerned, I'd told the truth and had hopefully helped a friend out.

I had followed Frankie Fraser into the witness box. Charlie's chances had not been helped after Fraser managed to turn the whole thing into a farce. On leaving the witness box, he told everyone that it was the first time he'd ever left court a free man. Okay, it *is* funny... until you put it into context. He was supposed to be a character witness for someone in a serious situation. Did he think that saying what he did would actually help Charlie? These were the kind of favours he could do without.

I left Woolwich that day with a lot of thoughts running through my head. I wasn't sure what the outcome would be of the trial. It wasn't looking good, but I still believed in a man being innocent until proven guilty. Charlie was on my mind. I felt I'd done all I could and now it was out of my hands. His whole future was at stake in that courtroom, though for a lot of people it was just treated as a day out. On my way home I thought a lot about the Krays and my relationship with the family. It had been a long time since my first meetings with them, a long time since I had contacted them as a fan... and that day I'd just stood up for one of the brothers as a character witness in court. That's how much our friendship had developed and I'm proud to say I was able to support them in court. I wasn't a mobster from the old days, but I was respected enough to be asked and it meant a lot to me. I know it meant a lot to Charlie that I had been there too.

I was unable to attend the rest of the trial, but as fate would have it, I could make it for the verdict. My football team always had an annual trip away and for the second year running we visited London. We set off mid-afternoon on Friday the twentieth of June and by seven p.m. my mobile phone battery was close to exhaustion with the news breaking that Charlie had been found guilty on both counts, and that sentencing would be delivered on Monday. I was devastated but if honest, I'd expected it. All Charlie could hope for now would be a lenient sentence.

On the day of sentencing the usual security was in operation, but this time we were made to queue up outside to make our way to the public gallery of court number one. I can only imagine this was for the benefit of the media who had gathered to capture us all on film. There were all the usual Kray fans trying to get their faces on TV and in papers but my respect goes to the loyal friends who attended – Dave Courtney, Christian Simpson, Les Martin and Kiwi Andy – and kept a dignified silence. Today was also the first time that I had seen Charlie's co-defendants. In stark contrast to Charlie who was immaculately dressed as usual, Robert Gould and Ron Fields were dressed in drab everyday civvies. Whether this was just pessimism on their behalf, I don't know. I'm sure they could have made an effort to look respectable if they wanted to, and it may have worked a bit in their favour. It is possible to pick a suit up for a few quid these days or a tie for even less. Maybe they were trying to avoid appearing like ruthless drug barons.

Charlie gave it one last throw of the dice with an emotional plea to the Judge and Jury. He was desperate – desperate to somehow convince them and also desperate for a way out. He knew his fate was sealed and had to say his piece.

"All my life I would advise people, particularly young people never to be involved in drugs. Juries have got it wrong before about me, and this jury has got it wrong. I swear on my son's grave I have never handled drugs in my life".

He was given twelve years on count one (offering to supply five kilograms of cocaine every fortnight for two years), and eight years on count two to run concurrently (helping to supply a two kilogram consignment). I looked at him as the sentence was read out. He was stunned, essentially given a death sentence. I think he knew it as well... it is certainly what everyone in that room was thinking.

Judge Carroll's retort was short and to the point, "Throughout this case you have professed your abhorrence against drugs. The jury's verdict has shown your oft-repeated protestations to be hypocrisy. Those who deal in drugs can still expect justice from the courts but little mercy." He appeared like the headmaster you always disliked at school. As far as he was concerned, Charlie was a Kray and he was guilty – end of story.

Gould received five years for his involvement and Fields got nine. Once sentencing was passed, Charlie turned and blew a kiss to Judy Stanley, then waved to all of us in the gallery. He was led down to the cells beneath the courtrooms to begin his sentence. That was it... over. We filed out of the gallery outside to the waiting media, and whilst the usual 'friends' waffled on about how they had known the Krays for years I quietly slipped away with Dave Courtney and the chaps for a few drinks in *The Albion*, something Charles James Kray would never be doing again.

On subsequent visits to Charlie, letters and phone calls, he told me in great detail about the events surrounding his arrest and eventual imprisonment. On my first visit to him he told me about the operation that had him recorded, set-up, entrapped – call it what you want – was called operation ACID. The first meeting between them all took place at the *Medallion Vert Hotel* in Moseley, Birmingham, on Thursday the ninth of May 1996. Present at this meeting were Patsy Manning (Patsy is from Birmingham and it was his sixty-sixth birthday party), Deano and George who had travelled together from London, Jack who had travelled from Newcastle, and Charlie. This was one of the times Charlie had asked me to come along and for reasons which I am now glad of, I couldn't make it.

Deano and Jack already knew each other in this scenario. They were the two undercover policemen from the North East. Patsy was a long time friend of Charlie's and the twins. As the meeting progressed, they had a few drinks and began to acquaint themselves; talking about times they had visited one another's hometowns and friends they had in common. Patsy and Jack discussed how depressing the atmosphere in Newcastle was until the mid-eighties when money was injected into the pubs and clubs of the Quayside. Jack claimed to have invested money in the area around ten years earlier and mentioned that Deano should bring Patsy up to Newcastle some time. Patsy said he'll use Jack's name when he is there in the usual manor of 'I'm a mate of Jack's... nudge, nudge' to get looked after.

Jack also claimed to have 'done some work' in London, but all this boasting was an obvious front to make himself more credible in his present company. He was talking the talk and bluffing about a fabricated criminal past. Charlie also mentioned Newcastle, telling of the charity event I organised that he and Tony hosted. He told them that he met Gazza's (Paul Gascoigne) family there and had his photo took with them and went on to tell them about me. I know this to be a fact. My name brought into the conversation – no matter how innocent – associated me with Charlie. I didn't know it at the time, but the police would most likely have been watching my movements. They would have been aware of me anyway, but would now be aware of my name for another reason because of Charlie name dropping me. As he told me this, I thought back to the night of the charity event. I remembered that we'd shared jokes about police being present... singling out a few people we said looked like coppers, but it was all in good humour. Now the irony was that we were most likely right. It would stand to reason that there would be a police presence, as Charlie and Tony in the same room were quite an attraction. I was frantically trying to think if I'd noticed anything out of the ordinary at the party but it was impossible. The whole night was out of the ordinary. All eyes had been on Charlie.

Their meeting in Birmingham was full of 'any friend of mine is a friend of yours' conversations. They had even discussed the twins themselves... Patsy reminiscing about the first time he met them in the sixties, around a week after arriving in London. I could imagine them both in their element discussing 'the days'.

Jack and Deano must have been convincing. They told of connections in Brussels and discussed a piece of work they had recently handled. It was a general bonding meeting of 'friends'. The criminal language was apparent – doing 'jobs' and 'work' is not the sort where you send in a resume and sit an interview. Such claims from an undercover policeman are to earn respect and trust within the group. Charlie told me that he had no reason to doubt their credibility.

Charlie loved to tell his stories about meeting this person and that person... he told them about Jackie and Joan Collins, Barbara Windsor, times he met Sonny Liston and what they talked about. He and Patsy took turns in re-telling one story about Charlie, the twins, George Raft and Rocky Marciano. They had got together in Bethnal Green and Patsy had been told by Reg to get over and meet them.

He got there as quick as he could in a taxi but missed out on a photo opportunity with them by one minute. Billy Daniels was brought into the conversation as well. Famous names... boxing... it was all déjà vu.

More déjà vu was about to come. As I was learning about these conversations after the trial, there were things that started to piece together. There had been conversations from these meetings on tapes, which were used as evidence and played to the jury at the trial. In one of these tapes, Jack was heard to ask Charlie if he wanted a signed football for a charity event to help raise money. If I were a gambler, I'd put money on it being the football I was asked to comment on in court where the signatures were all fakes. For such a large-scale operation, I would have thought that the signatures would be genuine. As I was hearing all this, I was kicking myself. If I'd been there maybe I could have sussed them out at this point – ask how they knew the team and other details which would have put them on the spot.

Charlie's memory for detail was impeccable. He could tell me every date they met, where they met, what they discussed – everything. It was like the museum curator confessing to a crime at the end of an episode of Scooby Doo. As he told me about the meetings, I couldn't help but wonder about the whole 'deal'. To begin with, I had been under the impression that he'd been innocent all along. Now I wasn't so sure. It was difficult to know what to think.

He told me that they stayed over at the hotel and the next day arranged further meetings. Jack and Deano discussed business in Amsterdam and 'a problem' over there where someone died suddenly. This was the first time where drug activities were hinted at. Someone dying suddenly, a problem and Amsterdam equals drugs and gangs to me. He didn't elaborate the story any further, but said that Jack wanted to do business with Charlie's firm because he had been 'let down' on a deal. He was interested in Charlie (cocaine) and smoke (cannabis) and the supply of it. Charlie (Kray), whether we like to admit it or not, had offered to supply a large amount of drugs to someone. The gist of the discussion was that Charlie said he could not discuss a price just then, but they would have to wait until further arrangements are made. It would be possible to arrange a regular supply of drugs in the near future. Charlie was enthusiastic about the whole thing. They exchanged phone numbers, Jack not wanting a lot of people involved... only he and Deano would be involved from their side, well, those two and the rest of the police force.

Charlie arranged their stay at the *Selsdon Park Hotel* in Croydon under different names. Apparently he'd seen O.J Simpson there before, "He was guilty as the day is long. I don't mind people getting a result, but not him." I wondered if this was because he thought that O.J was guilty all along but good lawyers had made sure he walked free. Maybe he was bitter that his own lawyer had not done the same for him, I don't know. Jack brought someone else to the hotel instead of Deano – another officer going by the name of Kenny from Manchester, but any friend of Jack's was a friend of Charlie's. Okay, so he had just met Jack to discuss drug trafficking and now Jack has brought someone else in on it who Charlie had never laid eyes on in his life... and this was alright with Charlie. It sounded odd... naïve that a drug trafficker would have such disregard for caution. They were talking tens of millions of pounds, not just a ten quid wrap of speed. I found it hard to work Charlie's logic out. He'd tell me all this so matter of factly... sipping his tea at intervals, leaving me hanging on his every word. I couldn't believe some of the details he was recalling. To me this was one of the most important Kray stories. I think more so because it happened in my time and I knew him when it happened – I was almost part of it too. It also has importance to me because, like all other Kray stories, it was controversial. The more Charlie spoke, the more amazed I was that we were not having this conversation in Broadmoor. Charlie told of his outlandish boastings about himself in Manchester where he lost a hundred thousand pounds on a deal. On hearing this, you may be hoping that drug trafficking is not Charlie's day job, but he told them that he sorted the problem out by putting 'five grand' up to eradicate the problem, which in gangland terms suggests only one thing. I'd rarely seen Charlie with more than a hundred pence in his pocket, let alone a hundred thousand pounds, or five thousand for that matter... it was just part of his personality, his trademark. Of course they didn't believe him. They may have pretended to believe him at the time, but in reality they would have known all his moves for some time and known it was a lie. It was all talk. I know from sources that they said a lot of his comments were "Bullshit... all big talk... not a word of truth in it." If Charlie was a big time drug dealer and they knew it, I don't know why they would laugh off his stories as false. It seemed to suggest that they knew Charlie was just talking the talk without walking it. The whole situation seemed to be one contradiction after another from both sides. He'd told me in the past that he knew the police had turned a blind eye to some of the minor crimes he'd been involved in and he knew he had been watched on several occasions, but this time it seemed he was oblivious to the fact that he was meeting up with police and saying he could supply them with drugs.

They discussed quantities, which Charlie said would be tonnes... a serious deal from the size of it. This interested Jack; he told Charlie that he could move a regular supply in large quantities, but the price of the cocaine would have to be right. I'm not sure what the norm is for cocaine deals, but if I were buying from someone who kept meeting up with me and repeating how big it's going to be, I'd lose my patience and go elsewhere for it. At no point could Charlie have sounded like he knew what he was doing... he just kept making the same promise to them over and over. I don't know whether it was a bluff or complete nonsense, or both. The police were quite prepared to wait for him to set the deal up, discussing it so many times on tape that he would incarcerate himself.

As the visit drew to a close, we embraced as we said our goodbyes. I felt sad for him and for what he had done. My visits from then on consisted mostly of conversations about the deal and the trial.

The next time we met, Charlie looked much different. His suntan had faded, his grey hair had grown through the dye and he had begun to look the old man that he was. He always looked healthy with a tan, adding to his flamboyant 'playboy' appearance. Now he just looked like any other man in his seventies. Straight into the visit and he picked up where he'd left off on the story. There were things he'd told Jack that really made him feel like a 'mug'. There was the part in the last visit where he mentioned the part about knowing the police had watched him in the past which he'd even told Jack, there was some other information he told him too. Charlie had a friend, an ex-policeman, who had told him this originally. Scotland Yard have a list of criminals whose phones they periodically tap for two weeks at a time. He told him one time; 'You're hooked up' which is why Charlie wouldn't discuss any business over the phone. Now Charlie could think back to their meetings and realise he'd been offering this kind of information to an undercover policeman. He'd start by saying he told Jack about being out with Denny Laine, formerly of Wings and The Moody Blues, then go on to tell me about a group called Phoenix who he had done a 'publicity thing' for around that time with David Bailey taking pictures for them. The group was going to play at the Royal Albert Hall and he was going to get tickets for Jack and Deano. If Dave Courtney was known as the *Yellow Pages of Crime*, then Charlie should simply have been known as the *Yellow Pages*.

We didn't talk much about the charity event where the football was auctioned, other than it was to raise money for St Christopher's Hospice where Charlie's son Gary had died. It was at *The Mermaid*, and he told me it was a good do. They met up again around a week after the charity event... Jack phoning round as he'd been 'away' doing some business in Brussels. He called Charlie from Newcastle Airport, telling him he'd met up with the 'Brussels Firm' soon after the party, which was why he'd disappeared for so long. Maybe he just had the week off to spend with his family, who knows?

Charlie told me something that made me laugh. When he'd arranged the hotel rooms for Jack and Kenny, he told Jack to see a friend of his there who would 'sort him out' – meaning he'd get a good deal. Jack didn't ask the bloke though, and so ended up paying the full price for the rooms which was ninety-five quid each. Patsy heard about this and said it was Charlie's fault and that he should have phoned up to arrange the rooms for Jack and not left it down to him. Jack just shrugged it off... well; it had all come out of the taxpayer's pocket anyway. Charlie was told that Patsy had said this and whether true or not, knew it was just to try to break their friendship up. It really meant nothing to him in the scheme of things.

Things got moving... Charlie and Ron Fields were invited up to Newcastle. Jack sorted some plane tickets so they could fly up with the idea that they would get together somewhere quiet to discuss business. Charlie contacted Ron about it and they flew from Gatwick to stay overnight in Newcastle. Jack made it clear he wanted it to be low profile with just Charlie and Ron, and none of Ron's firm. Then Charlie let rip with another bombshell – they asked for the airline tickets to be booked in their own names, Charlie Kray and Ron Fields. I later heard that the police were in their element over details like this. Here were two known criminals, each with a long history, travelling together to discuss drug trafficking and using their own names. Knowing the conversations that took place, actions were inconsistent with the use of common sense. Using their own names was hardly the actions of two major drug dealers. I assumed that even small-time criminals would have used different names; again it looks like the work of rank amateurs. Both men had criminal pasts and were still very much active, I'd have thought just to try to cover their tracks *slightly* would have been second nature to them.

They spoke on the phone for the next few days, until the twenty-sixth of June when Jack met Charlie and Ron at Newcastle Airport and they got into his four-wheel drive jeep. Along the way, Charlie mentioned that Fields had noticed a cream Vauxhall following them for quite some time, but they just laughed it off as paranoia. Still, they didn't seem too paranoid when arranging bookings in hotels and for plane tickets, as they were booked into the hotel under the same names as well. They made their way over to *The Linden Hall Hotel* in Longhorsley, near Morpeth, making small talk along the way. Charlie remembered they discussed things such as Fields getting married in September, and that his ex-missus had been a staff nurse who was always handy for 'patching people up'. Also they talked of a mate of theirs from the North East called Dingus McGhee who was serving time for killing two policemen. They even joked on with Jack saying that if he pulled into a quarry, neither Fields nor Charlie would get out of the jeep... they said they wanted it to be the start of their business relationship, not the end of it. They talked about bodies keep turning up in similar vehicles in London. I suppose at least in their present company, they were safe in that respect.

They reached the hotel; a big stately home out in the country, Charlie was well impressed with it. Kenny was there to meet them and also another bloke called Brian, who was part of their 'firm' i.e., he was an undercover officer too. Charlie and Field's room was obviously bugged. They'd had plenty of time to set microphones. On the night they had drinks and watched England playing Germany in the Euro '96 semi-finals and then on the Thursday morning they met up in one of the rooms to discuss the drugs deal.

Jack apparently started by saying they wanted cocaine and they wanted it regularly. Charlie told me that Jack and Fields discussed the purity of the cocaine at a 'wash up' of something like ninety to ninety-two per cent; Fields assuring him it was of high quality. Part payment was to be made up front with only those present at the meetings to be involved in it. Brian had suggested a driver might be used, though he would have no idea that it was a drug deal. Also, using their own driver would cut costs down. Fields said they could have five kilos to start with and Jack said they would want that every fortnight. They agreed a one-week timescale for Jack and Brian to raise the cash, and would contact Charlie if they got hold of it any earlier.

Jack and Fields discussed a price for five kilos – it was set at thirty-one thousand five hundred pounds. There was talk of other drugs too as they discussed buying and selling cannabis. As Charlie started to tell me the sort of prices and quantities they were discussing I couldn't help but think how foolish they had been. I have no doubt that the policemen were very good at their job... it must have been difficult, stressful, dangerous work for them. Charlie and Fields *were* setting up a major drug deal with them – there is no ambiguity there. There was no false evidence, tapes were played and it proved that they had discussed all this. There wasn't any way out as far as I could see. Charlie even recalled a veiled threat from Fields where he'd said the money had better be real – last person who tried to pay in fakes ended up in a Range Rover (hinting towards an *Essex Boys* style murder over counterfeit money). Okay, he was joking, but when we know he was saying it to policemen, it could be something else for them to look into.

The deal was set at *The Selsdon* in Croydon where the five kilos would be handed over and driven up to Newcastle. Brian and Jack were to bring money to pay for three kilos and settle the rest once they had sold some of the cocaine. This was in July of 1996, where there were a lot more calls and sorting out to be done for the imminent deal. Charlie, in true Charlie form, had told them he was skint and wanted to borrow an advance of five hundred quid for a trip to Birmingham. It was sent to him by registered post.

Each time Charlie told me of their meetings, whether face to face or in letters, he'd say what 'nice blokes' they were. Again, it just emphasises that they were good enough to fool these 'drug traffickers'. I always wonder if undercover police ever do genuinely like the people they deal with or if it is all an act where they really can't stand being in their company, like a *Donnie Brasco* scenario. Charlie always did have a love for story telling and name-dropping; he told stories to the police in confidence that others would never hear, as did Ron Fields. Things like well-known underworld figures having mental breakdowns while 'doing bird', unable to handle prison life and various other scams they were running... all of which they were kicking themselves over once they sat back and remembered all the conversations they'd had.

Tony Lambrianou phoned me a few months after Charlie started his twelve-year sentence offering me the chance to supply the security for a Gala Night in an Essex Golf Club to raise money for his appeal. I'd already had a letter from Charlie on the sixth of August 1997 after his sentencing saying he thought the appeal would be his last chance. I told Tony I would be proud to as long as I wasn't stepping on anyone's toes, namely Dave's. He told me I wasn't and that it was on Dave's recommendation that he had called me. I recruited the best of the best... John Lillico, Christian, Andy, Kiwi Andy, Darren Newmass, and a couple of Christian's mates.

The clubhouse was brand spanking new and the guest-list read like a who's who of gangland. There was Joe Pyle, Frankie Fraser, Freddie Foreman, Tommy Wisbey, Tony Chris and Nicky Lambrianou, Roy Shaw, Dave Courtney and Les Martin. There were the usual celebrities, Billy Murray, Ray Winstone (brilliant in *Lenny Blue*), Karl

Howmann, and Shane Richie. The Rockingberries provided the entertainment, and Frankie Fraser's wife Marilyn performed a couple of numbers too. The night was a great success and Tony raised a healthy five-figure sum for Charlie and his appeal. Les Martin was often looked upon as a bit of an oddball amongst the 'Kray Circle', and a lot of his so-called friends slagged him off behind his back. Les was the only one who would ask the questions and campaign on behalf of the Kray brothers; others may have had the intentions but he was the one out there doing it. His name is well known at the Home Office and for me he is one of the unsung heroes of the Kray story. After Charlie's trial and subsequent conviction he worked tirelessly on his behalf. Les had asked Christian and me to help him with the security at the court of appeal, as sometimes these events can get out of hand, especially if the appeal is successful and the conviction overturned. We accepted the invitation and were both present throughout the hearing.

Unfortunately all of his work was in vain. In February 1999, three judges at London's Law Courts – The Lord Chief Justice, Lord Bingham, Mr. Justice Ian Kennedy and Mr. Justice Jackson, rejected Charlie's appeal. He was told he'd be able to appeal against the length of his sentence once he'd served half of it. He had made a plea for mercy on the grounds of old age, but it was apparently up to the Secretary of State to release someone on compassionate grounds. There were plans to write to the Home Secretary, Jack Straw.

He was moved from Belmarsh to Long Lartin Prison and then to Frankland in Durham.

With him in Durham it meant that I was closer to Charlie than any of his friends or family and helped out by taking visitors to the prison from the station at Durham. When I had visited him earlier on in the year at Long Lartin, he had started to look his age as he settled into prison life. At Frankland Prison he looked unwell. As we talked he would

145

clutch his chest, sometimes pausing to catch his breath. I was very concerned for him; he was in obvious pain but would try not to show it. He would love to reminisce about 'that night' in Gateshead. It really had been one of the nights of his life and he had never forgotten the welcome that he had received from the Geordies. He had accepted his sentence now and knew in his heart that he would never see the outside world again. My only disappointment was when Charlie's ex-wife Diane came to visit him. I had arranged for her to be picked up and driven to the prison. Unfortunately I was let down, and so let Charlie and Diane down at the same time. It meant she missed half an hour of her visit, and it's something I've always felt bad about.

I had not visited Reg for almost six months when out of the blue he called me to thank me for what I was doing for Charlie. He never ceased to amaze me. Sometimes he could be completely insensitive and ungrateful, and then just when you didn't expect it he would surprise you. It was good to hear from him again though. We discussed our concerns for Charlie as he was not looking well at all when I had last seen him, I told Reg I'd do all I could to help Charlie out. It was hard to imagine right then, but the reality was that the Krays were dying out. Both surviving brothers were in poor health and in prison for what would surely be the rest of their lives. They remained eternally optimistic about their predicament. They had to... in prison you can never give up.

On my first visit to Charlie in Durham he asked me all kinds of questions about the policemen who nicked him. He wanted to know who they were, but I could not provide answers. He even employed private detectives to try to find out who they were. It wasn't that he wanted 'revenge' in the sense you may be thinking – nothing like that was ever discussed at all. What he wanted, was to find out who they were and find out as much about their past as possible. In short, he wanted to know if they had any skeletons in their closets... anything he could find to tarnish the reputations of these men, in doing so questioning the validity of the evidence against him. His appeal had been rejected and this was how Charlie wanted to try to beat the police. The manner in which he had been caught was for Charlie a bitter pill to swallow. He wanted to play as dirty as he thought they did... he wanted to find as much dirt on them as he could before launching his next appeal.

My next visit, we chatted more about the events that put him where he was. He still was thinking about the future though; he wanted out of prison desperately. The wheels were still in motion for his next appeal, and he told me of his birthday bash in 1996... the second time he'd asked me to make it to 'meet his new friends'. I felt worse now. I know he knew he'd asked me to Birmingham that night, but we both never mentioned it. We knew it would have been difficult. He spoke to Jack the day before, which was the tenth of June 1996. It was held at the *Wake Green Lodge Hotel*, Fethi's place. Ron Fields couldn't make it as he was 'waiting for a delivery'. Jack was bringing Brian down to it from Newcastle. Not much was mentioned of the party itself. He just went on to tell me that the drugs they were to supply Jack with were delayed, there were a lot of calls between them over the next two weeks and a lot of waiting around. Charlie remembered that Jack was asking for specific times which was annoying him, so he said he'd get Fields to tell him.

Fields called Jack to arrange further details. Apparently on 'business' calls, Fields would be called 'Mr. Floyd' and would give out the number of a safe phone box for Jack to call him back on. Good thinking, Ron. They agreed to meet and make the deal in a few days time and Jack phoned Charlie back to confirm. He also asked if Charlie could sort some rooms at *The Selsdon* again for them. There was some sort of problem when the two officers, Jack and Brian met up with Ron Fields to do the deal. Charlie was not amused by whatever it was, but as he had to keep his voice low it was hard to make out what he'd actually said. Basically, the deal didn't go according to plan and Fields had asked them to come back down in the next day or so. It was always difficult to make out the entire story as there were always officers around during visits and we couldn't let anything be overheard.

The deal was back on and they were to meet at Waltham Abbey. Charlie made sure he was never present at the drug deal. That part of it was not his scene, his involvement was just to introduce people and help set things up. Ron Fields and Robert Gould turned up at *The Swallow Hotel* at Waltham Abbey in Essex as arranged. Gould was part of Fields' firm. The 'deal' took place... they handed over two kilos of cocaine in worth sixty-three thousand pounds to Jack and Brian. Both Fields and Gould were arrested on the spot. Charlie was arrested at Judy Stanley's flat in Sanderstead.

I've heard so many different stories about the whole drug case since it happened. Some parts are true and others are plain ridiculous... others, I suppose we will never know if they are true or not. All I can do is provide the information that I know and leave it up to people to draw their own conclusions. Personally I think the accusations against Charlie were true. I also think he had grounds to protest that he was 'stitched up'. I can see both sides and that's how I want it to remain. I find it impossible to say that he was completely innocent. I could have believed it until I heard what went on at those meetings. Charlie only acted as a go-between to set the deal up... at no point did he handle drugs. I know that there were many things that Charlie said at these meetings that the police did not believe – that they knew he was making it up to make himself more credible in their company. This was no different to what they were doing. They were definitely out to get him, there is no denying that. Charlie was a talker. He was looking for any deal. He was old and a deal like this would have been his retirement package. I have no doubt that he would have sold Big Ben to them if they wanted it. They basically allowed him to talk himself into it. The way it dragged on and on only proved that he was no big time drug trafficker... but let's face it, Fields and Gould were arrested with the drugs on them. The deal *was* going ahead and it was all down to these meetings... all down to the big talk, the lies and seemingly inept means of bluffing his way through the whole affair.

Entrapment basically means to charm, delude or trick someone into doing something. They went for him, they charmed him... they deluded him into thinking they were Geordie wide boys who wanted to buy cocaine. He had not approached anyone to try and push drugs. Operation ACID must have been planned for some time. Undercover police could not have just infiltrated a gangland party one night wired up on the off chance that a coke deal would happen. It meant befriending people over a period of time (charm) and coming across as people of the same ilk (delude) in order to set up an elaborate deal (trick). I think they wanted Charlie Kray and he made it all too easy for them to get him.

But what could they possibly want him for? Why would they go after an old gangster who was still clinging onto the past and the legend that surrounded his name? This is where some of the rumours come in. It is alleged that the twins met Princess Margaret at society parties in the sixties. It had been alleged that 'substances' were present and pictures were taken – typical sixties parties but the photos would be damaging to the monarchy or anyone else present. It is also alleged that the Krays kept hundreds of files containing information about royalty, politicians and famous people – basically a huge collection of secrets about household names that could bring in millions of pounds in blackmail demands alone. These files are claimed to contain enough damning information to bring the country to its knees. Therefore, it was imperative that all three brothers remained locked up until their death.

It's no secret that the Krays knew a lot of influential people and in the sixties their rise to power had a lot to do with knowing the right people... more importantly knowing the right things about the right people. The files are said to still exist. True or not, it is a theory that regularly does the rounds.

Another rumour was that Peter Beaumont-Gowling had offered Charlie Kray to the police as part of a deal. Beaumont-Gowling was a restaurateur from Newcastle, and had big connections in the drug world. He served four years of an eleven year stretch for trying to launder five hundred and forty thousand pounds. It was drug money from cocaine deals. It is believed that he made a deal with the police to set Charlie up in exchange for his early parole. I don't know if this is true or not – it was certainly never discussed between Charlie and me. Beaumont-Gowling was shot dead in his Jesmond flat in Newcastle, an area known for its wealth. It was said that Charlie ordered the hit on him from his deathbed and that Reg had suggested it, wanting revenge on the one who'd grassed him up. I just think its another sensational story to link to the Kray Legend. Of course it *could* have happened, but it probably didn't happen... who knows. It is something that all three took to their graves.

It could just be that Charlie and Fields had been involved in this type of activity for some time and the police went after them. The way the deal went; the build up and the meetings, it is hard to imagine that they were experts in this profession though. Maybe they would have been better off going for real drug barons; the ones who own properties all over the world and turn over millions upon millions of pounds, the types who kill at the drop of a hat... who are feared and consider the use violence an everyday necessity. But instead they chose to go for a couple of blokes who never had much money at all, relying on favours from people all the time who never even thought to cover their tracks by using different names.

Charlie had been naive and careless in getting involved. All the signs were there that this was a honey-pot waiting for a bee... the ultimate sting. His partners in crime should have known better too. Charlie thought that if he did get caught it would be okay because he only introduced the two parties. In the eyes of the law, that is known as setting up a drug deal and not simply known as 'Ron this is Jack, Jack this is Ron'. He never physically handled drugs and made sure he had no part in the actual deal itself. Charlie was indeed always looking for a fast buck, but I'm convinced he wasn't trying to set himself up as the next Mr. Big. Les Martin is carrying on the fight to clear Charlie's name to this day.

Party Time

During the sixties, the good old days, there were parties every night. There was not the excuse of having to be up for work in the morning. It could be said that in Kray work circles, it was pretty much flexi-time all year. The twins were photographed with celebrities, well known faces, stars from stage and screen, sports stars... they loved having them taken at their clubs, and would always ensure that they were seen mingling with the people of the moment. This was the lifestyle they loved. It was what they had worked for.

Many events or social gatherings were held to raise money for charity, or to rephrase that, they were *advertised* as charity events. The charity did benefit at each event, but not as much as the twins did. It was their way of doing something for two good causes at the same time. In that respect, everyone was happy. What better way to raise their profile? They impressed and made money. It was the perfect set up.

In the early nineties, the Krays had their Second Coming... the film was out and Reg brought out his book, *Born Fighter*. Almost monthly a new book came out by a 'firm member' or an old friend and Reg was quick to spot the business potential in this renewed interest. They already had a tried and tested formula. It was obvious to Reg that what the world needed was 'Kray Nights'. Ron and Reg received countless letters week in week out from families with sick children (as well as dozens of con artists), and now the time seemed right to do something to help. They knew charity nights worked and there was no shortage of charities to help. After all... charity begins at home, doesn't it? Even if you happen to share it with a few thousand others. The time was also right to heal the rift between the twins and Charlie mainly because they needed something from him. They fell out with him over the film deal – the twins were not happy with the way Violet had been portrayed in the film by actress Billie Whitelaw. Ron had told me on a visit that she never swore like she did in the film. Because Charlie was an adviser to the film's director, Ron and Reg held him responsible for the script, dialogue, direction and the final cut. They needed someone to blame, so their one-man-production-company brother took the brunt of it. As part of their research, the Kemp brothers visited Ron and Reg, and they said they were pleased with how they were portrayed. For the rights to make the film the twins were paid a hundred and ten thousand and a further hundred and forty-five thousand was paid in royalties. When the film went on to gross three and a half million, they held Charlie responsible for not getting them a better slice of the action. Roger Daltry, front man of The Who originally owned the rights to *The Profession of Violence* on which it was based and sold the rights on to become the film. It's not as though they were given a bad deal, but when you feel you have missed out – you look for someone to blame. They had also fallen out over another matter. Reg was told there had been tee-shirts sold in London and other major cities in the country, including Newcastle. These tee-shirts were unofficial Kray merchandise with a picture of the twins on the front. Reg asked me to get to the bottom of it, which took three weeks of phone calls and a trip down to London... and it turned out that the tee-shirts were being manufactured in Croydon by none other than Charlie. I had no choice but to tell the twins and so the biggest pile of shit in the world hit the biggest fan in the world. Charles James Kray was now affectionately known as Mr. X.... every call, letter and visit they never mentioned him by name.

So, he had some making up to do and now he was given the perfect opportunity to do so. He would act as host and compere for Kray Nights, and in doing so Mr. X would once again become known as Mr. Kray. Reg was the king of manipulation and soon enlisted more fans to do his gofering. He just needed to click his fingers and people would come running.

It was now that I could look at my relationship with the twins and see how it had changed. I didn't see myself as a fan anymore and this was something I hadn't really stopped to consider before. I knew I was a fan before I'd met them and certainly was a fan in the early days but now I was part of their inner circle. I was a friend, an associate. If I didn't agree with something or not want to get involved, I told them so. I didn't just go along with anything. I could take from the friendship what I wanted and this helped me gain their respect. The relationship wasn't just a 'Steve do this, Steve do that'. It was like any other friendship. This led to a new set of gofers being brought in. I was only gofer to one person... me. Reg was smart enough to judge what people were like and what chain of manipulation he would utilise to his best advantage. A lot of people fell into the 'I'll do anything for the twins' category and that's all they were; people who would live off a slight notoriety because they earned them a few quid. Getting something out of it for yourself, favours in return, back handers, you name it – was what it was all about. It was also the networking I was interested in and contacts were one thing the twins were not short of.

As the party idea progressed, one of Reg's young gofers turned up on the scene. A Cockney kid called Gary and we did not get on. There was just something about him I couldn't put my finger on. Reg had this annoying habit of giving your phone number to anyone he took a fancy to. God only knows the amount of ex cellmates, and so-called old firm members who have called me up at stupid o'clock for a chat. So, sure enough, I received a call from Gary. He'd been enlisted by Reg to organise the venue, food and entertainment for the latest Kray Night. Reg had given him a list of numbers to sell tickets to, my number being one of them. It went something like this:

"Hello my name's Gary. I've been asked by Reg Kray to let you know about a party that I'm organising for him. Do you want any tickets? They're twenty-five quid each."

News to me, I told him. Again he asked if I wanted any. You know when you can dislike someone just by their *voice*? I told him I'd call Reg myself and hung up. He was just so cocky and irritating. The lack of respect showed that nothing had been thought through. I phoned Reg at Nottingham and left a message on his landing for him to phone me and two minutes later he did. I told him I was pissed off at this Cockney wide boy's attitude and pissed off that he'd give him my number. I didn't expect an apology and wasn't disappointed. The nearest to an apology was, "He's just a gofer. Doing some running around for me. I'll have a word with him and make sure you get your tickets for the do. How many do you want?" I told him I only wanted one and left it as that. I felt better for getting it off my chest but I didn't expect him to phone Gary at all. The next day a rather sheepish and respectful Gary phoned to get my address to send a ticket... I take it back Reg, you kept your word.

The ticket stated that it was a 'Gala Night'. I travelled down to London's East End not knowing what to expect. The ticket also said there would be television stars from *Eastenders*, *The Bill* and *London's Burning*... and that all proceeds would go to 'a little boy with muscular dystrophy'... sounded good. I arrived early at the *Tudor Lodge*. It sounds just like a grand English banqueting hall and when I walked into the place, it looked absolutely nothing like one. It was basically a social club without any pool tables in. I was one of the first there but within an hour the *Lodge* was almost full with two hundred people dancing to hits from the sixties. I cringed as Carl Douglas was wheeled out to 'sing' his only hit *Kung fu Fighting*, unsure if it was for real, then grimacing as I found out it was. At least Carl had turned up though. The celebrity turn out consisted of Carl, Mike Reid from *Eastenders* and

Kate Kray. There were a lot of disgruntled punters to say the least. I made a few useful contacts though; one was a bloke called Mike who looked just like John Gotti. He told me he owned a cab firm in Hackney and that he used to work for the twins. I nodded and smiled... I'd heard it all before. He said I could stay at his place whenever I was in London and I thought nothing more of it. I also met Frank and Noelle Kurylo who were friends of the family and were in the process of helping Reg with a few projects; I exchanged numbers with them too. I said my farewell to Kate Kray at the end of the night and told Mike Reid that he was much better in *Runaround*. I returned to my hotel happy that I'd been an invited guest and not a paying customer.

I was still quite intrigued about Gary. He'd organised this event and hadn't turned up for it, and come to think of it Charlie wasn't there either. When I was invited along to the next gathering, I questioned if it was worth the effort. Weighing up the pros and cons (no pun intended), I decided it couldn't be any worse than the last one. I booked my train ticket and called Mafia Mick to see I his offer still stood. It did. No hotel bill for me! The party was at a club called the *Guvner's* in the heart of the East End. Bare-knuckle streetfighter, boxer – all-round hardman, Lenny McLean had a share in this bar. The night for me was a great success... the circle was complete as I shook hands with Charlie Kray for the first time. Having spoken to him dozens of times on the phone I knew we'd get along fine. He introduced me to many of the faces as well as Dave Courtney, who was climbing up the criminal ladder with a knuckle-duster and a smile. As I was talking to Dave, someone tapped me on the shoulder. I turned to confront... a young lad with cropped hair, a dodgy suit and a gold tooth. I later found out that the phrase, 'all over him like a cheap suit' had it's origins in his wardrobe. He introduced himself as Gary and I shook his hand half-heartedly before turning back to Dave. I wasn't impressed with him on the phone and in person I was glad my gut reaction hadn't let me down. There were well over two hundred people crammed into the pub at twenty-five quid a head. This time though, they got value for money. In attendance were: West Ham footballer Julian Dicks, *Eastenders* star Steve McFadden, Shane Richie, boxer Jimmy McDonnell, actor Ray Winstone (amazing in *Sexy Beast*), Lennie McLean, Tony Lambrianou, Alec Steene, Patsy Manning, George and Andrew Wadman, Charlie Kray and his biographer Robin McGibbon and also Charlie's son, Gary. There were also many friends of the twins there: Scott Mytton, Dave Clarke, Colin and Andy Fanning, Christian Simpson, Ray Cann, Janet and Alan Alsop, Frank and Noelle Kurylo, Andy Gravonor, Eileen Sheridan-Price, Irene Hart, Ron Proffit, Kiwi Andy and Les and Ellie Martin.

For members of the general public, this is what it was all about. The parties were a chance to mingle with stars and rub shoulders with the gangland faces they had read or heard about courtesy of our mutual friends, the Krays. For any stars that turned up, they knew what to expect; they knew that they could relax and talk to people in a hassle-free atmosphere. The party was great and it seemed like there would be a lot of money raised. There had also been an auction of all kinds of Kray memorabilia including paintings that raised a further thousand plus. As the night wore on, I'd noticed Gary was in and out of the kitchen like a yo-yo. I just didn't trust him so I thought I'd investigate. As I opened the door slightly, I saw Gary standing with his back to me counting a large wad of cash and handing it out to two other lads. One of the lads was Paul who I'd met on a visit to Reg... the 'great burglar'. I could not believe what I was observing. People had paid good money towards what they thought was a good cause and here was this little tosser handing it out to two other tossers. At a rough guess, I'd say five thousand would have been raised at least, and here it was being divided up. I pushed the door wide open and Gary turned round like a startled rabbit... no, make that a startled thieving bastard.

"Alright geezer?" he said. "I will be when they give you that cash back." was my reply. Paul stared at me... "Reg said I could have it, so mind your own fucking business." That was it. I punched him straight in the face and turned to face the other two. I wanted them to try something... they stood there panicking. They knew I'd caught them out. Gary was squirming. Then he took out the rest of the wad and asked me how much I wanted... he counted a hundred out and offered me it. I just stared at them; long enough for any guilt to take hold if they had a conscience. I walked out and back to the bar to order a treble Jack Daniels and Coke. A few minutes later and the three rats emerged from the kitchen. Paul was defiant, "Wait till Reg hears about this, just wait." I was fuming, "I can't hear you cos your mouth is full of shit." I was still fuming as I stared over at them. Gary brought a drink over to try and calm the situation down; or to talk himself out of it more like. I listened to what he had to say and still wasn't impressed. He told me that Reg had told him to sort a few people out for coming; okay, some celeb's taxi maybe but not some ex-con who was just gonna shoot it up his arm. This had ruined what started out as an excellent night.

I made sure I told Charlie Kray all about what had happened. I didn't want to see this sort of behaviour again, they were scum as far as I was concerned. Charlie said he always thought Gary was bad news and thanked me for telling him. He was going to tell Reg the next day. I was still thinking about the incident as the party drew to a close. A lot of people had paid money under false pretences. I'm sure those who paid would like to have known who had ripped them off and tricked them. I could see that calling these events a 'charity' event was just a big con. Gary had no intention of giving any away unless it was to his friends. He was conning people, but he was also conning people by using the Kray name.

I got the train back to Newcastle the following day with Ray Cann. Ray is a genuine bloke (and not a bad tattoo artist either) who I became good mates with. We were buzzing with talk of the night before and I asked him if he fancied organising a party with me in Newcastle. We could invite Charlie Kray up, a few of the others from London, get some local celebs involved and do it for a Northern charity. We agreed there and then to work together. Ray had some contacts that could help us out and we both knew we could do it. Importantly we knew we could do a decent job. The first thing needed was a venue; Ray gave me the number of a lad called Davey Falcus who ran a social club in Bensham, Gateshead called *The Elysium Lane* and I arranged a meeting the next day. Davey was one hundred per cent behind us and willing to help however he could. The room was spot on... seating around a hundred and seventy people with enough room for a further hundred standing. What's more it had a long bar and a big stage with lighting. Perfect. It had everything we needed and Davey was letting us have it for free. We scanned the bookings erm... book, and made a provisional booking for July the eighth 1995. Here was the carrot I needed to dangle in front of the former Mr. X. All I needed to ask him was if he wanted to spend his birthday in the North East. He was hooked as I went through our plans, "As good as there, Steve", came the reply. Just two more hurdles left – the tickets and the buffet. A quick call to Steve in South London (a good friend of Reg's) solved the ticket problem and a bit of grovelling and a few promises to our respective families got the buffet sorted out and we were on the home straight. Everything was falling into place. Next up, I contacted the family I wanted the money we raised to go to. The Morans' were a close-knit family from Felling, Gateshead I was friends with father and son – both called Terry. I'd met them through football. Young Terry was a natural with the skill, confidence and commitment that he dreamed would one day earn him a place in Newcastle United. On Guy Fawke's Night, 1994, Terry was involved in an horrific accident. He was wearing a shell-suit that night and was standing too close to a bonfire. His clothes caught fire and he suffered eighty per cent burns. He was rushed to hospital and was not expected to survive the night. Terry was strong and pulled through... he was still in hospital when I contacted the family about the charity night. I told them it had the full backing from Reg Kray and that Charlie Kray would be in attendance. I warned them of the publicity, some good some bad, that the event would attract in the coming weeks. They seemed okay with it but asked for a few days to think it over properly. During that time I contacted a some local celebrities for their help: Boxers Glenn McCrory and Billy Hardy, footballers Paul Gascoigne, Lee Clark and Steve Watson all said they could make it. Soon after I got the green light from the Morans... it was all systems go for July the eighth!

Key to holding events was primarily about doing so for a cause. It was apparent that the Kray name could attract a lot of attention and holding events was a way of using that name for something positive instead of all the negativity that had surrounded it. That is what pissed me off about the Gary incident. He was using the name and the event to line his own and his friends' pockets. To do something like that is the lowest of the low... to claim that someone's money is going towards a charity and then keep it for yourself, it's hard to put into words. From my point of view, I saw it as a chance to put right any damage that this had caused. What he'd done wasn't made public because he is still around, but from my involvement in the incident I was keen to see a real charity event take place. Hearing the Morans say they were happy to accept made all the work worthwhile. From that moment on I was bombarded by phone calls from Reg about it.

There was still a few weeks to go and I thought the calls were slightly on the neurotic side, but hadn't considered the fact that Reg was locked up and always thinking about life over the walls and wanted to be constantly updated. Then out of the blue, Reg got one of his gofers to send me the money up to buy myself a mobile phone along with the message: "Steve buy a mobile phone. I'm sick of missing you at home. God Bless. Reg. P.S. Ring me with your number." It was a nice gesture... until you put '1995' and 'mobile phone' together and come up with 'house brick'. Within a week I was the proud owner of a top of the range phone, and boy did I milk it with the lads. Remember that vision of someone walking along the street with a ghettoblaster to their ear?... That was not unlike using this phone. I tried carrying it in my trouser pocket once but could only walk round in circles. I got some cards printed up to give everyone my new number and Reg would always call me on it knowing he could reach me. That was until he saw how much it cost him to call and he never bothered again. It was ideal for organising the event and gave me a number to stick alongside all the publicity. It seems weird to think back now... it wasn't that long ago that I was one of the first in the area to get a mobile phone, now it's unusual not have one.

The publicity side of organisation was what really gave me the buzz. Still does. Whether I'm in the limelight or promoting something, it's something I thrive on. There's a certain knack to getting coverage in all the local papers for the same event, and this time I cracked it. Give the same story to the morning paper and the evening papers on the same day and nine times out of ten they will both print it. Give one or both of them the story a day earlier and it's yesterday's news. So *The Chronicle*, *Journal*, *Sunday Sun* and good old *Gateshead Post* all ran with 'Krays to attend Charity Night'. Soon after the locals I had the national press calling the house brick for a story. The publicity worked well and within a week a hundred and fifty tickets were sold at ten quid each... a week later and still the brick was ringing until the event was a sell-out. Due to fire regulations, we were only allowed two hundred and ten people in the venue, so that meant that straightaway we had already raised over two thousand quid.

A week before the event I was nervous. I received another call from Reg asking how things were going and if the little boy was okay. I told him that everything was fine and that Terry was looking forward to the night. I think Reg telephoning contributed towards my nerves. This call sounded familiar though; I knew he was leading up to something with the usual tone and smalltalk... ready to spring something onto me when I was off guard. Then it came, "Steve, I don't want Charlie or Tony Lambrianou at the party, okay?" I couldn't control myself, was this bloke for real? "You're fucking joking Reg, the party is a sell out because of them." There was a long pause and then I knew he was serious. He said that I should do as he said or cancel the party and hung up on me. This sort of 'twist' was not uncommon, but his demand was outrageous. I called Charlie up immediately and asked what the problem was – he was as stunned as I was. He said he wouldn't let me down and would come up regardless of what Reg said. He didn't want to let Terry down either. I phoned Tony next and got a better insight into the problem. Reg had loaned Tony two portfolios to show someone who was interested in buying them. The portfolio was a limited edition photograph album released by the twins, which were retailing at two hundred and fifty quid. The bloke wasn't that interested and sent them both back to Tony, who only sent one back to Reg holding on to the other. Apparently he hadn't got round to sending it back and suggested this may be the reason. It made sense and it was the sort of thing Reg would spit his dummy out over. I put it to Tony that he sends the album to Reg immediately to smooth things over. As a compromise, he said he'd bring it to the event and I could send it to Reg... Result. I spoke to Reg again and explained what was going to happen; again saying it was a sell-out because of Tony and Charlie and he'd be bringing the album up with him.

"I don't fucking want Tony there. Tell the papers up there that Tony and me are no longer friends"... Non-result. Typical stubbornness.

I asked about Charlie and was told he was okay, but to make sure Tony was *not there*. I had no intention of calling the papers but to keep Reg happy, my brother Rob helped out. He designed an authentic looking newspaper layout with all the right typography and I acted as reporter on this 'gangland rift' exclusive. It looked spot on. I sent a copy straight to Reg who was over the moon with the article and the fact that I'd acted so quickly. I knew he would find out that Tony had attended but people had paid money for tickets and we could not disappoint. Reg would get over it anyway.

This left me in an awkward situation to say the least. I knew what Reg was like and I knew his ideas and plans could change at the drop of a hat. There was no way I was going to call the whole party off just because he suddenly changed his mind about it at the last minute. Everything was organised, the local and national press ran stories on it and it had completely sold out. Now he wanted it scrapped because Tony hadn't given him a few photos back? We'd raised twenty-one hundred quid so far and there was no way we could hand it back after we'd promised the Morans. All that planning and time and arranging to give the money to someone... then Reg wakes up in a bad mood so we have to cancel was not on. Again, this was another case of not being on the outside and knowing the full extent to what he was doing. You cannot just mess people around like that – famous gangster or not, it's not right.

Monday the fourth of July and everything is running along smoothly again. I was working as usual in the post office when three masked raiders burst in and attacked myself and a member of staff. Quite a lot of money and stock was stolen, but luckily I'd spotted them just before they came in and hit the alarm. It was all over in an instant but something like that stays with you forever. Luckily neither staff nor customers were hurt, just badly shaken. It's true that everything does slow down in that situation... it's like you are on autopilot, watching from a third person point of view. Until you have been in that position you can never fully appreciate how you will react. My advice to anyone is don't try to be a hero for a few quid; life is too precious. You mean nothing to an armed robber, especially if you get in his way. The reason I say don't try to be a hero for the sake of a few quid is that when the post office representative came to investigate, his first question was, "How much was taken?"... He did not even bother to ask if anyone was hurt.

In the last few days before the party, the Gascoigne family confirmed they would be attending, though were unsure whether Paul would be there or not. And then the day before the party, a message from Charlie on my answer machine to say he will be up later than expected due to family illness. I was still happy he was coming, but when it's out of your hands you just have to sit back and see what happens. Ray and me got some people together to help with looking after people; meet 'n' greeters. Basically we wanted every angle covered and wanted it to be a talking point for a long while to come. The biggest disappointment for me was that my mam, dad and Rob had already arranged holidays and wouldn't be able to make it. I knew they were thinking of me though and that was what mattered.

Then it was time... the big day. In the morning a package from Reg arrived. It was a recorded message from him to be played at the event. I played it through a couple of times and was happy with it; listening to him made me feel sad that he couldn't attend. I knew he was proud to be associated with this fundraiser, and I made sure I'd have a drink for absent friends on the night. The message was his way of being there and I thought it was a nice touch. I kept checking my watch all day and was convinced it was going backwards; it was taking forever for the hands to reach seven o'clock then they just seemed to speed up as the time neared. I put on my tuxedo and bow tie and headed for the *Elysium*, arriving with time to spare.

Inside there were already queues at the bar; all the usual suspects had arrived. Alan and Gordon Fanning, Scott Mytton, Andy Gravonor, Christian Simpson, Kiwi Andy, Dave Clarke, Steve Marshall, Gary the Gofer, Carl Carty and Sharon, Mad Marilyn, Les and Ellie Martin. Also a few of my closest mates... Dave and Mickey Butterfield, Halpin, Mickey D, Chris David Mark and Steven Liddle, Carl and Mark Douglas, Parker, Paul Donnely, Croany, Babbsy, Maccoy, Colly, Ballsy, the Clarkes, Browny, Weasel Wilcox, Moley, Wheatley, Steppy, Tappers and a couple of 'cool cats' called Toby and Britney... apologies for anyone missed out, I'm sure you'll point it out to me sometime.

Ray had Geordie, Simon, Alfie and Sean driving people to the club who'd spent all day travelling up. Then we got news that Paul Gascoigne couldn't make it as he was in the process of signing for *Glasgow Rangers*... some people will make *anything* up to get out of a party. His family brought some extra signed football tops up which more than made up for it. Nice one!

The Morans arrived with all of their friends. It was an emotional time for Terry as he'd just been released from hospital that week. His parents, Terry and Gillian were concerned that he'd be overwhelmed by such an event with everyone there for him, but we had reserved a large room for them to relax in. It was great to see them there; we were amazed at the recovery Terry was making.

Inside, the buffet looked amazing (thanks to Ray's wife Bev and other contributors including the Morans) and the place was really starting to fill up. All that we needed now was Tony Lambrianou and Charlie Kray. Tony was first to arrive looking dapper in... well, in a safari suit. He said he'd just got back from Kenya and had literally just rushed straight to Newcastle. I was wondering... had someone misinterpreted 'dress fancy'? We had another room for him and partner Wendy to get changed into their eveningwear. Phew, one down – one to go. The press had gathered at the door to get photos of the first Kray in the North East since the sixties and you could hear the buzz of anticipation from them as well as the punters. We had Kenny Dick djing and the place was jumping... then he mixed straight into a Sting record and our 'special guest' arrived. Neil Grant, a Sting lookalikie, stunned the crowd as he walked in as though it was his local. Within seconds he was being mobbed and could easily have pulled it off until he gave out his business cards with 'Sting Lookalike' printed on. Still, it was a good laugh and kept everyone in high spirits.

I received a message informing me that Charlie had arrived and was waiting in a car outside. I made my way to see him and as I approached, he got out to greet me. I can still remember it like it was yesterday, "Hello Steve, mate. How are you?" We shook hands as we greeted each other. Charlie was looking fit and well with his customary suntan. The photographers moved in and we were mobbed on our way to the club. Ray got the drinks in for Charlie and Tony and introduced them to a few of the North East faces while I told the press there would be a photo call in thirty minutes. There were a few groans from them as they had to get the story out that night, but that was how we wanted it. Next up, were the formal introductions. I took the microphone as Kenny lowered the music, "Ladies and gentlemen, if I can have your attention please. First I would like to thank you all for coming on behalf of Terry. I would like to take this opportunity to thank all of those people who have made this night possible. Now I would like you to put your hands together for our main guests of the evening... Mr. Tony Lambrianou, and Mr. Charlie Kray.

Ray was flanked by two lads to keep people back as he led our main guests into the lounge. They received a standing ovation that lasted a few minutes. It was a strange feeling to be standing there introducing these two people to a North East crowd. I'd known them both for a while now and for me the whole 'sixties firm' days never really registered anymore. To be in this position I could see in the eyes in a lot of people something similar to what must have once been in mine. It was an honour for me to introduce them, and it being the first time doing something like that it was something I'd remember for a long time to come. Ray led them to their seats where everyone wanting a photo, a signature, or a handshake besieged them. It was complete madness.

To say they were well received would be an understatement.

The music re-started, and then the buffet was opened and gone in an instant. The auction of signed Kray memorabilia and celebrity signed odds and sods raised a bit more cash and I must admit I enjoyed shouting, 'going, going, gone!' The most moving part of the night and the most silent was when it came to the playing of the tape that Reg had sent me. Once I had everyone's attention and the tape was in place, you could have heard the proverbial pin drop. The silence just added to the moment; it gave the impression that something historic was taking place. I pressed play and Reg Kray's voice crackled into life over the PA system.

"Hello friends there in the North East. I would like to thank you this evening on behalf of my friends Steve Wraith and Ray Cann and myself for the fact that you are present in support of our young friend Terry Moran. I would like to thank all of you and also the celebrities present and my brother Charlie for being host. I wish I could be with you there physically but I am with you in spirit and I hope that you all enjoy the evening as much as possible and I hope that the night is a success. I also wish to give a personal message to young Terry. Terry I would like you to know we are all here for you. We all love you as a person, and if there is anything I can do for you personally to make you happy I am willing to do so. Try to have happy thoughts and think happy thoughts and this will make you happy. I pray and hope that you will get better in the future and to lead a happy life. That's all for now Terry. And once again I would like to thank you all. Goodnight. God bless Reg Kray."

The tape fell silent. Looking around the room I could see that everyone was captivated. They were actually listening to *the* Reg Kray. Seamus Watson, a well-known face in Dunston, began to clap and as he did the rest of the room joined in as if awoken from a trance. It evolved into deafening applause. I was grinning. I would swear that Reg could have heard the reception he got that night; it was a proud moment for us all... the looks on the faces of the Morans, the message from Reg, Tony and Charlie showing up, the other celebs *and* all the punters.

As the cameras flashed again at the photo call, Charlie turned to me put his arm around me and said, 'Thanks Steve, this is the best birthday I can remember. It's taken me back. I've never had a night like this since the sixties." Comments like that also made the effort worthwhile. As the night drew to a close I lost count of the number of people who came up to me and shook my hand. The night just shot past me. It was amazing but exhausting... thank God for last orders. As people made their way out I counted the money. The grand total was two thousand four hundred pounds. The Morans were overwhelmed and asked me to donate the money to the Newcastle Burns Unit that had looked after and nursed Terry through the early days. How good did it feel to be able to do that? It's hard to explain. Okay, so we hadn't exactly raised millions but it can still go towards helping people.

Charlie was keen to go clubbing so we arranged a night out in *Julie's* nightclub for him on Newcastle's Quayside. He said his goodbyes, and as he was going thanked me again for 'the best night I've had in years'. With that he was gone. Ray, Tony and myself chose to wind down with a few select friends after hours in the club to reflect on what had been a successful night. The night had gone well, and without any problems. Then of course something had to happen... A young lad had apparently been making a nuisance of himself all night, and on more than one occasion had asked Tony absurd and insulting questions. To his credit Tony had ignored him. But the lad persisted and somehow found himself left behind in the club with us. It's hard to imagine what this lad was thinking; was he drunk, slightly eccentric, or did he have a deathwish? I'd put money on the latter but I dare say it was a good combination of all three with a large dose of stupidity for good measure. When he asked Tony whether he had ever slept with Ron Kray it was the straw that broke the camel's back which led to the punch that broke the tosser's face. Tony cracked him on the jaw with such force that it sent him flying into the wall on the other side of the room. It really was some punch. Tony had kept his cool for long enough and this idiot had tested his patience one time too many. I dragged the lad outside and made sure he was okay, then shut the fire doors on him. Now would be a good time to leave, the last thing I needed was the headline, 'Kray Firm on Rampage at Charity Bash'. We retired to Rays to chill out and boy did I need it.

In the run up to the party, Tony had mentioned it in passing that his mother was originally from Consett, and so, theoretically that made him half Geordie. He also mentioned the fact that he had never seen his mother's grave and did not know its whereabouts. So having the time and the inclination Ray set out on a mission to locate Elizabeth Lambrianou's resting-place. After a lot of phone calls and good detective work, Ray traced her grave to a plot in Shotley Bridge Cemetery. We took time out to visit the site, tidy it up and place some fresh flowers there. The day after the party we made the sentimental journey once again to the quiet leafy village but this time with Tony and Wendy. Once we had pointed it out we left them alone. As we stood back, it was quite a touching sight to see this former gangster and hardman pay his respects to his mother. He placed his own flowers around the grave and then said his goodbyes. He came over to Ray and me and after drying his eyes thanked us. It was a very emotional moment for us all. We said our farewells to Tony and Wendy and thanked them for coming. It was the end of an amazing couple of days and Ray and I had achieved everything we had set out to do and more. Like a jigsaw everything had fallen into place and we both knew that we couldn't have done it all without the support of our families and friends. Charlie phoned the next day to thank me again "One of the best nights of my life Steve." I felt content and a sense of righting the wrongs that I had witnessed in London.

After the success of arranging two charity nights at *The Elysium Lane* for my young friend Terry Moran I always said that I would never do another charity night again for the Krays. The second party for Terry was on the sixteenth of December, 1995. We did this for him as he gave all the money in the summer to the Hospital Burns Unit to show appreciation for the care that they had given him. Charlie was to play host and Tony Lambrianou came as a special guest. Running like clockwork, Reg phoned me two weeks before the party and asked me for the bar takings on the night. Again it was an outrageous request. I could not believe that he was doing all this again, but looking back it's quite easy to believe. Asking for the bar takings was something that would be done in the sixties and people would think nothing of it. Asking for the bar takings in the nineties was something Reg Kray would do and think nothing of it. I really thought this was a selfish act. Why was he doing it? I can only assume it was because he saw there was some money being raised for a charity and wanted a part of it. We already had the room free for the night and he expected the money that the bar made to go into his pocket. Things didn't work like that anymore; it was only the Krays who did. Time had moved on but they stayed firmly rooted in the sixties. If I had gone with Reg's suggestion I know I would have a lot less friends than I have today.

We argued over the bar takings on the phone and I hung up on him. He had me seething with rage. He rang back immediately swearing and warning me that he was pulling out and that I better not have Charlie there... Then he hung up. Jesus, at least he didn't say, 'my dad is bigger than your dad' first. I rang Charlie told him the crack and told him not to bother turning up. I didn't want to drag him into it as he took enough crap from Reg over the slightest things. I told him I would go ahead with Tony. Reg phoned the following day to see if I had agreed to his terms and I told him he could stick it. He was asking the impossible. I was doing this for Terry, not him. I informed the local papers that I would give refunds to those who had paid to see Charlie. I couldn't be any fairer than that. No one wanted one a refund and the party went ahead successfully. Reg didn't speak to me for around a month after that. Neither of us would back down. At the party we raised a thousand pounds, but they were beginning to feel like too much hard work. It wasn't just because of all the hassle that went with it or the constant arguments with Reg over money, but because the organisation of these nights was so time consuming.

In 1998 I had a rethink when my attention was drawn to another young lad whose family I knew well through the post office. Alan Hedley from Wardley had impaired hearing and a serious bowel disorder but still remained upbeat and cheerful. I admired his parents for the love and determination that they gave to Alan and I wanted to help them in whatever way I could. Three years had passed since the last party. I was still in touch with Ray Cann and phoned him to ask if he was interested in co-ordinating another party at the same venue. He jumped at the chance to do it again, as did Davey Falcus... he let us invade his social club again so we began to put our heads together. This would definitely maybe be the last one.

I already had an idea of what I wanted to do with the night and what I wanted to call it but would need Reg's blessing. I rang C-wing and waited only a couple of minutes for the return call. After the usual chit chat about how each of us were doing I told Reg of young Alan's health problems and that I wanted to put on a night in the North East with his help. I then explained that I wanted to call the night *The Firm Friends Reunion* as it was thirty years since their arrest in 1968. I wanted to hold it on May the eighth, which would be thirty years to the actual day. Reg was impressed with the idea. I asked him to compile a list of people who I could invite from his past. The wheels were officially in motion.

Local friend and DJ Kenny Dick agreed to do his usual turn with Premier Discos and my mate Paul Martin agreed to bring his band, *Cryin' Out Loud* free of charge to perform. We decided against a buffet and priced the tickets at a reasonable ten spot. Next up, a few calls to local footballers John Anderson, Malcom Macdonald and Mick Martin who all pledged their support and agreed to make an appearance for Alan. I couldn't believe how well everything was coming together. The venue, entertainment and now some football heroes... couldn't be happier. A few days later Reg phoned me again tb say that he wasn't too keen on the idea now. How out of the blue' I thought. He also wanted to know how much he could expect to make from the night. I told him that the money was all going to Alan and that none of the guests or acts were being paid, i.e., a *charity* event. I must have caught him on a good day because from that moment on he never mentioned it again. Instead Reg asked me to contact his wife Roberta to ask her to send up some merchandise to sell for him on the evening.

I liked Roberta. They had got married in July 1997. She had been arranging parties for a while herself since the marriage. I had no real interest in attending them anymore and when asked to help by Reg I said I could organise security for them and that was all my input could be. Roberta made the events credible again. She wasn't everyone's cup of tea but that's because she was doing things for Reg and not for herself. Reg had surrounded himself with so many idiots and 'yes men' over the years but many of them crawled back under their stone when she came on the scene. She had a good head on her shoulders both personality-wise and business-wise, and had a good nose for sniffing out certain smells which tended to come out of people's mouths instead of words.

For *Firm Friends* guests, Reg told me to use my discretion so I played safe and asked Roberta. I was given a list that included Frankie Fraser, Freddie Foreman and Tony Lambrianou. That was more than enough so I set about publicising the forthcoming event in the local and national press. I provided them with a photo of myself with the three principle guests and it went down well. After speaking to Fred and Tony and receiving confirmation that they would travel up with my old mate Christian, I called Frankie Fraser. I had met Frankie quite a few times and had always got on well with him. From the tone of his voice I knew he wasn't too interested so decided to leave it at that and wished him well. I rang Freddie and asked him if he knew of any of the old firm that would be willing to travel up. He said he would make a few enquiries but if all else failed that he would bring up a celebrity friend. I was intrigued.

Once the publicity had gone out I was swamped by calls for tickets. I contacted people who had attended previous nights and we were almost guaranteed a sell out. Good news for us and even better news for Alan. I had asked John Lillico to help arrange the security and he brought down a few of his mates from Ashington to help out. John also came with me to meet Freddie, Tony, Christian and the mystery guest when they arrived in Newcastle. The guest was none other than Gary Webster of television show *Minder*. Freddie had done us proud. They arrived in the afternoon so I arranged for a quick tour of St James' Park, which was much appreciated. As we were waiting to go into the ground an armoured security van was pulling in and Freddie had us in stitches with his comments, "Well that is good timing!" From the football ground we took our guests to the *Cross Keys* in Dunston where they received the warmest of welcomes from landlady Val. After a quick bite to eat and a chance to freshen up we were on our way to the venue. I was more relaxed this time than I had been previous occasions. We arrived just after seven o'clock and there were already a group of thirty people mingling. By eight o'clock the room was a mass of men suited and booted and women wearing their best evening dresses. This was going to be a night to remember. We had reserved tables for Alan and his family next to Freddie and the chaps as well as the ex-footballers. Alan loved it and it was great to see him enjoying himself so much. Again there was a long silence as I played Reg's taped message for the evening and then an explosive applause and cheering as the taped whirred to an end. There were endless photographs taken... flash after flash, and the night seemed to end all too quickly.

The night was a great success and raised a lot of money for Alan and for Reg with his merchandise stall. Instead of staying back at the club for a late drink we had been invited to a nightclub in Sunderland called *The Palace* by a friend of mine, Tony Currie. Somehow the words 'Sunderland' and 'Palace' just didn't seem right to me, but I was willing to give it a go. Tony was a doorman by night and a private detective by day and said that we would all be more than welcome in Sunderland. His friend had laid the taxis on, as getting there and back was my major concern. The club itself was huge and as we approached I recognised a few of the lads on the door, Andy Walker and Mickey Armstrong, who I introduced and they led us through the ravers to the VIP area upstairs. It was a great atmosphere... people wall to wall with most of them wanting autographs and pictures of Fred and Tony. I took time out with Christian, John and Tony Currie to toast a successful night. As usual there was an absentee, this time it was Dave Courtney. He was attending a wedding as the best man but promised he would pop up to see me the next day. After clubbing it we made our way back to the *Cross Keys* at about three in the morning and I sat up with Tony and Fred talking about the old days. They talked about how they felt about Reg and his continuing imprisonment. We stayed up for a couple of hours talking, and unwinding before we turned in. They were good to listen to. I could see in their eyes how they looked back on those days with some fond memories. They didn't really dwell on the bad times; it would have spoilt the night... just a couple of retired men talking about work.

We got the chaps up and out to the station for the eleven o'clock morning train to London. I had no sooner said my goodbyes to one set of friends, than I was back at the Central Station a few hours later to welcome in Dave, his wife Jenny and close friend Brendan to town. I brought John along and compared hangovers along the way... it's safe to say that I had possibly the worst hangover in the country that day. We filled Dave in on the previous nights events and he was gutted that he had missed out. I assured him that we would make up for it that night with a trip down Newcastle's legendary Bigg Market. We dropped them off at the *Cross Keys* into the capable hands of Val and made our way home to grab forty winks in preparation for the night ahead. With Dave in town and up for a night out there was no way you could be at anything less than a hundred and ten per cent fit. Saturday is always a good night out in Newcastle and this night was no exception. I had told all the lads that Dave was coming up, so with me there was Chris and David Liddle, Chris Parker, Ian Brown, Steven Spence, Arron Parker, and Anthony Halpin. Together with Ray, John and Graham Borthwick there was a nice little squad of us assembled together.

As a doorman, a good perk is not to have to queue at bars in the town you work but if you are out with a big group as big it is unfair to take the piss. So at each bar we went to

I asked the lads on the door before attempting to queue-jump if it was okay. We had no problems. Most of the lads were just pleased to meet Dave and Jenny and Dave loved the fact that people wanted to talk to him. He is usually a shy and unassuming person, but he must have come out of his shell for a few hours on this visit.

I had let Tony Currie know that Dave was in town and asked him if the offer was open to take him down to *The Palace*. Tony checked it out and said there would be no problem. He sorted the transport out and as last orders was called we found ourselves on the way to Makemland once more (Makems being natives of Sunderland). The club was jumping again as we made our way upstairs to the VIP lounge. It was only *foam party* night! Try to imagine a big bubble bath with a few hundred strangers and loud music. The club closed at two in the morning and we were amongst the last to leave. We watched as one of the lads (alcoholically and chemically enhanced) decided to mimic Germany's predatory football striker Jurgen Klinnsman's goal celebrations by diving headfirst into the foam from the balcony. The impersonation was perfect but his landing wasn't... he staggered from the foam with a gaping head wound. The rest of us were howling with laughter at the state of him but eventually managed to compose ourselves and help get the wound covered.

Whilst Klinnsman headed off to the Accident and Emergency unit we made our way to the *Cross Keys* and chilled out with Dave. Dave was in the process of writing his second book *Raving Lunacy* after the huge success of *Stop the Ride I want to Get Off*, and assured me that he would give me and the lads a mention. I'm pleased to say that he kept his word as he always does so am not ashamed of giving his books a free plug.

Doing the Door

The early nineties saw a big change in the direction my life was to take. I was losing interest in the post office business and couldn't see my involvement lasting much longer. My connection with the Krays and the friends I'd made was proving to be profitable and was taking up much of my spare time. Business with the twins and football seemed to be taking over, both developing from pastimes into occupations. I was also managing a Sunday League football team who over the years has included; Dave, Mark, Steven and Chris Liddle, Mark Collingwood, Andy Wilcox, Rob Wraith, Chris Parker, Anth Vickers, Davey Campbell, Marc Croan, Ian Brown, Joseph Collings, Fred Clarke, Neil Logan, Rob Lake, Anthony McGowan, David Ball, John Moore, Ade Fasan (RIP), Paul Grey, Dave Butterfield, Steven Spence, Arron Parker, Keith and John Armstrong, John Mole, Lee Gates, Kev Laskey, Mark Lockwell, Andy Green, David Walker, Brendan Mullholland, Willie Dryden, Thomas Pope, Davey Brown, Raymond Oshin, James Maccoy, Ian Laing, Paul Young, Steven Thompson, Mark and Carl Douglas, Ross Mcloud, Steven Roberts, Steven Clarke, and Paul Donnely.

Professional football was now receiving more media interest, especially with the increase in availability with satellite and digital technologies. Television and radio were always looking for different angles on a story and would often want a supporter to give his view on different issues. Eight times out of ten, they would ask me, as I had become an unofficial voice of the Newcastle United fans through the magazine. It was good to be asked about issues surrounding the club – also good to get recognised by fans as they would always ask me about what was going on at St James' Park and we'd discuss the latest signings and transfers. One of the interviews I was asked to do was BBC's *Newsnight* in the wake of the Hall / Shepherd saga at the club. This was when Freddie Shepherd and Douglas Hall (both club chairmen) went on an (alleged) massive drink and prostitute binge and were caught on video tape making derogatory comments about women from Newcastle and criticising United skipper, Alan Shearer. The media are well known for the ability to manipulate events and report comments out of context, so that the reported version differs from actuality. It is well known that men from Tyneside worship women and football. Whether Hall and Shepherd's comments were taken out of context or not was irrelevant... they said what they said and were guilty. They were on the television news, in the papers and people could read it all in black and white, pardon the pun. I lost count of the number of press interviews about Hall and Shepherd I ended up doing, I was literally walking from one to the next.

Newsnight... unfortunately Jeremy Paxman was on holiday, I was flown down to the studio in London and asked to give my opinion on the state of the club. Asked to dress smartly, I wore my best suit jacket (of the 'track' variety) trainers, jeans and had my head freshly shaved. I sat across from the interviewer with a studio link up to an intelligent and beautiful woman from Tyneside and ex-Newcastle striker Malcolm Macdonald. Newcastle United is one of the biggest clubs in the country with a massive following. The scandal caused outrage a lot further a field than just the North East; *Newsnight* was broadcast nationally. The interview went well with all three of us putting our points across as civilised grown-ups, then out of the blue the presenter asked me, "Yes Mr. Wraith but isn't it true that you would have the Kray twins playing for Newcastle United if you could?" For a second I was gob smacked, but I quickly retorted with, "Yes I would, but sadly one of them is dead, you should have some respect." Someone had clearly told him that I was associated with the twins and that it would be a great piece of television to ridicule me in front of millions with this question. All he succeeded in doing was confusing the watching audience who didn't know me. He just made me look cool, calm and collected. I thanked him after the show, hoping that his producer had shouted all the things at him I'd wanted to.

Like most young lads on Tyneside I was spending my money as quickly as I was earning it. Most of it was spent in local pubs, *The Ship* and *The Swan*. It was not uncommon for me to start drinking on Friday, have a lock in till Saturday morning, go home get some kip or go to the match if Newcastle were playing and be back in again for another session that evening. This had been one of the main reasons that Reg had given me a mobile phone – complaining that I was at the pub more than I was at home, which was probably true.

Spending time in my local pubs eventually led me into door work. Looking back now, there were a few factors that led me towards it. One of them was that I could never mind my own business when it came to a fight or an argument. I still can't. I always had to be there amongst it. I liked to stop any bother if I could, one way or another. Don't get me wrong – I have never been a fighter. I prefer to diffuse situations. Unfortunately some people enjoy themselves by going out to pick fights. I had the fact that I am physically big enough to step in on my side as well, which was definitely a bonus. It is a case of 'size matters' – a bully will think twice about having a go at someone his own size and will back down at someone bigger. If mates were having a drunken fight, my intervention could be a good excuse for them to call a truce.

Most bar fights are a one-way attack on another person who just wants to enjoy a night out. It is unacceptable that some moron who can't handle his booze can ruin someone else's night out – or ruin their life in some cases. If I could do my bit to help out, then I was happy. If only people would just think first..., it takes a lot more energy to pick a fight, have one, then live with the consequences than it does to shrug one off.

On nights out in Newcastle, I found it was getting easier to jump the queues outside bars. My face had became known because of television appearances and I became friends with a lot of doormen around town. My association with Newcastle United and the Krays was the perfect icebreaker. Conversation would start off with talk about football; see if I had any inside knowledge on The Toon (Newcastle United), and so on. Some doormen knew of me from my Kray association and we became friends through that, so I'd say it was an even spread. When talking to them I found that punters would mistake me for a doorman, so the progression into the line of work was inevitable. If the shoe fits... wear it. No one I have ever spoken to has said that becoming a doorman or door*person* was his or her number one career choice. No one. A lot of door staff will have a day job and do door work to earn extra cash; others have turned it into a full time career. Nearly everyone I know says they just 'fell' into it, but it always related to size, reputation and contacts.

On a night out with the lads in Newcastle one weekend when I saw Gary (a.k.a Lurch) on the door of *Masters*. We discussed the usual topic – football – then he asked me if I fancied earning a few quid over Christmas. One of the lads had broken his wrist and Gary wanted me to fill in, if I was willing to. I was game enough, and couldn't think of a better way of earning a bit cash than to be standing in a bar listening to music and looking at gorgeous women all night. It literally *did* sound like Christmas to me. My first shift was a Thursday night, which as anyone will tell you is as busy as a weekend in other cities. I was dressed in a white shirt, black trousers, Dr. Martins and a black bomber jacket. I felt and looked the business. Gary introduced me to the lads who would be watching my back and vice-versa. There was Irish, Buzz, Dave and John Lillico, who remains one of my closest friends. There were two key positions front door and back door, with buzzers and flashing lights to let you know where a fight had broken out. That night there was six fights in just over four hours, and this was a relatively tame night according to the lads. I loved every minute of it. It felt right and *definitely* felt like the start of something new and exciting.

The festive season is always a bit on the mental side. Once a year drinkers and office parties... everyone drinking too much, eating too much, the just out of school lad getting off with the middle-aged woman in the office and never living it down, being sick in the streets, in shop doorways... and remember, this is people *enjoying* themselves. Up until that Christmas I had been doing exactly the same thing (although I'll never admit to the middle-aged woman) and it was only then that I realised that there was more to life than spending my hard-earned cash on booze. It's really only when in this position that you can cringe for the first time knowing what you must have looked like. You can't beat Christmas time in Newcastle.

Then January comes and it is then the quietest time of the year. People realising they spent their entire wages and Christmas bonus in one go. A quiet period in door work means no work, as I had been the last in I was first out when shifts had to be cut; I lost my Thursday to Sunday shifts and was gutted. I hadn't been there that long but I missed it. I missed the adrenaline rush that I got when the lights and buzzers came to life and I missed the lads I was teamed up with. I still saw them on nights out though, so I didn't loose touch altogether. It was like getting bombed out by a girlfriend after a few weeks... just after that 'getting to know you' stage and everything is running smoothly. It was tough to deal with, but there were no hard feelings.

I left it for a while, until an old friend of mine George Poulter, telephoned in the New Year. He managed *The Filament and Firkin* as well as *Scruffy Murphy's* and asked if I would be interested in sharing the head doorman's job with Paul Tinnion. I thought about it and decided to give it another go. I had got the taste for it now and wanted to get back in and a head doorman's job had more credibility than relief work. By now Newcastle City Council had decided that all door supervisors should be licensed. This required four days training covering all aspects of the job, including fire regulations, health and safety, drug awareness, licensing laws and first aid. On the final day each potential doorperson sat a multi-choice test on what he or she had learned. I passed with flying colours and was given a weekend shift as joint head doorman on George's bars at the Haymarket end of Newcastle.

Paul Tinnion is the kind of doorman you would want in the trenches with you – always on the ball and not someone to mess with. On the doors, you need to know that your partner is going to be watching your back and isn't going to bottle it. With Paul by my side I never had to worry. He's one of the best to work with and over the weeks and months we handled every situation that came our way. The bars weren't as hectic as *Masters* had been at Christmas but nevertheless we had our fair share of bother. The Haymarket is not very far from St James' Park, so football matches always brought trouble our way. Never anything too serious though; it was always outweighed by the Newcastle fans who would talk to me about the beautiful game. Of course, I had to bear a bit of verbal abuse from some of the supporters as well. It was water off a duck's back though, I am aware that you can't keep everyone happy and one thing every fan is, is an expert on football. You just can't win – 'sticks and stones' as the saying goes. There were plenty good blokes as well as bad blokes who would come in... and we can't forget to mention the ugly ones.

Doormen in general have a bad reputation, but I'd say it's been getting a lot better in recent years. They were considered by the public to be paid thugs who chat up women and give any man who looks at him the wrong way a good hiding. You got a problem with that, eh? Have you? Joking aside though, that's' how things *used to* be and that's how the name 'bouncer' came about... and it wasn't that long ago. Bouncers were feared and unfriendly – in a word, bullies. A bouncer would probably intimidate you on the way into a bar so you wouldn't cause any bother inside. If you caused anything, they would clear house, throw people out and hurt as many as they could along the way. That's why they were there and they enjoyed it. You wouldn't talk to a bouncer – ever. They were unreasonable... *everything* was settled through violence, because it was the only language they understood. Blokes would see them as a challenge and again, that's how a lot of fights broke out. The same thing was going on all over the country, bars were getting bad reputations, which meant cities were getting bad reputations. Put a thug on the door to keep the peace and there will be only one outcome.

It was getting out of hand so the council and the police force called for a change of image. They wanted to rid the bars and clubs of bouncers and bring in 'doormen' who went on to become door people, which is why the licensing initiative was set up. What publicans wanted now was a customer friendly doorperson – someone who would talk to the customers, and eject them if they misbehaved with reasonable force. There is always a better atmosphere if you greet someone as they approach as opposed to growling at them. Progress... back then, bars were nothing like they are today. Now it's all about designer labels, designer furniture and designer drinks – a bar is about image and attracting clientele – not about cheap booze and punters. With that, you need the right people on the doors. It's PR now more than anything – conduct instead of conflict.

I learned very quickly that doing the door was as much about front as it was physical size. Never back down when you have made a decision because it shows weakness, always maintain eye contact with a customer who you have a problem with, be aware of who that person is with, and most importantly make sure someone is watching your back. You need balls, brains and *then* brawn. In my late teens I studied drama at college – acting has always been an interest of mine since learning that I was named after Steve McQueen. Working on the doors, I could see that another element to the job was acting, in the sense that you have to become a different person. You need confidence in yourself and what you are doing. You may not be the toughest person in the world, but the way you act will play a big part in whether you will need to prove it or not. Once you put your clothing on, you start to become the role itself. There was an episode of *Faking It*, a television series on Channel 4, where a doorman and an acting coach trained a young lad. The idea was to place a middle class Oxford graduate in a fish-out-of-water situation and see if he could convince the public and head doormen that he was for real. He pulled it off and was actually good at it! At one point, there was an arranged confrontation to test him and he didn't back down. He proved he had the front to stand up to a big bloke, although if things had kicked off, they may have had to change the programme's name to *Breaking It*. Skills are required to diffuse situations verbally but physical skills are needed when the peace talks break down.

I was making regular trips to London to see the chaps, all friends I'd made through my contact with the twins. If I had not become so close to Ron and Reg, then meeting and networking with the likes of Dave Courtney would never have happened. Being connected to them opened a lot of doors sociably, and having friends of friends is always useful. The doors being open sociably soon were open economically too. Through Dave, I was doing regular shifts on the doors at *Diamonds* club in Hackney and also at the *Ministry Of Sound*. Working at *The Ministry* gave me a taste for club life. I loved everything about it and it was a lifestyle that I got used to quite easily... with him by your side, resistance is never an option. I considered moving to London full time but was advised by Dave that I should stay up North and make my mark. I decided to take his advice. I could see what he meant. Down there Dave is a big fish in a big pond but it took him years to get where he is. Newcastle is a major city but is still the right size to be able to make a name for yourself.

Back home, I made further enquiries for club work. A couple of months had passed when Mike, the manager of *Legends* nightclub in Newcastle, called me to offer some work. I jumped at the chance and four hours later I was signing on the dotted line with Geoff Capes' (*the* Geoff Capes) security firm. What Mike had neglected to tell me was that the previous doormen had just been sacked and that the police were keeping a close eye on the club. It's sometimes nice to know these details when you start a potentially dangerous job. It was common knowledge that the doormen had been running the club by their own set of rules, which basically meant that customers were getting beaten to a pulp on a regular basis with the security tapes going missing each time. Also the club had gained a reputation as a place for drugs so the inevitable police raid was on the cards. They had stormed the club with over a hundred and fifty officers, but to their embarrassment caught no dealers and only a handful of people for possession.

The ex-doormen were not happy despite receiving a substantial settlement, and they made us work hard for our money. The first couple of days passed by without incident; the calm before the storm. Paul Tinnion soon came on board, it give me a lift to have a mate there with me. Because of the trouble from the ex-door staff, Paul and I were now looked upon as outcasts amongst the door fraternity and were subsequently barred from most bars in the city centre with the threat of a good kicking if we tried to visit. I'll admit now that each night was a nerve-wracking experience. I changed my route to and from work, was careful not to let anyone know my address or telephone number and I even gave a false name to people I talked to in the club. That's how I had to live. Paranoid maybe, but you cannot be too careful in this game.

Although some of the threats lacked any real danger, you have to take each one seriously because one day someone may just call your bluff. You have got to look after number one and even a half-hearted threat by some numpty on the street had to be considered. I'd thought about calling in some favours from friends down South, but this was my own fight – I couldn't call for back up at the first sign of trouble.

As time went by the threats died down and we had weathered the storm. There had been a few run ins, but as the months passed, the lads from other bars started to respect the fact that we had all stood our ground and not bottled it. I suggested to our boss that he lift the ban on doormen entering the club now that the trouble had cooled down. We could let them in so long as they surrendered their licence to us while in the club. He agreed to it and again we'd made our job that little easier. For many reasons you can't afford to have doormen as enemies when you work as one. It's bad enough having enemies, but doormen need allies – you can't have any bad blood in your own city. Our bans began to lift one by one and I was soon able to go for a pint in Newcastle again without having to look over my shoulder. Special mention must go to those who stood their ground and watched my back at *Legends*. They were Paul Tinnion, Johnny Miller, Vaughn Basset, Maria Gillon, Mark Higgins, Simon McGhee, Biff, Adam, Naz, Andy, Gareth, and Amanda Scott.

The job can be messy at times and it's not uncommon to see a broken bone or some blood spilled at least once a week. Mix testosterone and alcohol together and it often equals bad behaviour. Then there's the stag parties, hen parties, fancy dress parties, the air guitarists, the stage divers, the indie kids, people being sick, drinking sick, covered in sick, falling in sick... you name it, we've seen it. The 'incidents' are always the best part. A few incidents a night are a lot better than having to fight. Just because we work the doors does not mean we look forward to fighting.

The best part about the job for me is some of the surreal sights that you can have a good laugh about even years afterwards.

Monday nights were student nights at the club. Love them or hate them but it's their debt that pays our wages. Working a student night would have been all right if it wasn't for the students. There was always a Jeremy from the rugger team whose daddy owned most of the world and would have us all sacked for chucking him out. You got used to it though – each time you were told they would be earning four times as much as you in a few years, you just had to be tolerant... and be prepared for exactly the same speech next week. I'd always laugh to myself, knowing that in a year or so they may be asking if I wanted large or medium fries. Kicking out time on a Monday night had to be seen to be believed; Whitney Houston would never have sung that song if she'd ever came to *Legends*.

Then there was Posh Ron. Just add enough alcohol and he'd start stripping! This went on every week so we were used to it after a few Mondays, but it starts to get boring after two semesters. I remember the last time..., the usual routine after a few pints, the final sock kicked off... then we gathered his clothes up and hid them. We had no choice but to escort him out... into the snowy January night. There were still people queuing to get inside so he kept them entertained until the police came to offer him their hospitality. We handed his clothes over to the police and made sure we kept the videotape in case they needed it for evidence. Clearly you have to be bright to get into University, but common sense and streetwise is something that mustn't have been on their curriculum. There was a restaurant upstairs in *Legends* that would double up as a VIP room every weekend for celebrities, so on Mondays it was just business as usual up there. I'd stand on the stairs leading to the VIP area and could guarantee that people would want to get upstairs to mingle with the stars. I'd play it cool saying I shouldn't really let them in... but we all know that money talks. Five quid usually bought them the privilege of watching people eating a meal.

Life wasn't always fun and games at *Legends* though. There were always the odd scuffles, but I wouldn't say it was worse than anywhere else. It was mainly visitors to the city that would cause trouble as opposed to the regulars. Every June in Newcastle we have *The Hoppings*; this is where the Gypsies come along and transform the town moor into a huge funfair with rides and stalls for a full week – and they loved causing trouble in the club. I remember one Thursday in particular as a few of the doormen were late into work leaving only three of us on duty, Johnny, Paul and me. Inside there was a group of lads from Edinburgh out on a stag night – doing as Scotsmen do, and doing a good job of it too. It was a laugh. Thursdays were a bit quiet in there so it livened the place up... then of course the Gypsies arrived to put a dampener on the whole night. Within five minutes the Gypos had introduced themselves to the Scots in a non-too-friendly way, which caused the Scots to do that other thing they do well. We were told over the radio that there was a fight in bar one, so Paul and I went to investigate with Johnny staying on door duty. We needed more doormen, but rule number one is never leave the door unmanned. We legged it down to bar one and there were twenty blokes beating the piss out of each other. With no time to think, we had to get in amongst it and sort it out as quickly as possible. I was dragging the Gypos out while Paul had his hands full dragging the Jocks out. It was total mayhem. As we were rag dolling them up the stairs, Simon and Vaughan arrived and without any questions began hauling them out too. It was one of the only times at work where I've actually had to hit anyone; a record I'm quite proud of. In that situation I had no choice. One of the Gypos had decided to bite my arm so I caught him with a big uppercut and floored him with a left. I had to move fast because if he'd drew blood, I might have turned into one.

The introduction of CCTV cameras was the end of the road for some doormen. Security had to be stepped up for everyone's protection so they were put in clubs and on the streets. People may protest about privacy but Big Brother has been watching us for years now – cameras have made places safer. There are pros and cons... you can be caught skiving or doing anything you shouldn't be doing, you could be getting attacked and need to know who it was or you could be blamed for attacking someone when you were nowhere near. I personally think cameras are a good idea. In pubs and clubs, every time a punter was thrown out he'd go to the police and say he was assaulted. Most of the time it would be only his pride that got hurt, but now doormen could prove their innocence too. Just after the cameras were installed, I was in *Legends* on a night out as a civvy. I was standing just off the main dance floor with Richie, Graham, Curly Keith and Iraqui Alan enjoying a few drinks and having a good time when a fight broke out. It happened too quickly to even call it a fight really, but it was enough to give someone a broken nose. Doormen are never fully off duty; I caught what happened out of the corner of my eye and rushed over to the lad. He was in a bad way and being surrounded by clubbers, bright lights and dry ice must have added to his confusion. Irish Mark was working the door that night so I called him over to help out. By that time the injured lad's mates had crowded round to see what was going on... and to ask what I'd done. Ever tried convincing a bunch of drunken lads that you didn't hit their mate when you even have his blood on your shirt? Well I have and it's impossible. My mates wanted to get involved but it wasn't worth it. It was made worse when Irish Mark arrived and got the unofficial story of what happened from the hostile 'witnesses'. Innocent until proven guilty?... Never. Not in these situations. It's always the other way round and the only one who could clear my name was falling down drunk *before* the punch. His friends were never going to let it lie, so I decided to leave before it became a bad night for everyone.

The following night, I arrived for work and was told the manager wanted to see me. He said there was no work for me that night – I was suspended for assaulting someone last night. Brilliant. The police had been called after I'd left and the same story was given to them. It was a nightmare. The manager had to give them my name and now I was a wanted man who'd fled the scene of a crime... it was getting better by the minute. I told the manager that I didn't do it and I was actually trying to help the lad. I remembered the cameras were now in the club and told him to look through the tapes because he didn't seem to believe me. The police had taken the tapes and I was suspended without pay. I couldn't believe it. I just had to roll with it for a week until the police got back with the tapes and – surprise, surprise – I was innocent and had actually tried to help the lad out. It was great to get the not guilty verdict, but it had cost me two hundred quid.

I'd been working at *Legends* for almost two years when I made one of the worst moves in my life. I decided to move to Sheffield. I had met a woman from Sheffield on a night out with the chaps in London and fell head over heels in lust. I travelled down to Sheffield for a couple of weekends on the trot to see her. She was ten years older than me, had blonde hair, blue eyes, and a cracking figure... and just happened to be a millionairess.

I was sucked in by the whole thing – who wouldn't be? Within three months I had proposed for the second time in my life and I had got to the stage where I was handing out invitations. It was obvious to everyone else which head I was thinking with, but I couldn't see what they could. I had walked away from my life on the door and employed another member of staff to cover for my absence at the post office. The magazine was on its last legs and I convinced myself that the retired life was for me.

What was I on? My mates had met her and tried to warn me about her, but lust is blind. She gobbled me up, spat me out and almost cost me everything. I will never forgive her. One of the first incidents was when she was photographed with *the* Nicholas Cage entering a hotel after a night out. Luckily the *News of the World* covered the story, so everyone I knew could read it and ask me about it. My mates loved it! I mean, it's not that often that your mate's fiancé plays away with an Academy Award winner, is it? She denied everything; I forgave her, thus becoming Steve Naïve. I had reporters hounding me for days on that one.

After all that she started throwing huge tantrums, claimed she was pregnant, then said she'd miscarried... I really was finding it difficult. The 'honeymoon period' was well and truly over by now. She was taking Prozac, which in theory should have been making things easier. I don't think it was actual depression she had. It was aggression, not depression. When we reached the lowest point, we decided to go on holiday to repair the damage... her treat, she wouldn't hear of me paying. It suited me fine, I didn't want to throw my money away on a potential holiday in Hell and anyway, she had some making up to do. We visited Greece and the first couple of days went really well. Amazingly well. We were back on track. Day three was a slight contrast. It could have been planned but it seemed so out of the blue... She told me that she didn't love me, didn't want to marry me, hated me, and was going to tell all of her family that I had been unfaithful so that they would hate me as well. I think she must have had a secret stash of 'don't beat around the bush' pills too. Her family didn't like me anyway, especially her daughter so I knew they would believe her.

I had all I could take from her. Three days into a holiday, she's made a story up about me – now, will her family believe it or not? There was no way I was going 50 /50 so I decided to phone a friend. I called my mate Paul Donnely in England and asked him to book me on a flight. That was it; I was leaving her and going home. I packed my things as best I could into two carrier bags and took some money out of the safety deposit box in the room. I was just about ready to go when the apartment door burst open and the bitch came at me with a bottle. I tried to duck out of the way but with two bags in my hand was an easy target as she cracked me across the head. She started to claw my face as I dropped the bags. I grabbed her arms and pushed her onto the bed. She came at me again so I shoved her as I made for the door. This time she banged her arm on the rough surface of the wall and it started to bleed. I paused... she looked down at her arm and smiled... squeezing the graze and rubbing the blood onto her face and through her hair. I was watching her, panicking, but didn't know what my next move should be. She was starting to look like a *Chainsaw Massacre* victim right before my eyes. Now she made for the door and I knew I couldn't let her leave the room. To anyone who saw her it would look like I'd tried to murder her. I blocked her exit so with no way out, she ran to the bathroom and locked herself in. Now was my chance. I was out of the room, down the stairs and into a taxi before you could say Anthony Perkins.

Instead of taking a direct flight I took a cross-country flight to Athens and flew to Luton. I had three pounds left in my pocket when Paul picked me up later that day. I had never been so happy to see one of the lads. She returned home full of stories about my womanising ways and how I had stolen thousands of pounds from her. To top that, she tried to turn Reg, Charlie Kray and a few of the other London faces against me. She knew all the same people down there as I did, but if they believed her, I'd be in serious trouble. As soon as I was able to give my account of what had happened they were happy that I was telling the truth. I do owe Dave Courtney a lot though. He believed me from the outset and was one of those who tried to tell me that she was bad news. Thanks Dave.

My family welcomed me back with open arms, glad that I'd had the sense to get away when I did. Now I had to get my life back in order. I thanked the girls at the post office,

resumed my shifts and told all my mates – ding, dong...
the psycho's gone. They were glad I'd seen the light and
had made the right decision at last. Another decision
I made was to sell the post office. I'd worked there for
almost a decade, and always saw it as my safety net. My
heart wasn't in it anymore. I needed a clean break and by
selling it I would be able to get on and do other things. I
called a family meeting to discuss it and they soon realised
that I was doing it for the right reasons. My grandparents
were upset at first as it had been in the family for nearly
four generations, but they gave me their support.

My jobs on the door were gone after my excursion to
Sheffield. Basically, I'd severed my ties thinking I'd never
return, so I had to eat a lot of humble pie with Capes
(although you'd think he ate it all judging by the size of
him). My job at *Legends* had been taken but I was offered
work in other bars. It was good to get back into it and
with bars springing up all the time; there is never any real
shortage of work. I was taken on at *The Union Rooms*,
working with Gordon, Eric, Mark, Simon, Gary, Amanda
and Alex.

I was working again but still had itchy feet – I couldn't
seem to settle. I even took a door job while on holiday in
Ibiza with a few of the lads. The first couple of days were a
laugh as I caught up with friends I'd met on my last visit.
I also made some new friends at the *Star Club* now called
Eden. It was just as well... there was a lot of friction between
the lads and me by the end of the first week. It was nothing
too serious, but I thought it was best not to rock the boat
and created a bit of breathing space between us. I took a
doorman job at *Eden*. This was the sort of breathing space
I needed. The lads were bemused at my decision to work
but I was sticking to my guns. I teamed up with James, the
only other English lad from Nottingham, and a Swedish
steroid freak by the name of Magnus. The manager of the
club, Mario, explained to me that the hours werefrom
eleven-thirty at night till six-thirty in the morning and

that I would receive the equivalent of sixty quid cash in hand. Result! Working the door abroad is so different to back home in England. It's far more relaxed and not half as much trouble. The only real trouble was when I had to hit someone who went for me as I tried to calm him down one night. It turned out that he was the Governor of Ibiza's son, his dad being the one who granted licences for clubs. It was a close call but ended up fine in the end. It was just like those early days at *Legends* all over again... so, okay, sometimes they *actually can* get you shut down.

The next night was foam party night with Boy George as special guest DJ. About an hour into the night a cockney bloke tapped me on the shoulder and asked me to do him a favour. He was in his mid forties, tight curly hair and very tanned. He introduced himself as Tony, a partner in the club. He had arranged for a film crew to visit the club and record an advert for the *Ministry of Sound*. He wanted me to look after them and the girl who they would be filming for a TV commercial. After the formal introductions, the story unfolded... I was to carry Lisa, the star of the advert, on my shoulders onto the dance floor where she would be performing dance moves to the camera. Within five minutes I was completely caked in foam, in fact choking on the bloody stuff as the director asked me if I could try and look as if I was enjoying it. Take two. I know I said earlier that I'd acted before, but this was a little *too* Stanislavski for my liking. Like a trooper I managed to battle on till the end with her safely on my shoulders. The director was happy, I was soaking wet with aching shoulders, and Lisa was looking forward to a blossoming career. The director promised to supply me with a final copy, and a few months later I got one. Unless you are looking for me you can't even see me on the advert but at least I know I was there.

I toyed with the idea of staying in Ibiza and giving up on my life back home for a while. I had enjoyed my time there and decided that if things didn't work out for me in England then I would return the following year and pick up where I left off. I said my goodbyes and decided I was going to give it another go on the doors again in Newcastle. I wasn't too sure what I wanted out of life. Working in Ibiza was great because it was a different world. I knew I could never leave Newcastle altogether though – it's the best place in the world. Ibiza was a good time to gather my thoughts and find myself. There was the saga with her from Sheffield, leaving my door jobs, heading out on holiday, finding work there... I needed to decide what direction I was going in.

In Newcastle I left my number with a few people to get some more nightclub hours. I was offered work at *Chase*, a new bar on Newcastle's developing Quayside. A trendy bar, more hours and better money... going once, going twice... sold to the man with the baldy head. I thanked Capes for giving me work when I needed it and left *The Union Rooms* on good terms. The Quayside was a welcome change to some of the places that I had worked and the lads there had years of experience under their belts. Graham, Richard and Keith had worked there since the bar had opened and I was accepted straight away. At first I was there on weekends only but as Christmas drew nearer I gained a lot of weeknights. There was also the promise of other work with the company that had signed me up. I was soon given a head doorman's position at their other bar, *Jonny Ringos*, more hours and more money... and soon after I was given six nights a week at *Sea*, a new night club on the Quayside. I've worked there on and off over the last few years working with a good bunch of friends, Alan Scott,Wayne Keepin, Steve Leng, Terry Grey, Mark, Julie, Peter, Clyde, Heta, Nigel White, Billy, Barry Dorner, and David. It took me twelve months to get my life back together, but I'd done it and I promised myself that I would never walk away from any job like that again, because I might not be as fortunate next time.

The trips to London carried on. I'd meet up with Dave Courtney and his mates; Mad Pete, Bulldog, Brendan,

Seymour, Wish, Marcus Tucker, Andy, Lou and a New Zealander by the name of Christian Simpson. Christian is a real character. Like me, he read about the twins at a young and impressionable age and sympathised with their plight. Living day to day in New Zealand, he wanted to speak to one of the twins to pass on his respects and offer his help in whatever way he could. He read an article about the Kray family, which said that they still had the same solicitor. He left a message at the solicitors office for both Ron and Reg saying that one of their great aunties had died and left the twins a huge sum of money by way of inheritance. Christian waited for a reply, which came a lot sooner than expected. Within an hour Reg wanted to know more about the money. The news had also had an effect on Ron, who had reacted badly to a change in medication because of the stressful news. Christian panicked and when quizzed further by the family's solicitor he buckled under the pressure and had to tell the truth. The solicitor was far from amused, even when Christian explained that all he wanted to do was to speak to the twins and wish them well. No sooner had he put the phone down than it rang again. It was Reg. He said that it was an irresponsible thing to do and he should have known better. He then asked him how old he was; when Christian replied that he was sixteen, Reg told him to learn from the experience and that if he was ever in England, that he should come and see him. The call ended with the usual 'God Bless' and now Christian was even more determined to make further contact. He came to Britain as soon as he could and is now highly respected amongst the chaps. Apart from Dave Courtney, I have to say that Christian is one of the closest friends that I have met through the twins.

I'd stay at Dave's flat in Woolwich, South London. The life down there was amazing. Now if you think your life is hectic you really want to try living Dave's for a few minutes. His wife Jenny has her hands full with the kids – Jensen, Beau and Courtney, but she still finds time to answer the phones, make countless cuppas and cook meals for the never ending guests that pass through – and that's *before* looking after Dave! She really is one in a million. Dave has been called *the Yellow Pages of Crime* and it was easy to see why. Dave has a friend in every major city and by picking up the phone can help you out without having to get out of the Jacuzzi. I felt that I had to earn my keep when I was down there, although Dave said it wasn't necessary. I took my door supervisor course in Wembley and gained my certificate and badge, which now enabled me to work legitimately, instead of what I'd been doing on earlier trips. I worked at a few pubs and clubs for Dave mainly filling in when his places were short of cover. Places such as the *Ministry of Sound* and *The Aquarium* were becoming third and fourth homes to me now. If I wasn't working at them you could guarantee I'd be drinking in them. I was really neglecting my jobs, friends and family back home but at the time I didn't really care. I was having too much of a good time to even think about home, which looking back sounds pretty bad. I was messing around with drink and women; doing the whole 'live fast, die young and leave a baldy corpse' lifestyle. I also picked up work doing personal security for a lot of famous people such as Elton John, Robbie Williams, The Spice Girls, Michael Flattely, and soap stars Steve McFadden and Martine McCutcheon. They always ranged from good fun yet hard work to being a complete nightmare and incredibly hard work. Stars would never fail to amaze. They can be down to earth and friendly or the complete opposite. I always got on well with Steve McFadden – he's a top bloke.

During the day in London, I made my money debt collecting and being teamed up with Christian Simpson, we always had a good laugh along the way. Often you can tell when you are introduced to someone whether they are for real or not, and in the Kray circle there were a lot of fakers. Chris is the genuine article. At the time he had just got fixed up with a new flat after a rather hair-raising first experience on his way onto the property ladder. Reg had always told him that he would set him up with a place to stay if he ever came to England, so Chris took him at his word. Reg asked Gary (one of his many gofers) to sort it, and surprisingly he had sorted it within a week. "Five hundred pound for the first months rent and it's all yours geezer!" Christian was a little wary, but after reassurance from the gofer that Reg and Charlie had sorted it, Chris paid the money. Although Gary did look like a used car salesman, you still wouldn't buy one from him... so handing over five hundred quid to him would never feel right.

That night, Chris got a taxi to his new home – imagine his surprise as he found it actually existed and the key actually fitted and turned in the lock. Now imagine his surprise as an axe-wielding Turk greeted him as he entered what was also *his* house. The Turk was pretty far from being delighted. He swung at Chris a few times, narrowly missing his head as he dived back into the taxi and tossed the keys out of the window. The driver needed no encouragement to step on it at that point. The gofer was a hard man to find for the next couple of weeks, but when he finally surfaced, he refused to pay the money back saying that Charlie had it. As we got to know more about Gary we realised what a scheming little toe-rag he really was. I've always been a great believer in 'what goes around, comes around' – I just don't believe that you can go around walking some kind of walk, pretending, and hope to get away with it forever. What Gary did with Chris – ripping him off or 'doing a Rickerby' as it's known in the North East, is the lowest of the low.

Debt collecting is to me a job like any other. It has its ups and downs and you can sometimes wonder to your self 'why on earth am I doing this?' – just like any other. Although we had some laughs along the way but I never did see it as a positive career move. In recovering any debt there are always some people who will take a little more persuading than others. There was one guy who had ripped a friend of mine off to the tune of ten thousand pounds. The lads and I were asked to get what we could and we would be given ten per cent each for our troubles. The bloke in question owned a taxi office in the Edmonton area North London but decided to do a disappearing act... along with the ten grand. We had to find him and retrieve the cash or property to that amount. Now if you do a Rickerby on such a large scale you would make sure you moved away, or at least lay low for a while (or wear disguises in public, not go out 'jogging' or organise boxing events) Not this bloke. He actually set up a new taxi firm just three miles from his old place! Amazing. Outside his new empire stood a gleaming silver BMW. I'm no expert but I knew that this was worth our wages, so the lads and me entered the office for a chat. I have always been a good talker, or a gobshite as some would argue, so it was up to me to explain the situation to our friend. The rest of the lads all six foot tall and wide with an array of sporting bats and clubs stared menacingly to prompt him into a friendly solution.

The jobs always paid well, but there was considerable hassle. I'd have to work with learners a lot of the time who turned out to be walking liabilities.

I remember one job with a learner where we got no answer at a house. I went round the back to investigate while he stuck a shopping trolley through the front window. Great intimidation technique... if Dale Winton is putting the frighteners on someone.

The job could sometimes be quite dangerous too. I have only ever been *slightly* hurt on a job. It was a simple cash in hand job where the bloke in question attacked me with his mother's walking stick before she joined in with him. He paid the money in the end and we all had a nice cup of tea afterwards, but it was another wake up call to think about calling it a day. I could laugh about fighting the bloke then having to restrain his mother, but the job was losing its appeal.

Hanging around with Dave always made me forget about

my day jobs. His life is one big adventure and it's great to be a part of it. One night there was a 'tip off' call to say that someone he had a score to settle with was in a club and would be there till the early hours. So together with Dave's best mate Tucker, we set off to this club to look into settling the score. Along the way Dave had been making a few calls – which is nothing new – but the calls were all about an old Motown record called *Strollin'*. We reached the club where a rave was in full affect, glow sticks, whistles, white hats and gloves... the lot. Dave had a word with the security on the door, and then... well, and then nothing. The lights came on, the music stopped, and the doormen started parting the clubbers like the Red Sea. Suddenly the speakers crackled into action once again, and all the clubbers looked on in confusion as *Strollin'* began to play. I followed Tucker and Dave towards this big bald bloke loitering next to the DJ stand. In Dave's words it was 'the bollocks' – like a scene straight out of a Scorsese film as we walked through the club, honing in on our prey. As we neared the fat bald bloke, Dave pulled on his knuckle duster and within a second fatty was out for the count. We strolled back out shaking hands with all of the door staff on the way.

Dave Courtney had become Public Enemy number one in the eyes of the Metropolitan Police, they were determined to have him one way or another. They tailed him and photographed us all at every opportunity. It was like a game of cat and mouse and I found it quite amusing that the Met were wasting taxpayers money at first, but as it continued I thought it was a disgraceful waste. The police spending thousands of pounds on surveillance equipment just to take pictures of a bunch of blokes was a waste of money and police resources to me. They kept watch across the road from a pub Dave owned, *The Albion*. They were on the second floor of an old Youth Hostel and had been there for weeks watching all the unspeakable atrocities such as pool playing, drinking and the odd game of darts. We were all there one night when Dave told us to 'watch this'. Armed with a tray of lagers and bar snacks, he crossed the road and asked the receptionist to send the tray up to the police officers on the second floor and if they fancied a game of darts they were more than welcome. Within minutes the police had packed and fled the building... another victory for Dodgy Dave! I know I was photographed throughout this period, but it didn't bother me. I was not a major player, I was just a friend.

Back in Newcastle, work began to take off. Because of the personal security I'd done in London, I was always top of the list when pop stars or sports stars were in town and wanted a hassle-free night out. One club had been pre-warned Robbie Williams may or may not be showing his face after his gig at the Newcastle Arena – then he turned up with thirty of his entourage in tow. The management had asked us to look after him and his own security firm, so first up I had to ask a lot of clubbers to clear some room, which didn't go down too well. Of course I was just doing my job as usual, but this was something I have never agreed with. One thing I've noticed is that the stars who love mingling and meeting people are always more down to earth and there are no problems, whilst those that make a fuss and not wishing to talk to fans generally causes animosity. Which it did. Each to their own though. Robbie and his guests made themselves comfortable and started drinking like there was no tomorrow... the Champagne stocks were the first casualty. Robbie was being a pain, jumping around all over the place like a little kid. If he'd been anyone else he'd have been out on his backside, but these superstar-international-pop-idols are good for business no matter how irritating they are. It was a tough job to keep people (mostly women) back from trying to get close to him, and it was made that bit tougher when they even began to offer me sexual favours in return for turning a blind eye... mostly women as well. Just as things started to calm down, the cheeky chappy jumped up and sang *Angel* and sent the entire club into a frenzy. I was glad I wasn't part of his personal security team, as they would have quite a job on their hands. I couldn't imagine babysitting like that on a full-time basis. The next day there were reports in the local newspaper that Robbie had bought everyone in the club a drink. It amazes me where they find these stories.

Steps (where are they now? Bless 'em) caused trouble in their own unique way when they visited the club. There weren't as many followers as Robbie, but it was still quite hectic all the same. We were asked by their security team not to let anyone take any pictures of the band. This really was mission impossible. The usual suspects tried to gain entry to the VIP area and were given the usual answer. The manager had now started switching his phone off when VIP's were in because these people would phone him up in another desperate attempt to get past us. As expected, people took photographs, the security team started to cause trouble with our punters and we were expected to pick up the pieces... just another example of the sort of behaviour that gets stars bad reputations. I dare say that a lot of the punters had bought their records, maybe been to the gig and now were pleased to see the band in their local nightclub; surely the odd photograph wouldn't hurt.

Whilst still doing club security, received an offer to work on the door of *The Groat House* in Newcastle's Bigg Market. I couldn't let this one pass. I love the Bigg Market, and *The Groat House* is just a kick up the arse from where I took that first job at *Masters*.

People often ask me what I get out of doing the door. Well it's simple... it is a means to an end. It pays my bills, keeps a roof over my head, and gives me good spending money. I'd say that one of the best things about door work is meeting people. I have had some laughs and met some characters that I wouldn't have otherwise met – punters as well as colleagues. I also met my fiancée, Dawn, while working on the doors. It was through knowing the twins that I got into the whole security game, so I suppose in a way they indirectly had a hand in me meeting Dawn. If my jobs ended tomorrow, I'd be glad that I'd got so much out of doing the door. You can't beat it.

Funerals

The day started just like any other. It was the seventeenth of March 1995. I had opened the post office as usual and went through my daily routine of serving the first few customers and then when it was quiet again, retiring to the back-shop for a cuppa and a read of the paper. I always had the radio turned up high on Radio One or Virgin... as I sat down to glance at the headlines the top news story was announced across the airwaves. "Former Eastend gangster Ron Kray has died." He had previously suffered from chest pains and had died of a suspected heart attack. He was sixty two years old.

The news knocked me out of my routine. I was numb. I turned the dial on the radio from station to station to confirm what I had just heard. I couldn't believe it but it slowly began to sink in. Ron had passed away at seven minutes past nine at Heatherwood Hospital, Ascot. Only a couple of days earlier I had sent him a get-well card. Everyone knew of his illness. Death may be inevitable, but it is often unexpected.

It did not take long for the phone to start ringing, but for a change I was lost for words. I asked the journalists to give me a couple of hours to absorb the news before I answered their questions and made comments. I needed to make some phone calls of my own first. I phoned Reg then Charlie and then Frank and Noelle Kurylo, Janet Alsop, Gary the gofer, Brad and Kim.

It was still sinking in the next day, when predictably the papers were full of stories about the twins. I had declined to comment to any of the major tabloids in case I was misquoted. I did talk to the locals... *The Journal, The Chronicle* and *The Gateshead Post* whose journalists I knew I could trust. During all this, my mate Ray Cann the tattoo artist contacted me to see if I intended to go to the funeral and that he would be willing to give me a lift there and back. I had not even thought about the funeral at this point, but I agreed and thanked Ray for the offer. I had already got to know Ray well from our early involvement putting the charity events together and now we were good friends. Over the next few days the newspapers carried a different headline, or different slant on the Kray story. It was a feeding frenzy. They ranged from Ron's alleged last words, to a statement he had made before his death that he was the evil twin and that Reg should be exonerated of all blame. For many it will have made for an exciting read, for me it simply hyped up the Kray Legend, and could only be detrimental to any plans of imminent release that Reg may have had.

Four days later Reg called me with the details for the funeral. The conversation was as follows, "Hello Steve, Reg here have you got a pen? (I had) good. The funeral is Wednesday, March twenty-ninth. Make your way to *English's Funeral Parlour* for nine-thirty; your name will be with the security staff. I want you to make sure you get there. If you can't for whatever reason, be at St Matthew's Church for eleven, I will make sure you are on the list there as well. I'm organising the service, so you will get in".

I told him that Ron would be proud of him for all he was doing and for being strong. He agreed, saying he was now at peace. He had others to call, so after his usual 'God bless' he was gone.

I noticed he was a lot calmer than he had been on the day that Ron died. Reg seemed to have come to terms with his brother's death and was at peace with himself for a change. He seemed to be coping well with it. I phoned Ray and let him know that Reg had asked me to attend the service. He would start making the relevant arrangements... time off work and use of a car for us to travel down. I then phoned Michael Russen, the taxi company owner who I knew in East London, and asked him if it would be okay for us to stay at his flat overnight. No problem. He too seemed excited. Okay, I see the attraction of a Kray funeral and all that goes with it... but to be excited about a funeral? Never mind. My next call was to the local florists. My mate Fitzy's wife, Colleen, worked at *Sarah Gaskins* in Newcastle and said they would custom make me a wreath, whatever I wanted for a discounted price. I appreciated the gesture. I had given the wreath a lot of thought and had decided that a cruise liner was appropriate, as Ron had told me on my first visit that that was his dream to go on a round the world trip. I only wish that his dream had become a reality. But he was free now – free from the torment that had imprisoned him.

The day before the funeral Gary phoned me to organise meeting on the day. Nine-thirty at the Funeral Parlour were Reg's instructions so I arranged to meet Gary fifteen minutes earlier. He did not seem too clear on the arrangements – if he was so close to Reg why did it seem that I was telling him things for the first time? I had suspicions about Gary and his relationship with the Kray family, I decided not to dwell on it for the time being. Mid-afternoon, Ray picked me up in a borrowed car, and after a quick photo-shoot with the wreath for the *Evening Chronicle*, we set off on our long journey to London. We met up with Mickey Russen at Scratchwood Service Station at the end of the motorway and he drove us the rest of the way into the heart of East London.

There was a lot on my mind that night. Funerals are always horrible things to have to go through, but gangland funerals will always lack that certain emotion you are used to. Gangland funerals are foremost a sign of respect by major figures from all over the country. It is a form of etiquette. All cultures have rules, the funeral marks the fact that the person had influence and people want to travel to show their support. There are different levels of intimacy... I knew Ron well and knew that I was there for my own reasons.

My first job the next day was to write out the card that

would accompany the wreath. I wrote, 'You always wanted a round the world cruise. Now you are free enjoy it, Steve Wraith, Ray Cann, Michael Russen.' Radio Newcastle had asked me to speak to them that morning on their weekly phone in programme with presenter Mike Parr. I had done a lot of shows with Mike so was prepared for his line of questioning. His stance was,

'Why mourn the death of a psychotic gangster?' I told him and the listeners back in the North East that Ron had been a friend and that his past did not concern me. I knew him now, not as he was in the sixties. Due to the medication and that he had been institutionalised for so long, he was a different man to the one the public had read about. My comments apparently caused uproar with the listeners and phone-lines were jammed all day with people wishing to voice their concern about that 'naïve, misled youngster'. Radio Newcastle had never had it so good! The Krays were never going to get good publicity for anything. They are icons of underworld Britain... to mourn Ron instead of saying 'good riddance' the moral majority of listeners were saying I didn't know what I was talking about. I knew more about it than most of them, so I did not let it bother me.

We left the flat at eight forty-five that morning. Ray drove while Michael gave directions. I sat at the back with the wreath. As we drove through the streets of East London, I thought about the day ahead and felt honoured to be part of it all. I was surprised at how quiet the roads seemed to be as it was rush hour in London... then we hit gridlock a quarter of a mile from Bethnal Green road where *English's* was situated. The roads that had been so good to us looked as if they were going to let us down. Somehow we managed to push our way through the traffic, and with Mick's local taxi knowledge we reached the funeral parlour with a few minutes to spare. We pulled up outside behind a police cordon and got out to lay our wreath. The first thing that struck me was the number of people, gathering to witness another chapter in the Kray's storybook unfold. It was an amazing sight – like a state funeral. People pushing to get a glimpse of anything... reporters and camera crews... police all over the place. It was at this moment I realised that I had finally walked into the books that I had read all those years ago, if that makes sense. I had read every book about the Kray twins and their associates and now I was part of one. I was not just a bystander... I was a family guest. The security was impressive. They were massive – all with as much jewellery as Mr. T, all immaculately dressed and very mean looking. Leading the operation was Reg's close friend Mr. Dave Courtney. As we mingled amongst the who's who of the underworld, we could hear the cameras clicking across the road. Photographers were perched, balanced and clinging on for dear life from different vantage points, all trying to get the best picture for tomorrow's papers.

I laid the wreath next to Reg's floral tribute, which read, 'To the other half of me'. As I stood up, I shook hands and embraced Dave. There was no sign of Gary, so as Ray parked the car Mickey and me nipped to the nearest cafe for a cuppa. Once Ray had parked up, I cleared it with Dave to allow Ray and Mick into the parlour; as we waited outside. It was impossible to walk anywhere at a normal pace. We just had to stand in line and shuffle in as best we could. I could still not take in the numbers of people that were congregating. The flashguns and the clicking of shutters rattled through the air again as a prison van pulled up outside. It turned into the alley adjacent to the parlour... all eyes were on it, but no one emerged. God knows how many rolls of film were wasted in those few seconds. There was confusion until a dark Peugeot pulled up with Reg handcuffed to a well-dressed screw as the passengers. He was led quickly and quietly into *English*'s as the crowd cheered. The authorities obviously wanted to get him in unnoticed, which was an impossible job. Reg Kray was back in the East of London once more.

We managed to get into the funeral parlour after around fifteen minutes of uncertainty and were shown to the room set aside for friends and relatives. A few familiar faces had already arrived in the shape of Frankie Fraser, Tony Lambrianou, Charlie Richardson and of course Charlie Kray. I also saw Alan and Janet Alsop – we were now good friends after sharing visits to Reg. I introduced them to Ray and Mickey, before I beckoned one of the funeral directors over. I asked him to tell Reg that I had arrived and within a few minutes he re-appeared and and took me to see him. I was led down a small corridor to an old oak panelled door on the left hand side. He pushed the door open and said, "You can take as long as you like, Sir."

My jaw dropped. Instead of seeing Reg, I was now alone in the room with Ron's body in his coffin. I looked back and the door was closed behind me. It was no mistake. He was in a large oak coffin, his hair swept back and immaculate, as usual. He was dressed in a crisp white shirt and silk tie. Even in death, I thought to myself, he looked dignified and dapper – every inch the well-dressed gangster. I know undertakers are experts at making the dead look good, but all the strain and mental torture which had been etched on Ron's face in his latter days had disappeared without a trace. It was like he had been wearing a mask and now it had been removed. He was free at last; he was completely at peace. I did not feel sad seeing him in the funeral parlour. I felt sad for the fact that he had died in prison. I felt sad for Reg and for Charlie, but in a way happy for Ron. I put my hand on the coffin, said my own goodbye and left him for the last time. The funeral director had been waiting for me outside and led me back to another door on the opposite side of the corridor. As he opened the door, Charlie Kray spun around, "Steve, good to see you mate, thanks for coming down, it's a long journey." I shook his hand, and he pulled me towards him and embraced me. Standing next to him was Reg, handcuffed to a middle-aged prison officer.

He stepped forward bringing the officer with him, and put his arm around me as best he could, "Steve thanks for coming, how are you?" He seemed calm, just as he had on the phone last time we spoke, a lot calmer than I thought he would be. *English*'s had put on a lavish buffet for Reg, but food was the last thing on anyone's mind. Reg then patted me on the head (he was always amused at my lack of hair) and asked, "Who have you come with?" I explained that I had driven down with Ray and met up with Michael and that we were staying at his place. Quick as a flash he asked, "What about Bulla Ward? Is Bulla here? Is he coming?"

Bulla and Reg had fallen out in the sixties. Bulla was a tough bloke and laughed off one of Reg's punches one night in *The Regency*. There were not many men who could withstand one of his punches, so to save face Reg took out a knife and carved Bulla's face up. He regretted the fall out and had asked me to get him there to make the peace. To be truthful, with all that was going on I had forgotten to ask Mickey whether he had managed to get in touch with Reg's old mate, and whether he would be attending the funeral to pay his last respects. Michael claimed to know him, and had tried in vain to contact him before the funeral. I had tried as well but to no avail.

Thinking quickly I replied, "He'll be here Reg, paying his respects. Reg, I know he will." Reg smiled, and then asked, "Has he forgiven me?" I didn't quite know what to say. "Yes Reg, he's forgiven you." What else could I say on the day of his brother's funeral? "Good, good. Well thanks for coming Steve, I'd like you to go and see Ron now. I'll be in touch. In fact you ring me later tonight, I'll let the staff know your going to call, take care and God bless. Thanks again for coming."

He kissed me on both cheeks and embraced me. It was quite a moment, something I will never forget. Charlie repeated the farewell, saying, "I'll see you for a drink later on, Steve." The same funeral director was waiting for me outside the door, and began to lead me down to see Ron's body. "No, it's okay mate, I've already seen him." I said. He apologised before taking me back to re-joined Ray and Michael in the friends and relatives room. I think they had felt a bit out of place standing alone. I told them that I had been with Reg and Charlie and had been taken to see Ron. It was then that the whole emotion of the day hit me. I had always wanted to see the Kray brothers together, but not like this. I wiped a tear from my eye as we waited for others to pay their final respects to *The Colonel*, and express their sympathies to his brothers.

By now Dave was close to having a blue fit, "I'm fighting a losing battle. I've got old blokes trying to get in here, saying they are old friends of Ron, Reg, Charlie and any old uncle you can think of. I can't let everyone in for God's sake." I didn't envy his job one bit, but I knew that if anyone could pull off the biggest organised funeral since Winston Churchill's, then he could. Once everyone had paid their respects, the wreaths were loaded on to the glass horse-drawn carriage and the twenty-two limousines, which were to follow behind in procession. The horses were black and beautifully dressed with long black plumes protruding from their heads. We were ushered from the parlour and as we made our way outside the flashing from the cameras dazzled us once more. There was pandemonium outside. Things were beginning to happen. Dave told me to make sure that I got into a car... it didn't matter which one. We made our way down to the eighth car; a black, six-seater top of the range limo. No expense was spared. The cars were immaculate inside and out and each one was decked in floral tributes (Our wreath remained with Reg's tribute alongside Ron's coffin throughout the day, and could be seen clearly in photographs in most national newspapers the next day). Inside our car were Ray, Michael, Janet and Alan Alsop and me. The driver started the engine and with the rest of the procession we were off on our long journey, first to St Matthews Church in Bethnal Green, and then on to Chingford Mount Cemetery in Essex to the Kray family plot.

It was an unforgettable journey. We had only to travel approximately three quarters of a mile from the parlour to the church, but it took over forty-five minutes. The crowds of people were ten deep, all leaning and peering over metal fences, which had been put up by the police. I stared out at all the people. It was the sort of mania that's normally reserved for rock stars or movie idols... certainly not the sort of admiration the authorities would expect the public to bestow upon a notorious murderer. Cries of 'We love you' and 'Good on you Ron' could be heard; whilst in the distance the clip clop of the horse's hooves weaved their way to our first port of call. I wondered what was going through Reg's mind as we passed along roads and streets that he had not seen for the best part of twenty-five years, and how he would feel as he passed along the street where he and Ron once lived. As we neared the church, I caught a glimpse of Patsy Palmer (Bianca from the BBC soap *Eastenders*) paying her respects. The East End of London had changed so much since Reg had been taken away from it, and as we finally reached St Matthew's I promised myself I would ask him how he had felt about what he had seen. The scene when we reached the church was unbelievable. It was bedlam... simple as that. Roughly twelve hundred people had gathered outside the church gates and many were chanting, "Free Reg Kray. Free Reg Kray!"

I led the occupants of our car towards the church doors. Reg had arrived about two minutes before us and was already inside. At the doors the orderly queuing system for friends and relatives had been reduced to a free for all. At one stage it looked like we would not get in. There was a public address system set up for those outside to hear the service, and I did not want to travel all that way to be stuck outside. I noticed the funeral director and luckily he remembered me... he ushered the five of us to the front of the crowd and into the church. The pews at the back of the church were all that was left, but I saw Dave and he waved me over.

The coffin was carried into the church by Johnny Nash from North London, Teddy Dennis from the West, Charlie Kray from the East and Freddie Foreman from the South.

Close friend Laurie O'Leary also helped take the coffin in. Frankie Fraser had originally been asked but felt that his height may be a hindrance. Frank Sinatra's *My Way* played as the coffin was placed alongside Reg. The atmosphere was tense as the service began, the smell of incense hanging heavily in the air. Reg, Charlie and Dave had masterminded the day's events to Ron's specification and it was running like clockwork. Throughout the service Reg remained handcuffed to the officer. It did not seem to bother him too much. The officer was just there with him as opposed to trying to be heavy-handed. Every so often Reg would place his free hand on top of the coffin in a moving display of affection. But why handcuff a man who had no intention of escape? Why humiliate him? Was it a political statement by the Home Office that this man would never be free? Whatever the reasoning, to me it was inhumane. Okay, the officer was just doing a job... if they wanted to, they could have handled the situation differently and let him mourn without being chained to someone.

Sue McGibbon read out messages and telegrams from well-wishers. She also read out a message from Reg. It went, "My brother Ron is now free and at peace. Ron had great humour, a vicious temper, was kind and generous. He did it all his way, but above all he was a man, that's how I will always remember my twin brother Ron."

As the service ended, Ron's coffin was carried out to Whitney Houston's song, *I Will Always Love You*. I don't think there was a dry eye to be seen in the rows and rows of hardmen. As Reg left the church he winked at our group... he was bearing up. It was bedlam once more as we made our way back to the car. The five of us held onto each other as we made our way through the swaying masses. It was all too easy to get split up as journalists, television and radio interviewers threw questions at us. I was not interested in commenting, not today of all days. I noticed a few others such as Patsy Manning, a close friend of the family, were willing to stop for a chat.

When we eventually made it back to the car, our driver was a little stressed out to say the least. Someone had climbed into our car and refused to move. The driver had tried to explain to him that he was in the wrong car, but he would not have it. After a quiet word in his shell-like, he left to find another car and more people to annoy. Drama over, the driver started our six mile journey to Chingford Cemetery... take two... enter nutcase door left. The front passenger door was pulled open and in stepped a middle-aged woman who was madder than a coach load of Hatters at a magic mushroom convention. Her name was Georgina and was armed with Valium in one pocket and half a bottle of whisky in the other (for Reg apparently). She told us a tale of woe – she was supposed to marry Ron before he died and told us a few other things I can't remember. The driver looked back for some kind of assistance, but as the procession of cars had already started to move, I told him to drive on. We would have to take our unwanted passenger with us. As the car pulled away we all exchanged anxious glances in the back of the car, as Georgina said, "We were going to have kids you know." This was going to be a very long six miles indeed.

This gave me another excuse just to sit back and watch the crowds. Young people, old people... hundreds upon hundreds had gathered just to catch a glimpse of the brothers. There were many memorable sights throughout the day from that limo rear window, nothing more memorable than the sight that greeted us at the Bow Flyover. Construction work was taking place, yet the whole workforce had downed tools and were standing in a line by the roadside, hard hats off and heads bowed... it was one hell of a sight. I can only imagine how Reg and Charlie must have felt. As we reached Chingford, it had taken one and a half hours to travel six miles, though with Georgina in the front, it felt like one and a half days.

The horses pulling Ron's hearse had struggled up the steep bank leading to the cemetery gates and we followed them in. By now we were almost used to the strobe-effect lighting from the constant photographs and the pushing and pulling of the crowds. As we followed the road to the family plot our hitchhiker decided it would be a good idea to walk the rest of the way. There was no argument from any of us. The surrounding fence to the cemetery had a lot of holes in it and I was shocked to see people, many of them kids, clambering through. If ordinary people had made it to the graveside we might not gain our place next to the family. I need not have worried. There were so many people around the grave, but they all kept a respectful distance as Reg first laid flowers on his mother and father's graves, and then his wife's. He paused a little longer there, his face full of sorrow and regret.

Just then I felt a hand on my shoulder, it was Dave Courtney looking less flustered than he was earlier outside the funeral parlour. He asked me to look after Charlie for the rest of the day and make sure he wasn't hassled by anyone. I told him I'd be honoured.

We made our way to where the family had gathered directly behind Charlie and Reg. There was a tremendous feeling of grief... then looking around, I began to wonder. It seemed a lot of people were there out of curiosity or to somehow enhance their stature from their association. There were 'tourists' – people just there to be a part of it all – staring at Reg all the time, studying his face for reactions and witness the London gangland boss cry. As the vicar read the last rites and Ron's body was finally laid to rest the cameras flashed en mass for the last time. Ron Kray was the centre of the world's attention even in death. He would have loved it. Reg threw the first piece of soil down onto the coffin and then arose, and then, one by one we all did the same. Reg then turned, embracing Charlie, shook hands with Freddie Foreman and then out of the blue turned around to me and said, " Thanks for coming Steve." He stretched out his hand and I grabbed it. This time it was my grip that was the strongest. Reg was finally drained of all energy. "I'll be in touch Reg." With that he was led away, pausing to say some more goodbyes.

As Reg left I stared in disbelief at people, who will remain nameless, photographing the activities at the graveside. A number of people who I used to respect, lost it that day. After one last glance at Ron's grave, we all returned to our limo. All of the wreaths lined the pathway to the grave, hundreds of them and we paused to read as many as we could. We finally found our wreath, lying alongside Reg's. To me it symbolised how close I had become to the Kray family and was glad to see it was still next to Reg's.

The driver had been told our destination... *The Guvner's* public house was the venue for the wake. Without the lovely Georgina, our journey seemed to be quicker and we arrived at the wake within twenty minutes. There were already quite a few people in there and I could see that it was soon going to be packed out. It was a typical London boozer – dim, cramped, but with wet beer and good conversation. Already there were people such as Frankie Fraser, Freddie Foreman, Charlie and his son Gary, Tony Lambrianou, Dave Courtney and of course Lennie McLean.

Lennie was still known as *The Guvner of London* and when I him again at the wake I did not need to introduce myself. Lennie was the sort of bloke who would remember a name and its always good when that happens. I never got the chance to meet up with Lennie again before his untimely death, but followed his acting career with great admiration. The man was a real gent, a legend, and someone who I was proud to call my friend.

Tony Lambrianou was a member of the Kray firm and was one of the few who stood by the twins, receiving twenty years as his "reward". I'd read his book, *Inside the Firm* and got on well with him. This was the first time I had met Tony... soon after he introduced me to Freddie Foreman and before long I was talking with Frankie Fraser, Charlie Kray, Freddie and Tony about Ron, Reg and their memories of the old days.

Charlie Kray was the perfect host as usual, smiling and chatting to everyone who was there and thanking them for coming. He told me it had been a great send off for his brother and that he would have loved it. As we spoke, the early evening news appeared on the large television screens. A hush fell upon the room as people watched the first pictures from the funeral. The cameras only proved what I had already thought – that Ron Kray had received a funeral normally reserved for Royalty. Thinking of Charlie's words... it was true, he would have loved it. It was the best send off a man could ask for. There were tributes and messages from rock stars, TV stars and movie icons. The streets were full of mourners and well-wishers, people who were just dumbstruck by the whole thing, all his friends and media people from anywhere you care to mention. It was the ultimate two-fingered gesture to the authorities as he had the popularity to bring the nation's capital to a standstill.

As the night progressed I had my photo taken a few times, but did not really consider it to be appropriate at a wake. Lennie had called me over for one and there were others taken as well. I bumped into Tony Lambrianou again as he was about to leave. We wanted to make sure we kept in touch so we exchanged numbers and he promised that he would call.

By the time I finished talking Michael had left, Ray was bored to tears and Georgina had blagged her way in. It was late now so we had one last drink and decided to return to Newcastle. We made it back early the next day and I went straight to bed as soon as I got home. Just as I was drifting off the phone rang – it was Reg. I was surprised but pleased to hear from him in such a short space of time.

"Hello Steve, I'm just ringing to thank you for coming down to the funeral. I was in a daze for most of the day to be honest, but I'm pleased it went well. Anyway was Bulla Ward there? He was wasn't he! Bring him to see me okay? My units are running out I'll have to go. God bless."

He did not give me the chance to answer. I decided to leave it at that. He may have known that Bulla wasn't there when I told him... or knew he wouldn't turn up. He probably decided to leave it till the next day. I know Reg had been through a lot lately and I had much sympathy for him. At least to hear him like this on the phone, I knew he was getting back to his old self. I'd smile to myself after such 'conversations'... we were similar in some respects. We were both stubborn. It was as if we could not let the other have the final word on particular issues. I think he knew that I would not be enquiring about Bulla again – he just needed to make his point.

Charlie had been moved again, this time to Parkhurst . He had been in Frankland prior to this and was moved because he was suffering from chest pains and on visits he had been struggling to catch his breath. He had been happy at Frankland and had made a lot of friends there through me.

The Home Office decided that Parkhurst on The Isle of Wight was the best place for him, as it was in close proximity to St Mary's Hospital. He was taken down from the high risk prisoner status, to a Category B prisoner so his health could be monitored if need be. I wrote to Charlie as soon as I heard that he had been moved, just to let him know that I knew his whereabouts and was thinking of him. He phoned me to let me know that he was okay and that he appreciated everything that I had done for him during his stay in Frankland.

He finished by saying that he would be in touch soon

and that he would sort out a visiting order for me in the next few weeks. This was the last time that I spoke to him. Charlie's health worsened further... when the Home Office gave permission for Reg to visit him, I knew that Charlie's days were numbered.

On the fourth of April 2000, Charles James Kray passed away, with Diane and Reg at his bedside. He had heart problems, which had developed into pneumonia. He was weak and physically frail. He was seventy-three years old. Reg was devastated, he later told me that he was so overcome with guilt that he begged Charlie for forgiveness on his visit. I called Roberta to pass on my condolences and would have to sort out the arrangements for travelling down to London for what would surely be another big send off.

Ray Cann and Graham Borthwick telephoned and along with Ian Freeman we made arrangements to travel down.

I arranged the wreath for the funeral once again through Fitzy and Colly. It was in the shape of a diamond and had the word 'geezer' underneath it. The local papers were on hand to get some shots of us picking the wreath up and ran a story on it. Graham drove us down to Dave Courtney's in Plumpstead, South London the night before.

There was something else on my mind other than the funeral as we made our way down, the woman from Sheffield I had a previous relationship with. She was now with someone else, a man I had met many times before and had a lot of respect for. She told her new man that I had beaten and robbed her, that I had called *him* an old dinosaur and that I said he was past his sell by date. I had to laugh; this was like schoolyard stuff, but in the whole scheme of things she was trying to ruin my reputation and get me beaten up in the process. Her new man was a very well-known face in London – a hard man with a fierce reputation. Through third parties I heard that threats were being made and I took them seriously. I had to. I was concerned that matters were getting out of hand. She was telling all sorts of lies but I was powerless to shut her up. I was not frightened, but knew I would have to be a little more cautious on my trips to London, starting with the funeral. As if there wasn't enough to do and think about on a day like this, now it would be impossible for me to relax. I was concerned about a confrontation at my friend's funeral. I would keep a safe distance from him and hope he would soon see what she was doing.

The funeral had been delayed but with Reg making the arrangements you could guarantee that the day itself would run like clockwork. It was going to be a long day. I only managed a couple of hours sleep the night before at Dave Courtney's before I was awoken with a cup of tea and a cockney, "Whey aye man ye bugger ye know!"... Dave had been practising his Geordie accent. Dave explained that the lads were all meeting here at eight-thirty to leave in convoy at nine-thirty a.m. He had that sparkle in his eye so I knew he had something up his sleeve, I was sure we would all know in time. By nine a.m. the rest of the lads were suited and booted and ready to go.

Dave let us have his white Rolls Royce for the day with his personalised number plate "BADBOY" while he went with Brendan and Seymour in his new Jag. Mad Pete had the privilege of driving Dave's Roller, while Graham, Ray, Ian and myself were his passengers. Nine-thirty struck on a bright spring South London morning and right on cue Dave's well-rehearsed plan came into affect. *The Satan's Slaves* are a motorbike chapter and have bases up and down the country and all over the world. Dave knew a lot of the members of the various chapters and built up some strong friendships with them and had arranged for six of their top men to ride as outriders to our convoy of cars making sure that we all had a safe journey all the way to Bethnal Green and *English's Funeral Parlour*.

It was a strange feeling this time round for me. Five years ago when Ron had died, I had been naive and was still quite new to this way of life – still meeting people and still finding my feet I suppose. Back then; if I'm honest, I was still getting a buzz from it.

Now though, I felt sadness for Reg. He had seen this happen to both his brothers and each time he was the centre of attention. I never thought this was fair. It was also sad that Charlie had died a prisoner and not a free man. Regardless of his crime and his sentence – being in prison at that age ground him down immediately.

With Charlie there was still the spectacle of it being a Kray funeral. Charlie was a well-loved and respected bloke; he was also well-known for his love of parties and good times... Champagne Charlie. Again this funeral would be seen as another event. Reg's popularity was evident. All the up and coming hardmen were there, the top boys from each town and city... something like this is an opportunity to get their name and face known. A perfect chance to gain notoriety... not a criticism. I had been there, done it and printed and sold the tee-shirt. I had lived it. I had not only met the three brothers, I had became friends with them and stood by them through the years.

We reached Bethnal Green in good time with our escorts doing us proud much to the bemusement of other traffic and the local constabulary. Outside the parlour were a lot of familiar faces, and I introduced Ray, Graham and Ian to Bruce Reynolds, Frankie Fraser, Freddie Foreman, Tony Lambrianou, Charlie Richardson, and a few of the other lesser known faces. Once we had shook hands with the chaps we put our wreaths in place and went for a drink. I had a tip-off that because of 'that' woman from Sheffield, I would not be welcome at the church. Apparently she knew the people responsible for security and I would not be allowed in. I told the chaps that I would go to the church alone but they wouldn't have it. If we were going then it was all for one and one for all. I appreciated their solidarity. We finished our drinks and made our way back to our cars only to be stopped in our tracks by an announcement on a megaphone by the police officer in charge. There was a gas leak on Bethnal Green Road and he wanted to limit the traffic travelling to the church by car. We would have to walk the half mile or so there and back. It was a sunny day so there was little or no complaint. We looked like a mini army all suited, booted and crombied up walking through the heart of East London with Dave leading the assault with what he refers to as his 'Knights of the Round Table'. The Knights, of whom I am proud to be one, are his best friends from different parts of the country, based on his fascination with King Arthur. His house is based on Castle Camelot, and he even has the moat and the drawbridge. He has twelve seats at the round table in his dining room.

We had not been walking long and could see the church in our sights when it happened... taking us all by surprise. He had either been following us or lying in wait for some time, silent... then he attacked. A Yorkshire Terrier jumped out from nowhere and went straight for Ray attempting to chew his leg off. It lightened the moment as we made our way through the already swelling crowds. Dave got us through the gates and we began to make our way past the flashing lights of the press and up the steps to the church. I saw Rob Davis on the door, I knew him well and had a lot of time for him. He knew about the 'situation' I had found myself in and we were both keen to avoid any fuss. I was there simply to pay my respects. Reg had not entered the argument one way or another, so Rob was able to make an on-the-spot decision. The church was packed to the rafters and I stood at the back of the church with Dave and Ray as I had done five years earlier for Ron. Because the church was so packed and due to the circumstances I did not get a chance to speak to Reg and let him know that I was there. He was on his own now and I wanted him to know I was there and thinking of him. My mind was soon put at ease though. Ray handed me an order of service and said, "Reg thanks us for coming down". Ray had managed to slip to the front and let him know we were there. Reg shook Ray's hand, hugged him and told him to tell me thanks. I smiled inside. He knew we were there and that meant a lot to me. He knew he had friends there. We may not have been in touch as often now, but he knew. We were still close. The service was very much like his brother's with the hymns *Morning Has Broken* and *Fight The Good Fight*, and there were readings from Sue McGibbon and Freddie Foreman's son Jamie. He had a lot of supporters.

Charlie's body was carried from the church to Shirley Bassey's *As Long As He Needs Me*, and just like the last time, all eyes were on Reg to study his reactions. We formed a line of honour outside the church as he was placed back in the traditional black hearse for his journey to the family plot in Chingford, Essex. We returned to our cars and once our escorts gave us the nod we were off. Making our own way to Chingford rather than following the procession of cars, we arrived in good time and took our place on a hill overlooking the graveside waiting for Reg and Roberta to arrive. He'd seen his mother and his two brothers buried while serving his time. At each one of them he'd been handcuffed to an officer... and each one was getting harder for him to bear. I would have thought this funeral was the one to make a few allowances, but obviously the law is the law.

As Charlie was lowered into the ground I felt a lump in my throat. I'd had a lot of good laughs with Charlie, as I had said at his trial he was the perfect host and a gentleman, and I knew I would certainly miss him. I felt close to him because we'd socialised on many occasions. It wasn't just prison visits for a few hours at a time, it was a friendship of talking on the phone and meeting up and going out together... and he was the best there was for a night out. Charlie was the type who would do anything for a friend. He had a tremendous lust for life and to see him die in such circumstances left a bitter taste. Everyone was outraged that he was put in prison but when we now knew just how little time he had left made it worse. Our floral tribute had been the perfect words to describe him:

Diamond Geezer.

As the crowds of onlookers dispersed, a man shouted out "Three cheers for Reg Kray... hip, hip..." The crowd reacted accordingly. With that Reg shook the hands of those around him, kissed Roberta and was whisked away. That night we watched the funeral coverage on TV, and then I showed the lads around the West End as Dave and Jenny had a prior engagement at a boxing event with Ian Freeman.

Travelling back the next day, I picked up the papers to see all the coverage of the funeral. As with Ron, it had taken some time for the realisation to sink in. Charles James Kray was dead. When you see it in the papers and on TV like that, that's when you know it happened. On the day, it's just like you are on autopilot, like it is going on but not actually real. When you see yourself and friends in that third person situation in the media you *know* you were there and you *know* it did happen. The headline of one paper proclaimed "And Then There Was One"; the Krays were dying one by one, and now Reg was the last of the family line.

I had to work that night and because of the traffic on the way back I didn't have time to go home to rest or change clothes. I was shattered. When I finished and could finally get home I had a message from Reg waiting for me. "Hello Steve, Reg Kray speaking. Thank you, and thank your friends for taking the time to come down South to Charlie's funeral. You are a good friend. I'll ring another time, God Bless." I played the message over a few times and I admit I shed a few tears. For all his faults, this man had had to cope with his entire family dying whilst he was in prison. He had to deal with the despair, anguish and torment that the death of a loved one brings but he had to deal with it under different circumstances to most others. There was the build up in the newspapers as a Kray death looked imminent. Then he had to make all the arrangements and to deal with the pressures of all the media attention

– being in the spotlight throughout the service only to be taken straight back immediately afterwards. Prison can be a lonely enough place but now he really was alone. It showed more than anything how strong his character was and I for one hoped that he had enough fight left in him to beat the system, gain parole and spend at least a few years of freedom in the arms of the woman he truly loved.

In the year 2000, Reg had his parole hearing. To be fair, for all Roberta's hard work I could only see Reg becoming decategorised and not a release programme. A lot of stories had circulated about Reg's health, and I'd been asked on numerous occasions by my friends in the media to confirm that he was fit and well. As far as I was concerned there were no problems. You can't always believe what you read in the papers, but there had been a lot of coverage over the last year and a half of Reg's frequent trips to the hospital wings at both Blundestone and Wayland with what was described as an irregular stomach complaint. Some reports suggested ulcers, others a possible cancer. Reg although admitting to the pains, assured us all that it was nothing to worry about, and that he had faith in the doctors he'd been dealing with.

I wasn't convinced. In April at Charlie's funeral Reg had looked pale and it was quite noticeable that he had lost weight. A lot of observers put this down to the worry and stress that he'd endured with Charlie's illness and his parole board hearing. Our worst fears were confirmed when in September it was announced that he had been admitted to hospital in Norwich for tests. The reports at first were a little unclear and then Roberta dropped the bombshell... Reg had undergone exploratory surgery and a cancer had been detected. He had only weeks to live. I sat and watched the story break on the lunchtime news and still couldn't believe what I was hearing. As I watched and was taking it in, journalists started phoning me wanting some reaction to the story. I told them I was shell-shocked and that the Home Secretary should show immediate compassion and release Reg so that he could at least taste freedom before he passed away. Reg's solicitors Mark Goldstein and Trevor Lynn re-iterated what I had said when they were interviewed on later bulletins. The Sunday papers carried haunting images of a frail Reg lying in his hospital bed with tubes leading from his torso, his breathing aided by an oxygen mask. It was a sad picture to have to look at. He looked very ill. He *was* very ill. He was dying and yet he was still considered to be a danger to society.

How could a Home Secretary justifiably keep this man incarcerated? My comments were carried in the *Sunday People* where I was named as Reg's surrogate son, which I found quite amusing. The pictures of Reg were all over the papers as the exclusive stories began to break. They were a far cry from the Reg Kray that the public remembered, which is why I thought that they probably helped his cause for support. I'd sent him a card, as had Ray who was quite keen to visit him. I was not so sure. I had distanced myself so much from Reg in recent months I felt almost hypocritical, or like a ghoul wanting to see the last dying Kray on his deathbed. I decided against it. It'would be good to catch up with Reg and see him one last time. I'd moved on since those early days. The last time I'd seen him was at Charlie's funeral. I still thought of him as a good friend – it's not that we had a falling out or decided not to speak; it's just that we had drifted apart over the years. To rekindle what once was just seemed false to me. We had the sort of relationship now where we both knew we supported each other regardless of whether we were in constant contact or not.

I sent him a letter wishing him well and expressing my hope that both he and Roberta could enjoy what little time they had left together. I didn't know what else to say. Have you ever tried to write a letter to someone who is dying? It's not easy. Jack Straw, the Labour Government's Home Secretary, bowed to public pressure and released Reg on compassionate grounds a few days later. But, although a free man Reg was confined to a room in the hospital which was smaller than his prison cell in Wayland. Basically, the world knew he was dying and the Government decided to let him die on the outside. The cruel irony is that he could never be free; he couldn't go out and enjoy a walk or do something he'd been longing to do for thirty years. Reg was delighted at his 'release' and was said to be celebrating with a bottle of Moet and some Henry Winterman Cigars. Good on him, he deserved it. I phoned the hospital and left a message for him... I left my number and hoped now that I could speak to him for the last time.

Not a day passed without a new 'Kray Exclusive' in the newspapers. The tabloids in particular seemed to love the fact that the last of the Krays was dying. It was sensational in their eyes... Reg was a ready-made story they couldn't wait to exploit. It was sick fascination, which I found very disturbing. One particular paper carried it's stories under a sub-heading "Death Of A Gangster", where is the respect or the dignity in that I ask you? I suppose a lot of people would say that Reg brought it upon himself by courting the press for years, but everyone should be entitled to privacy in their dying days. I had still not spoken to Reg by the time he was considered fit enough to leave his sickbed in Norwich Hospital. He was moved to a honeymoon suite in the *Town House Hotel* in Norfolk. The room as you would expect, was beautifully decorated with a four-poster bed and an idyllic view of the river and the surrounding countryside. It had always been Reg's wish to have a house in the country where he would be able to take long walks and enjoy the simpler things in life. This hotel room would be as close as he would get to realising this dream. It may have come at the wrong time for him, but he was out of prison.

His condition had worsened, and as each day passed he was visited by many of his old gangland associates as well as old enemies to make their peace. Laurie O'Leary – good friend and Kray biographer, Joe Pyle, Freddie Foreman, and Frankie Fraser all paid him a visit. The rumours still circulated... reports suggested that Reg only had six months to live, but they turned out to be wrong. I tried to contact Reg one last time by leaving a message and my telephone number with the girl on reception at the hotel. She let me down, the message I learnt later was not passed on, just like my other at the hospital. Neither Reg nor Roberta were aware that I had tried to contact them. The news the next day came as no great shock or surprise. On Sunday October the first, 2000, Reg Kray the last of the notorious Kray Brothers died, aged sixty-six. Amongst those at his bedside were Freddie Foreman, Joe Pyle, Johnny Nash and Roberta. Over the next few days there were yet more rumours; this time surrounding the funeral arrangements.

The lead up to the funeral were not the set of circumstances Reg would have wanted. The chaps were adamant that Reg's dying wish was that they were pallbearers and that his send off was to be a mirror image of Ron's. Roberta maintained a dignified silence throughout this period, refusing to be drawn into any dispute. Reg's body was taken back to Bethnal Green in preparation for the funeral with Wednesday October the eleventh to be the day he'd be laid to rest.

The pallbearers were not to be old gangland figures but people who Reg had grown close to through his years of imprisonment. Close friend and former cellmate Bradley Allerdyce, music promoter Bill Curbishley, and Tony Mortimer singer and songwriter from former teen favourite band at the time, East 17. They had already been asked and had agreed to carry the coffin with others to be confirmed. There would only be a handful of limos for very close friends and what was left of the family. Others would have to make their own arrangements. This was another direct snub to the old school who still maintained that it wasn't what Reg wanted. It's something I can't comment on. From what I understand, Roberta was steering him away from gangland to have the normal life he'd wanted for so many years. In fairness to the chaps, Reg was part of gangland and he always would be. They wanted to give him the best send-off possible. I honestly don't know what Reg had wanted, but it would not have been for his friends and wife to start squabbling. It was appropriate that the wishes of his wife were respected.

I decided to travel down to London on the six a.m. train, and reached Kings Cross just after nine. I made my way to Bethnal Green via the Underground. It's hard to describe my feelings as I travelled. I'd had three hours on the train to do my thinking and I'd done a lot more prior to that. It bothered me that it had to end like this; that I would be attending just like any other civvy. It bothered me that I was not a part of it, not seeing friends and bothered by possible rumours that people may have heard. Up and out of the station I strolled past *The Blind Beggar*. I stopped and paused to look at it for a second... the place where Ron had shot George Cornell. It felt strange. The first killing that led to their downfall... the times Ron had described it to me... it all seemed like a lifetime ago now.

I continued past it and reached Bethnal Green Road just after ten am. I was dressed smart but casual, and had decided against a wreath. I simply wanted to pay my respects and be seen at the funeral to show any of the chaps that doubted my side of the story. I popped into a cafe for some much needed breakfast and flicked through the *East London Advertiser* which carried an eight page pull-out on the East End's most notorious family. From there it was on to *English's Funeral Parlour*. It was unusually quiet. The faces I was expecting to see were not there. Roberta seemed to have got her wish; the likes of Freddie Foreman and Tony Lambrianou were conspicuous by their absence. Frankie Fraser was there as was former train robber Bruce Reynolds with his son Nick; Billy Murray from TV show *The Bill* was the only 'celebrity' on show.

The service was at St Matthew's as it had been for his brothers. I shook hands with a few of the chaps and watched as Reg's coffin was loaded into the hearse. I had decided to walk alongside Reg to the church, quite an emotional journey as Reg stopped off at 178 Vallance Road for the last time. Although the crowds were nowhere near the same in numbers as when Ron and Charlie had been buried, they were still big enough to cause a lot of the mourners to be delayed and to miss the start of the service. It seemed to be a different affair than what anyone was expecting. The church was still packed to the rafters as the vicar told of how Reg had turned to God, and the hymns which had been recited at the other two funerals were given an airing again. There was a feeling of déjà vu... maybe because it had only been a few months since Charlie had died. There were a lot of strangers in the church, which I put down to the fact that once again the security had failed miserably in getting the right people in. A lot different to how Dave had ran things in 1995. Outside the church I bumped into Bruce and Nick Reynolds again. They were with Andy Jones, curator of the *Crime Through Time Museum* in Gloucester, and offered me a lift to the cemetery. The lift turned out to be in a beautiful red Bentley, which had had one previous owner... none other than Mr. Terry *Eurovision* Wogan.

The journey to the cemetery was a long one. The police seemed intent on separating the cars and we ended up in a traffic jam and arrived at the cemetery just after the hearse. Outside the big gates there were people – friends of Reg – being held back by police officers. Obviously the police were only acting on instructions, but whose instructions it was remains a mystery to this day. To not let all his friends in seemed a bit harsh to me. I decided to go it alone and thanked Bruce, Nick and Andy for the lift and we promised to keep in touch. Both Bruce and Nick were keen to come to Newcastle when they released their books later in the year, and I told them I would be only too pleased to help them with any publicity.

As the gates finally opened, the crowd of mourners surged forward and I caught a glimpse of a bald head and a cigar... there was only one person it could be. It was Dave and the boys... Ray, Ian, Seymour, Brendan, Christian, Wish, Welsh Bernie, Scouse John, Bulldog, Rob, Marcus, Piers and Big John. I shook hands and embraced all the lads. They were pleased to see I'd not lost my bottle. We made our way towards the Kray plot, and we waited on the hillside overlooking the grave. Reg was carried to his final resting place as we gathered. The vicar performed the Last Rites and the last of the Krays was lowered down into his grave. With that Roberta and the other close family said their thanks to those around them and they were gone. It was all very different. I think the lack of 'spectators' was down to the fact that there was not another Kray brother in attendance to look at. Reg was always a crowd-puller at the others just because he was Reg Kray and people wanted to say they had seen him. As far as friends go, it was apparent that there had been a falling out of some sort. Some of them had decided to stay clear, which must have been a tough decision to make. Looking around, there were plenty new faces on the scene just like the last two.

The wake was to be held in the heart of the East End. I decided not too push my luck and instead travelled in style with Dave and the lads in a couple of hired vintage cars back to a boozer in South London to give the last of the Krays a good old send off. My mate Gary, who makes cash as a *Jaws* look alike from the *Bond* films, made the journey back to Newcastle with me later that night. I finished off my day with a couple of swift ones on Newcastle's Quayside. I'd distanced myself purposefully to avoid a scene at my old friend's funeral. The feud with the gangland figure passed and on a recent trip to London we shook hands and the past behind us.

My Kray connection had now died along with the last brother. I have had my ups and downs just as I would in any friendship but I know they all died knowing they had me as a friend. That meant a lot to me. The friends I made along the way remain my friends today and I am privileged to have good memories of all three of the Kray brothers. I was proud to be their Geordie Connection.

The Final Curtain

I've always wondered how I would sum up my experiences. The Krays played such an important part in my life and writing this has made me realise that they still are a big part. I got to know them while I was growing up and from knowing them I grew up with life experiences that I would not have anticipated. I was learning all the time, even though it didn't feel like it and I suppose my life with them put me on the fast track to adulthood.

The Kray brothers are now gone but never forgotten. I don't think they will ever be forgotten. They will always be remembered by the classic photograph taken by David Bailey. It's one of those iconic images like Che Guevara or Jim Morrison's 'young lion' pose – mysterious and haunting. They defined an era in Britain – a time of change. I think that change was the most important factor in their rise to fame. If it had not been for a change in the country's economy, the chances are we would never have heard of them and they would just have been another couple of fighters on the cobbles of the East End. They were around at the right time career-wise – that's the important part. The country was incredibly vulnerable and in particular, the city where they lived. The war years meant they could establish themselves, just as all the other criminals were, but they had to excel above all the others. It just happened; they weren't waiting to move in. It was fate. The economy changing after the war meant they could achieve a lot more than they could have in poorer times. There were clubs, the gaming industry and fortunes to be made.

In another place, let's say Newcastle for instance, it may have been different. Newcastle did not undergo the same bombing campaign as London did. Communities up here were still intact and still strong. We were not weakened and morale was not at an all-time low. It was different in London, especially the East End. I don't think that the statement, 'They kept crime off the streets' is strictly true. As mentioned previously, the people in the East End did not have that much to steal. People didn't feel safe; they felt scared.

This book does not set out to glorify violence, gangsterism or anything else the Kray brothers were a part of. They had done all that before I was even born, and those were the crimes they were serving time for when I met them. My interest in them came in my teens when I was enthralled by their infamy. My memories of the twins are from their days in prison and of Charlie, outside as well as inside. I can't try to sell the idea of the twins as a pair of angels who knew they had done wrong and were remorseful about it. We must also bear in mind the memories of some other people's lives that were changed by the Kray brothers... the people they shot, stabbed, fought with and beat up, the families of the people they killed, those they extorted money from, the people who feared them – people who were just trying to make a living the honest way. They functioned well in their heyday because they were twins. No one had come up against anything like it before, and possibly never will. They became a classic case study for twin relationships... another reason why their name will live on.

My experience of the twins was always as separate entities. It was interesting for me because they were similar in many ways, yet different in so many others. I'd never set out to write a book that looked at their lives when they were in their prime and were running the East End side by side with the firm. That's been done and happened long before I knew them. Nor would I set out to analyse them as twins and their actions, citing scientific studies and say why they did what they did – that's best left to psychologists. My intention from writing this has been to tell a story from a different perspective, make my own observations and share them. I believe I've had memories of the three brothers which are worth sharing.

My relationship with Reg was of a father son nature. We talked about football and women, we argued over money, and nine times out of ten I did the opposite to what he told me to do. He could be pig-headed at times but I'll always remember one classic line he came out with. In discussing the duration of his prison sentence he once said, "I would have spent less time behind bars if I'd killed Mother Theresa." He was also the king of manipulation. Ron was the one in their heyday who has all the gophers, but behind bars, it was Reg. He could be a nightmare at times and I don't think he was aware that 'sorry' was a word, never mind what it meant. Ron and I would chat a lot about the old days and people from his past. I suppose my relationship with him was likened to the role a granddad takes when he tells you about his time as a soldier in the war. Ron certainly took me through his war in graphic detail on some visits. Rather than the beaches of Normandy, Ron's battlefield was the East End of London where he commanded his troops from *Fort Vallance*. My most memorable conversation with Ron has got to be the time he described the killing of George Cornell so vividly. My visits with Ron were good as they were full of conversation without constant interruptions. He could be very volatile. Like Reg, his moods were known to change in an instant. He never had a problem with ordering executions one day and shrugging them off the next. Along with that, Ron had the most wicked sense of humour. Charlie Kray was like a devilish uncle who wanted to take his young nephew to the West End and show him how to be a ladies man. I cannot ever remember having a bad night out with Charlie. He was great company and a joy to spend time with. I would say that I miss him the most because the time we shared wasn't always limited by visiting hours, and the fact that Charlie actually took the time and effort to visit me in Newcastle. I wonder whether Ron or indeed Reg would have had they been at liberty.

Charlie too was an excellent laugh. It was sad to see him deteriorate in the end, and even sadder to see it happen in prison. I would have been interested to see how my relationship would have developed had all three brothers lived for another ten years apiece.

I'd certainly say they succeeded in what they set out to do... they became famous. By whatever means possible, I think in the end, Charlie became a victim of his famous name. That's one of the big regrets I have from my relationship with them – not being present in Birmingham when Charlie was introduced to the Geordie policemen. I would have been able to sniff them out (no pun intended). I'm sure of it. He would have been sussed out some time earlier after his name kept cropping up in tapped phone conversations which had led to the convictions of other traffickers. I say victim of his own name as in sentencing, Kray gets twelve years for introducing the people who want to do business, and the other two accomplices received nine years and five years for actually handling the drugs. The drug industry is run by extreme violence and fear, not by a few old men who lived by the old code of never using weapons. Maybe if I'd met up with these 'businessmen' and alerted Charlie, the whole Kray story may have had a somewhat happier ending.

As for getting involved with the twins and the chaps I don't regret it for one minute. Why should I? I'm a law abiding citizen. I pay my taxes, have no criminal record and have worked continuously since I left school. I value the experiences I had with the Krays. I think I learnt much from my eleven-year friendship with the brothers. I certainly learnt a lot about them and a lot about what was going on in the underworld. I learnt about business, about trust and how to spot a fake; I also learnt that there are some good and bad people out there too. In those terms, it's not that different to what I would have learnt growing up on the streets of Felling – but the stakes were a lot higher. Knowing the Krays was a lesson in friendship.

I never anticipated it going as far as it did, but was glad it happened. As in any friendship, there were good times and bad but it was something I had to get used to. I don't really think that the twins had that many genuine friends when it came down to it. I'd say that the ones who stuck by them since the old days were their true friends. There were plenty people around them who were only too willing to sell stories, photographs, enhance their own reputation by association and take all they could from the Kray name.

Some may say that I'm no different. Everyone is entitled to an opinion. I never planned anything other than meeting the brothers – the rest just happened. The most important thing I learnt through it all was that crime almost certainly doesn't pay. The authorities will always catch up with you. This was true of the Krays and most of the people they surrounded themselves with. I was unique in that circle as I was never introduced as 'Steve; a good burglar from Newcastle,' or 'Shooter Steve from the Felling'. I was just Steve, friend of the twins. I was young and a bit naïve but I'm the person I am today largely through knowing them. It was through them that I drifted towards security work, which is something I have now made a career out of.

In the end, all that the twins had left was the legend. It consumed Reg to the point of filming a deathbed interview. It was a shock to see how the cancer had reduced this former muscular gangland figure to a frail bag of bones, but the actual show summed the Krays up in one word – Money. They loved making it, but the enjoyment was spending it.

I can almost hear the twins now, "A book? Good, good. What's our cut? We'll go seventy-thirty in our favour." I'm sure they would have approved it. The Legend lives on. God bless, Steve.

Acknowledgements

Thanks to the following people for their help and support.
Stu Wheatman, Martin Ellis, Steve Parnell, Ian Horrocks,
Tony Furby, Ian Duncan, Eddie Rutherford (RIP), Raul,
Alan and Colin Fanning, Scott Mytton, Andy Gravonor,
Neil McKay, Linda Richards, Ross Gregory, Ian Willis,
Roger Woodcock, Dylan Younger, Robin Perrie,
Robin McGibbon, Eric Mason, Laurie O'leary, Les Martin,
Peter Yeats, Dave Courtney, Ron, Reg and Charlie.

Special thanks to my parents John and Celia, grandparents
John, Elizabeth and Cecilia and my brother Rob for
encouragement, and last but not least Dawn, the love of
my life for keeping my feet on the ground and being my
soulmate.